Kentucky Remembered
An Oral History Series

JAMES C. KLOTTER and
TERRY L. BIRDWHISTELL
General Editors

Bert Combs the Politician

An Oral History

George W. Robinson, Editor

THE UNIVERSITY PRESS OF KENTUCKY

Paperback edition 2008
Copyright © 1991 by The University Press of Kentucky

Scholarly publisher for the Commonwealth,
serving Bellarmine University, Berea College, Centre
College of Kentucky, Eastern Kentucky University,
The Filson Historical Society, Georgetown College,
Kentucky Historical Society, Kentucky State University,
Morehead State University, Murray State University,
Northern Kentucky University, Transylvania University,
University of Kentucky, University of Louisville,
and Western Kentucky University.
All rights reserved.

Editorial and Sales Offices: The University Press of Kentucky
663 South Limestone Street, Lexington, Kentucky 40508-4008
www.kentuckypress.com

The Library of Congress has cataloged the hardcover edition as follows:

Bert Combs the politician : an oral history / George W. Robinson, editor.
    p. cm.—(Kentucky remembered : an oral history series)
  Includes bibliographical references and index.
  ISBN-10: 0-8131-1740-2
  ISBN-13: 978-0-8131-1740-9 (hardcover : alk. paper)
    1. Combs, Bert T., 1911–   —Interviews. 2. Governors—Kentucky—Interviews. 3. Kentucky—Politics and government—1951– I. Robinson, George William, 1926–   . II. Series.
F456.26.C66B47   1991
976.9'043'092—dc20
[B]   90-19970
ISBN-13: 978-0-8131-9229-1 (pbk. : alk. paper)

This book is printed on acid-free recycled paper meeting
the requirements of the American National Standard
for Permanence in Paper for Printed Library Materials.

Manufactured in the United States of America.

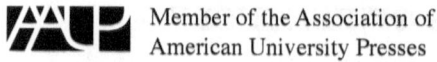 Member of the Association of
American University Presses

Contents

General Editors' Preface   vii
Preface   ix
Interviewees   xiii
Introduction   1
1. The Preparation: 1911–1954   8
    The Road to Law   8
    Law Practice and War   15
    Judge   18
2. The 1955 Gubernatorial Primary: Political Baptism   28
    The Selection   28
    The Campaigner   35
    Shelbyville   44
    Chandler v. Combs   50
    The Agony of Defeat   58
3. The 1959 Gubernatorial Primary: Political Maturity   62
    The Decision to Run   62
    Combs v. Wyatt   72
    The Merger   77
    The Team You Can Trust   83
4. The Combs Administration: Political Reality   93
    Advice and Counsel   94
    The Sales Tax   100
    The Merit System   106
    Toll Roads, Parks, and Tourism   111
    Appalachia   118
    The Truck Deal   121
    Election Campaigns   137
    Leadership   150
    Taking Government to the People   159
    Innovations   162
    Potpourri   165
5. Aftermath   171
    Law and Politics: 1963–1967   171
    The Federal Court   180
    The 1971 Gubernatorial Primary   187
    The Combs Impact   200
Notes   205
Index   207

General Editors' Preface

Kentucky is a national leader in the field of oral history, and over the past decades thousands of interviews have been collected. *Kentucky Remembered* is designed to bring into print the most important of those recollections. Each volume focuses on a particular subject and is prepared by an expert in that field.

Oral history is, of course, only one type of source material, but by its very nature it provides insights into the personal and hidden aspects of history. It lets readers experience the full range of the drama that is involved in the historical story. Oral sources provide a vital thread to the rich fabric that is Kentucky's history.

This volume is the first in the series and amply demonstrates the value of oral history. In studying one of the state's most important governors of the twentieth century, George Robinson of Eastern Kentucky University has skillfully selected from a large number of interviews the most pertinent parts and has fashioned them into a fascinating narrative. Each person, including Bert Combs himself, adds details and examples to the existing story. New insights into Kentucky's politics and people emerge on almost every page. Here, too, are the sound and the fury—and the humor—that traditionally have been a part of the state's political past. In short, *Bert Combs the Politician* is a fresh story, one to be savored and enjoyed.

James C. Klotter
Terry L. Birdwhistell

Preface

The Bert Combs oral history project from which these excerpts have been taken was completed between 1978 and 1980. A grant from the Kentucky Oral History Commission provided funds for travel and equipment used. Professor William Ellis of Eastern Kentucky University assisted me with the interviews, conducting approximately one-fourth of them, while Professor William Berge, then director of the Oral History Center at Eastern Kentucky University helped guide us both in our efforts.

My interest in Combs stemmed from work I did between 1974 and 1980 preparing his gubernatorial papers for publication. Impressed by the extent and breadth of the Combs program and by his personal identification with so much of it, I found myself wanting to know more and more about his life outside gubernatorial circumstances. For example, how had he prepared himself for the responsibilities of public office? How did his contemporaries evaluate his performance, his personality, his intellect, his honesty? Was Kentucky different because of Combs? Did politics change Combs?

Motivated by these and other questions and intrigued by the evolution of oral history as both an investigative and preservationist approach to historical understanding, I concluded that an oral history project would be an appropriate approach. Combs was agreeable to such a study. I had in hand a long list of Comb's acquaintances. William Berge was there to help me draft a project request and William Ellis, who was doing research in Kentucky history anyway, agreed to help me with some of the interviews.

It is important to stress that I did not embark upon the project with a specific goal of publication in mind. I had no thesis to prove or disprove. All I wished to do was to preserve on tape as much information about Combs as possible. I did not expect to find out everything, nor did I really know at the beginning what direction the interviews would take. Some patterns emerged quickly, however, and a general formula developed. An outline was prepared, and then questions were designed to prompt as broad a series of responses as possible, so that future researchers might find something useful to enhance their knowledge of twentieth-century Kentucky history.

More than sixty people were interviewed, some more than once, and Bert Combs, himself, eleven times. The selections here are drawn from the recollections of more than fifty people. Each tape includes questions and responses, but the questions have been deleted from these reproductions to conserve space. In some instances there have been slight changes in the spoken word, but in no case is the expressed meaning altered. It is worth noting, also, that what appears here is but a small percentage (no more than 10 percent) of what each participant contributed. The complete record on tape is currently housed in the Eastern Kentucky University Archives and is available to the public.

Excerpts that appear were chosen because they touched upon important aspects of Combs's career, revealed his character, exemplified personality traits, and suggested reasons for his actions. They also frequently showed the interests and rationale of the interviewee.

The organization is broadly chronological, encompassing five chapters. In Chapter 1, focusing on Combs's largely nonpolitical early years, some of the factors that prepared him for the future are established. Chapter 2 explores the circumstances surrounding the unsuccessful 1955 gubernatorial primary. In Chapter 3 the central focus is upon conditions that led to success in the 1959 gubernatorial primary. Chapter 4 deals with major achievements during the Combs administration and some of the events surrounding those achievements. Chapter 5 examines the years after the governorship, culminating with the gubernatorial primary in 1971.

Like most historical studies there is a sense of incompleteness about this one. Although no one rejected the opportunity to participate, contributions from certain key players are missing. In particular, Earle Clements, Wendell Ford, Joe Leary, Henry Ward, Ned Breathitt, and John Whisman proved to be unavailable. Their comments would have enriched the total product.

But the case of Earle Clements was unique. The former governor initially agreed to participate with the stipulations that an experienced Kentucky politician conduct the interview and Combs be present at the time. Though this was an unorthodox procedure I did secure Combs's (somewhat bewildered) assent and made plans to

Preface

have an interview conducted. I assumed that I would be allowed at least to observe, perhaps to turn the machine on and off, but it did not matter because Clements in the end, never agreed to any terms. Perhaps he never intended to participate.

A description of those whose contributions do appear is provided following this preface with special focus on their roles during the Combs administration and at the time of the interview. The length in minutes of each interview is also provided to underscore that what appears in this book is but a small sample of the material housed in the Bert Combs Oral History Collection.

The interviews themselves were conducted in business establishments, government facilities, people's homes, and, occasionally, on campus at Eastern Kentucky University. Usually the interviews lasted between one and two hours. In every case the interview was conducted to allow for varieties of responses. Most, though not all, of the participant interviews were completed prior to the series with Combs himself. This helped to highlight some areas for Combs to discuss if he chose to do so.

All the Combs interviews took place in his Louisville law office on the 26th floor of the Citizens Plaza Building in late afternoon. We discussed topics that I initiated although there was a general chronological flow from the first interview to the last. Before turning on the tape recorder I always gave Combs some idea about what I wanted to cover so he could collect his thoughts. At no time did Combs appear reticent to comment on anything. Never did he tell me to turn off the tape recorder so he could speak off the record. His explanations, narratives, justifications, and elaborations were not aimed just at me or the world that might listen. They frequently seemed to be self-directed as he recalled, reconsidered, and pondered out loud. He accepted responsibility for mistakes he had made and took a measure of credit for results that he had caused. He never ridiculed the actions of others nor did he blame anyone other than himself for apparent inadequacies. His wry sense of humor and an ability to laugh at himself showed up again and again. He was never on the defensive about anything. He always seemed to be quietly confident that as he had wished, he had left significant footprints in the sands of time.

It is important to remember that this is an oral history presentation. There are some factual references drawn from contemporary *Louisville Courier-Journal* accounts to help provide background details, but other sources were deliberately not used to heighten emphasis upon oral expressions. Some differences of opinion are reflected about the progression of events, the relationship between one person and another, the importance of one development over another, and the reasons why certain results ensued. Obviously a full-blown historical study would consider oral history as only one of several sources to be used. It would recognize the difference between recollection over a twenty- or thirty-year period and records dating from the time of the events. Oral history adds to, but does not replace, other data.

It is equally important to note that the written transcriptions of oral commentaries can never fully represent the verbal expression. It is impossible to appreciate fully the personality and the meaning of oral expression unless that expression is heard as well as seen. No researcher should ever accept transcribed data without checking the original source.

Based as it is on the Bert Combs project, this study is arranged to fit important stages in the life of Bert Combs. Thus the commentaries appear where they deal with those stages. Though Bert Combs has had a distinguished career as a practicing attorney the center of the study bears upon his political endeavors, concentrating heavily upon his gubernatorial administration. The background material provided, therefore, deals primarily with political patterns and events in Kentucky adjacent to his political successes and failures.

George W. Robinson

Interviewees

Phil Ardery Louisville, Kentucky; April 17, 1979; 53 min. A candidate for the U.S. Senate in 1946 who lost to John Y. Brown, Sr., in the primary. Ardery was an attorney active in support of rural electric cooperative associations. He supported Combs in 1955 but endorsed Harry Lee Waterfield in 1959.

Fontaine Banks Lexington, Kentucky; March 18, 1980; 51 min. A member of the Kentucky Department of Education (1956–60) who was an administrative assistant to Governor Bert Combs and Governor Ned Breathitt (1960–67). In addition, Banks was the president of Appalachia Regional Hospitals, Inc. (1968–75), and a senior vice-president of Excepticon, Inc. in Lexington when he was interviewed.

Robert Bell Ashland, Kentucky; April 27, 1979; 86 min. An executive assistant to Henry Ward who was also commissioner of the Parks Department (1950–54 and 1963–67) and an executive assistant to Lieutenant Governor Wilson Wyatt (1959–60). In addition, Bell served as deputy state highway commissioner (1960–63) and commissioner of Revenue (1963). He was secretary of the governor's cabinet (1974–75) and commissioner of the Bureau of Natural Resources (1975–78). At the time of the interview he was a consultant for the Ashland Petroleum Company.

Barry Bingham, Sr. Louisville, Kentucky; April 2, 1979; 88 min. Long-time editor and publisher of the *Louisville Courier-Journal and Times* (1930–71). Bingham died on August 15, 1988.

John Y. Brown, Sr. Lexington, Kentucky; November 19, 1979; 103 min. A former member of the U.S. House of Representatives (1933–35) and the Kentucky House of Representatives (1946–54) who was an unsuccessful candidate for the U.S. Senate seven times. He died June 16, 1985.

Wendell Butler Frankfort, Kentucky; February 5, 1979; 80 min. A teacher in Metcalf County public schools (1931–36) and the superintendent of education in Metcalf County (1938–42). After serving as a Kentucky state senator (1947–51) Butler was superintendent of Public Instruction of Kentucky three times, and commissioner of Agriculture two times, between 1952 and 1975. He was the secretary of the Education and Arts Cabinet when he was interviewed.

Tommy Carroll Louisville, Kentucky; June 7, 1979; 80 min. An active member of the Young Democrat Club of Kentucky in the 1950s and the organization chairman of the Democratic state campaign in 1962 and 1964. Carroll served as campaign coordinator for Ned Breathitt (1963) and was legal counsel for the Kentucky Democratic Central Executive Committee (1964–65). He also served as chairman of the Jefferson County Democratic Executive Committee (1964–68), finance chairman for the Jefferson County Democratic Campaign Committee (1969), and treasurer of the Kentucky Democratic Campaign Committee (1972).

Albert B. "Happy" Chandler Versailles, Kentucky; November 20, 1979; 56 min. A former Kentucky state senator (1929–31), lieutenant governor of Kentucky (1931–35), and United States senator (1939–46). Chandler served two terms as governor of Kentucky (1935–39 and 1955–59).

Bert Combs Louisville, Kentucky
Interview 1	April 24, 1979	61 min.
Interview 2	June 19, 1979	109 min.
Interview 3	July 27, 1979	62 min.
Interview 4	September 18, 1979	96 min.
Interview 5	November 14, 1979	60 min.
Interview 6	February 18, 1980	61 min.
Interview 7	March 11, 1980	60 min.
Interview 8	April 8, 1980	62 min.
Interview 9	September 16, 1980	60 min.
Interview 10	October 21, 1980	78 min.
Interview 11	February 24, 1981	80 min.

Robert Lee "Slick" Combs Middlesboro, Kentucky; July 25, 1979; 87 min. Bert Combs's brother and a member of the Kentucky Highway Department (1934–43 and 1960–67). Combs was also employed in coal industry businesses in Harlan and Manchester (1943–60) and was retired when interviewed.

Interviewees

Robert Cornett Lexington, Kentucky; June 21, 1979; 48 min. A member of the Kentucky state budget staff (1951–55) and director of the Department of the Budget for Kentucky (1960–66). Cornett also served as director of both Area Development for the Appalachian Regional Commission (1966–68) and Special Projects for the Council of State Governments in Lexington (1968–77). At the time of his interview he was in private business.

John Crimmins Louisville, Kentucky; September 11, 1979; 48 min. The chairman of Organization for the Democratic party of Jefferson County for seventeen years. From 1971 to the time of his interview he was the alcoholic beverage administrator for Kentucky.

Harry G. Davis Frankfort, Kentucky; February 22, 1979; 75 min. Executive secretary to Governor A.B. Chandler (1955–59). Davis was secretary to the Kentucky Wholesale Liquor Distributors thereafter.

Martin (Mike) Duffy, Jr. Louisville, Kentucky; October 15, 1979; 74 min. A member of the Kentucky Senate (1951–67) and veteran leader of the Jefferson County Democratic party.

Ed Easterly Frankfort, Kentucky; May 8, 1979; 120 min. A member of the Kentucky Associated Press (1931–56) who also served as its head (1951–56). Easterly was press secretary to both A.B. Chandler (1956–59) and Bert Combs (1959–63) and the vice-president for public relations for the Appalachian Regional Hospitals until he retired in 1974.

Edward Farris Frankfort, Kentucky; February 22, 1979; 62 min. The chief assistant to Governor Earle Clements (1948–50) and Governor Lawrence Wetherby (1950–56). Farris later was in private business and served as a legislative representative for consumer finance and insurance industries (1960–76). At the time of the interview he was a distilled spirits administrator and a member of the Kentucky Alcoholic Beverage Control Board.

Jo Ferguson Louisville, Kentucky; April 30, 1979; 108 min. A former assistant attorney general (1948–56) and the attorney general (1956–60) of Kentucky. Ferguson also served as commissioner of the Economic Security Department (1960–61) and has been in private practice since 1961.

Edward Fossett Frankfort, Kentucky; September 20, 1979; 56 min. A former law clerk for the Kentucky Court of Appeals (1957–

58) and assistant attorney general (1958–60). Fossett served as a legal assistant (1960–62) and chief administrative assistant (1962–64) to Bert Combs. Later he was an attorney for the Kentucky Department of Insurance (1972–77) and at the time of the interview was an attorney for the Department of Education.

J. David Francis Bowling Green, Kentucky; June 1, 1979; 77 min. A former county judge for Warren County (1950–54) and former commonwealth attorney for the Eighth Kentucky Judicial District (1955–59). Francis later served as chairman of the Kentucky Public Service Commission (1959–67) and was a circuit judge for the Eighth Kentucky Judicial District when he was interviewed.

Walter Gattis Frankfort, Kentucky; February 3, 1979; 56 min. A former professor of political science at Centre College in Danville (1948–54) and Eastern Kentucky University in Richmond (1958–60). Gattis served as a member of the Danville City Council (1953–54) and as a budget analyst for the Kentucky Department of Finance (1955–56) and for the state of Ohio (1956–58). He was the commissioner for the Kentucky Department of Personnel (1960–67) and the personnel program auditor for the Federal Department of Health, Education, and Welfare (1967–71). He was the assistant director of the Bureau of Government Services at the University of Kentucky (1971–73) and the director of the Personnel Department for the University of Kentucky Medical Center (1973–75). At the time of the interview he was personnel director for the Administrative Office of the Courts. He died on January 26, 1989.

Polly Gorman Frankfort, Kentucky
 Interview 1   March 21, 1979   60 min.
 Interview 2   May 9, 1979   44 min.
Gorman was secretary to the superintendent of Public Instruction (1954–59) and then served as secretary to the commissioner of the Finance Department (1959–60). She was appointments secretary for Governor Bert Combs and Governor Ned Breathitt (1960–67) and administrative assistant to the president of Eastern Kentucky University when she was interviewed. She retired in 1977.

Lambert Hehl Newport, Kentucky; February 16, 1979; 62 min. The former deputy tax commissioner of Campbell County (1953–56) and city attorney for Crestview (1956–59). Hehl also served as a Kentucky state senator (1959–63) and commissioner of Campbell County Fiscal Court (1963–73). He was county judge of Campbell County when he was interviewed.

Interviewees xvii

Sara Combs Kaufman Lexington, Kentucky; June 8, 1979; 57 min. One of Bert Combs's three sisters.

Gil Kingsbury Fort Mitchell, Kentucky
Interview 1 March 27, 1979 51 min.
Interview 2 April 19, 1979 47 min.
A member of the news department (1941–59) and later vice-president of public relations at WLW radio in Cincinnati. Kingsbury was a member of the Kentucky House of Representatives (1958–60), the deputy highway commissioner for Kentucky (1964–65), and a member of the Better Roads Council (1965–66). He worked in public relations for the University of Kentucky (1966–68) and was self-employed in public relations when he was interviewed.

Arthur Lloyd Lexington, Kentucky; January 24, 1979; 60 min. A former principal of Webster County High School in Wheatcraft, Kentucky (1926–28) and professor at Vanderbilt and Morehead State universities (1930s). Lloyd served as director of Public Assistance in the Kentucky Department of Public Welfare (1935–41) and was a member of the U.S. Army during World War II (1941–45). He was the vice-president and managing director of Burly and Dark Tobacco Export Association, Inc. in Washington, D.C. (1945–47) and the director of the Legislative Research Commission of Kentucky (1947–55). He later served as adjutant general of Kentucky (1959–63) and was retired at the time of the interview. He died in 1987.

Robert R. Martin Richmond, Kentucky; March 14, 1979; 73 min. A former superintendent of Public Instruction (1955–59) and commissioner of Finance (1959–60). Martin was later the president of Eastern Kentucky University (1960–76) and a state senator at the time of the interview. He retired in 1985.

Jack Matlick Louisville, Kentucky; June 13, 1979; 52 min. A former editor and general manager of *Kentucky Farmer* (1940–60) and manager of the Kentucky State Fair and Exposition (1945, 1947–48). Matlick served as commissioner of Conservation for Kentucky (1960–68) and was retired when interviewed. He died March 21, 1986.

Robert Matthews Louisville, Kentucky; April 9, 1979; 56 min. A former assistant attorney general (1955–59) who was chief administrative assistant (1959–60) and commissioner of Finance (1960–63) under Governor Combs. He later served as attorney general for Kentucky (1963–67) and was in private law practice when interviewed.

William May Frankfort, Kentucky; December 18, 1979; 60 min. A twice-defeated (1943, 1947) candidate for lieutenant governor who became a promotions executive for Aerojet General, a subsidiary of General Tire and Rubber Company (1947–51) and later established his own engineering firm, Brighton Engineering, in Frankfort (1951). He was chief executive of Brighton when interviewed. He died in 1986.

Henry Meigs, II Frankfort, Kentucky; February 8, 1979; 41 min. A former private attorney in Frankfort (1945–60) who became judge of the Forty-eighth Judicial District of Kentucky (1960–83).

Cattie Lou Miller Frankfort, Kentucky; April 5, 1979; 110 min. A secretary to Governor Earle Clements and Governor Lawrence Wetherby (1947–55) and executive assistant to Governor Combs (1959–60). Miller worked in public relations for the Louisville Chamber of Commerce (1955–59) and was a commissioner of the Kentucky Department of Public Relations (1960–67). She served as executive assistant to Lieutenant Governor Wendell Ford (1967–71) and was later commissioner of Personnel (1972–76). She was executive director of the Kentucky Crime Victims Compensation Board and executive director of the State Board of Claims from 1976 to the time of her interview.

Harry B. Miller Lexington, Kentucky; September 7, 1979; 56 min. A long-time leader of the Fayette County Democratic party and a member of Bert Combs's advisory committee in the 1959 gubernatorial race. Miller has been in private practice in Lexington since 1948.

J.R. Miller Owensboro, Kentucky; September 13, 1979; 90 min. A long-time member of the state Democratic Central Executive Committee (1946–73) who served as chairman of the Owensboro Democratic party (1953–55) and the Democratic chairman of Daviess County (1960–64). He chaired Wendell Ford's campaign for governor (1971) and served as state Democratic chairman (1968–73). He was an uncontested mayoral candidate in Owensboro when interviewed.

Ruth Murphy Frankfort, Kentucky; September 28, 1979; 151 min. A former organization and methods examiner for the Department of Economic Security (1948–56) who served as an administrative assistant to the commissioner of Personnel (1960) and as executive secretary to the commissioner of Commerce (1960–64).Murphy was an administrative assistant to Governor Ned Breathitt (1964–67), an executive assistant to the crime commissioner (1967–71), and executive secretary to the clerk of the Court of Appeals (1971–75). She was retired at the time of the interview.

Foster Ockerman Lexington, Kentucky; March 26, 1979; 40 min. A member of the Kentucky House of Representatives in the 1950s. He was also a former commissioner of Motor Transportation (1960–63) and was in private law practice in Lexington when he was interviewed.

John Palmore Frankfort, Kentucky; March 29, 1979; 90 min. A former prosecuting attorney (1949–53) and city attorney (1953–55) for Henderson, Kentucky. Palmore served as commonwealth attorney for the Fifth District Circuit Court (1955–59) and has been a judge on the Kentucky Court of Appeals (renamed the Kentucky Supreme Court in 1976) since 1959. He served as chief justice of that court twice (1966–67 and 1977 to time of interview).

John Ed Pearce Louisville, Kentucky; April 16, 1979; 75 min. A reporter and editor for the *Louisville Courier-Journal* from 1946 to the present.

Earl Powell Owensboro, Kentucky; July 13, 1979; 81 min. A former assistant attorney general (1953–59) and deputy attorney general (1959–60) who was a commissioner of the Department of Economic Security (1961–65). He operated a life insurance business in Lexington (1965–71) and was vice-president of Citizens' Security Life Insurance Company of Owensboro, Kentucky, at the time of his interview.

Ed Prichard Frankfort, Kentucky; February 21, 1979; 62 min. An adviser to Governors Clements, Wetherby, and Combs who had been a law clerk to Felix Frankfurter at the U.S. Supreme Court (1939), a member of the Justice Department (1940–42), and on the staff of President Franklin D. Roosevelt (1942–45). He died on December 23, 1984.

Julius Rather Lexington, Kentucky; October 24, 1979; 51 min. A legal assistant to Governors Combs and Breathitt (1960–64) who later shared a law practice with Bert Combs (1964–67) and is now in private practice in Lexington.

Bobby Combs Rehm Versailles, Kentucky; September 19, 1979; 80 min. One of Bert Combs's three sisters.

William Scent Louisville, Kentucky; April 16, 1979; 50 min. A former director of the Department of Revenue (1951–55) and commissioner of Revenue (1959–63) who was also United States attorney for the Western District. Scent was a practicing attorney in Louisville when interviewed.

Jay Spurrier Frankfort, Kentucky; September 21, 1979; 46 min. A supporter of Harry Lee Waterfield in 1959's gubernatorial race who was vice-president of Public Relations for Kentucky Utilities when he was interviewed.

June Taylor Frankfort, Kentucky; September 11, 1979; 62 min. A former member of the Department of Economic Security (1941–45) and the Department of Education (1945–50) who was later a secretary to the state treasurer (1955–59), an assistant to the secretary of State (1959–63), and executive secretary to Governor Ned Breathitt (1963–67). Taylor was the assistant to the commissioner of highways from 1971 to the time she was interviewed.

Samuel Van Curon Frankfort, Kentucky; January 27, 1979; 65 min. The editor of the *Harlan Daily Enterprise* (1942–60) and the *Frankfort State Journal* (1960–76). Van Curon was a member of the Eastern Kentucky Regional Planning Commission (1958–60) and a president of the Kentucky Press Association and the Associated Press Editors' Association. He was retired at the time of his interview.

James Ware South Fort Mitchell, Kentucky; March 2, 1979; 62 min. A former city attorney for South Fort Mitchell (1946–50) and Kentucky state senator (1958–65) who served as majority leader (1960–64) and president pro tem (1964–65).

Harry Lee Waterfield Frankfort, Kentucky; February 28, 1979; 84 min. A member of the Kentucky House of Representatives (1937–47) who later served two terms as lieutenant governor of Kentucky (1955–59 and 1963–67). Waterfield was retired when he was interviewed. He died on August 4, 1988.

Lois Combs Weinberg Hindman, Kentucky; March 1, 1979; 53 min. Bert Combs's daughter.

Lawrence Wetherby Frankfort, Kentucky; February 10, 1979; 62 min. A former judge of the Juvenile Court of Jefferson County

Interviewees xxi

(1943–47) who served as lieutenant governor (1947–50) and governor (1950–55) of Kentucky and was a member of the Kentucky state Senate (1965–71).

Dix Winston Owensboro, Kentucky; July 14, 1979; 81 min. A reporter and political writer for the *Paducah Sun-Democrat* (1950–56) who handled publicity for Bert Combs in the 1955 campaign for governor. Winston also handled publicity for Earle Clements's 1956 U.S. Senate campaign. He was a technical writer at IBM in Lexington (1957–59) and later an administrative assistant (1960–61) and deputy commissioner of parks (1961–62) to Governor Combs. He worked for the Big Rivers Electric Company in western Kentucky (1962–76) and was executive director of the Henderson County River Port Authority at the time of his interview.

Wilson Wyatt Louisville, Kentucky; September 27, 1979; 56 min. A former mayor of Louisville (1941–45) who served as campaign manager for Adlai Stevenson (1952 and 1956) and was a former lieutenant governor of Kentucky (1959–63). He was active in the Kentucky Democratic Committee and the Democratic National Committee. He is now an attorney in Louisville.

The following persons were contacted but were unable to be interviewed:

John B. Breckinridge	Joseph Leary
Ned Breathitt	Mrs. Lennie McLaughlin
Earle Clements	Carl Perkins
Owsley Stanley Combs	Rumsey Taylor
Wendell Ford	Henry Ward
Felix Joyner	John Whisman

Bert Combs
the Politician

Introduction

Bert Combs was governor of Kentucky from December 1959 to December 1963. The only other elective state office he held was a 1950–1955 term as judge of the Court of Appeals, the highest court in Kentucky at the time. He never served as an elected public official again after 1963, yet his political impact upon the commonwealth extended far beyond the few years he spent in office. To be the central figure of a study such as this suggests that he was uncommonly important to the development of twentieth-century Kentucky, and he was. Other Kentuckians held both judicial and elective offices of prominence, but there were striking and distinctive features about Combs's endeavors. Other judges who shared the bench with him were duly impressed by his judicial qualities at both the state and federal level. Most regarded him as a judge's judge. Yet, surprisingly, he was also effective as a political leader, something judicious-minded figures frequently failed to manifest. And he was popular not just at the beginning of his gubernatorial term, when most governors are praised, but also at the end when most governors are damned. It was a popularity that helped immeasurably to elect his chosen successor, Ned Breathitt, to the governorship. That no governor in Kentucky's twentieth century has been able to name and elect a successor before or since testifies further to Combs's appeal.

In part this attraction derived from a succession of notable accomplishments during Combs's governorship. Unprecedented support for public education, a road-building program that linked eastern and western regions as never before, promotion of parks and tourism—all represented investments in the future. These achievements alone were noteworthy but Combs's impact upon Kentucky was more extensive because of how he accomplished them. Combs believed that the majority of the people of Kentucky were guided by common sense. If they had adequate information, they would normally respond in an intelligent manner. Thus everything in the elaborate Combs program received maximum publicity in newspapers, speeches, press releases, and state-sponsored publications. There was no atmosphere of secrecy surrounding administration policy.

The same could be said for Combs, himself. He was as open to people and their ideas as any governor before or since. He might not always act upon every suggestion he received, but he did listen. He inspired great loyalty among his associates. He had genuine respect for and interest in the opinion of others, and he was considerate and fair in the decisions he made.

These personal traits not only contributed to his spectacular popularity while governor but were factors behind his continuing attraction. They are the reasons why many Kentuckians continued to regard him as the real leader of the Democratic party for the next eight years, even when he was a federal circuit court judge. Combs did more than preside over passage of significant legislation while governor. He fostered a new spirit in Kentucky. He inspired people to be proud of their state, to believe in themselves, and to look to the future with optimism about their fortunes and the fortunes of the commonwealth. The new spirit, in fact, may be his most singularly important contribution to twentieth-century Kentucky.

Born in 1911, in Kentucky's eastern mountains, Combs was the oldest surviving child of Steve and Martha Combs. He had two younger brothers and three younger sisters. His mother had been a school teacher before marriage. His father, a part-time farmer and logger, devoted much of his time to politics. He was perhaps the principal Democrat in solidly-Republican Clay County. Schooling was important to both parents and all the Combs children were provided the opportunity to finish high school. At the same time the home environment was one in which reading and serious concern for events outside Clay County were always promoted.

Graduating from high school in the mid 1920s, Combs seemed to have little opportunity for further advancement. The family had no money for college expenses and Manchester did not offer a wide variety of occupational pursuits. But Martha Combs was resourceful, and with the help of her friends he was able to enroll at Cumberland College. Later, Steve Combs proved to be equally resourceful in helping his son to secure employment with the state of Kentucky in the early 1930s. In each instance, the capabilities, skills, and intelligent temperament of Bert Combs impressed those with whom he

Introduction

studied and for whom he worked. The years in Frankfort broadened the young man's outlook and brought him new acquaintances.

Able to save enough money from his state job and encouraged by his parents, Combs went on to the University of Kentucky and was graduated in 1937 with a law degree. It helped that his mother's brother was Dean of Men at the university, but Combs, in his own right, distinguished himself as a student, finishing second in his class. Upon graduation, Combs married Mabel Hall, whom he met at the university. After a brief stay in Manchester, where he practiced law, Combs moved to Prestonsburg, where he established a law partnership with a former fellow law student. There he learned the rudiments of law and litigation in the field, became acquainted with other lawyers, and established himself as a "comer."

World War II interrupted that pattern. In 1942 Combs went into the army and eventually secured a commission as an officer in the Judge Advocate General Branch. His service included a stint overseas in the Philippines where he helped prepare evidence against Japanese war criminals.

Discharged in 1946, Combs returned to Prestonsburg with Mabel and a family of two small children born during the war. He resumed his law practice with a new partner and prospered enough so that he and Mabel were able to build a house for which they had been saving since 1937. In addition, Combs for the first time became involved in local politics. He served briefly as city attorney and commonwealth attorney and identified with Floyd County efforts to elect Earle Clements governor in 1947. At the same time his enlarging law practice brought him into contact with members of the Court of Appeals, all of whom were impressed by his legal talents.

Thus when the judge of the Court of Appeals from Eastern Kentucky died in 1950, other members of that body were unanimous in their recommendation that Combs be appointed to the vacancy. Since Governor Lawrence Wetherby was a part of the Clements organization that Combs had supported earlier, the post was his if he wanted it. The decision to accept was not easy, however, because Combs was earning five times what the state paid its jurists, and he would have to move to Frankfort to perform his duties. After considerable thought he made the commitment and, in effect, set in motion the process by which he would eventually become governor of the state.

The appointment lasted only until the fall of 1951 when he had to stand for election. Former governor Simeon Willis decided to run against him. Combs's subsequent victory, a narrow one over the better-known Willis, established for him a reputation as a vote-getter, and his work on the court inspired praise from fellow jurists around the state.

Initially Combs rented an apartment in Frankfort while serving on the Court of Appeals and returned to Prestonsburg on weekends to be with his family. After his election in 1951, Combs and family moved to Lexington and he commuted to Frankfort.

He was living in Lexington when Governor Wetherby called upon him to be the administration candidate for governor in 1955. Once again Combs was presented with an unexpected opportunity. After the initial shock wore off he agreed to make the race. Opposed by Albert B. "Happy" Chandler, he faced the most effective state campaigner of the twentieth century. By his own admission, Combs was not a good candidate. He had little or no experience with the rough and tumble stump-speaking politics of that era in which Chandler excelled. Combs did learn a lot about techniques, how to meet people, and how to tell stories, but not soon enough to offset the Chandler appeal.

Combs also learned a lot about Kentucky: its problems, needs, resources, and hopes. He surmised that Kentuckians wanted and deserved more services from government and concluded that state revenue should, therefore, be increased. Chandler, on the contrary, insisted that he could provide any and all necessities without a tax increase. Chandler won but soon found it necessary to obtain a sharp raise in income taxes for the state.

Stung by what he believed to be Chandler's misleading campaign tactics and supported by a sizable number of Democrat legislators with similar feelings, Combs determined to run again. The 1959 primary that ensued quickly turned into a three-cornered affair with Chandler's candidate, Lt. Gov. Harry Lee Waterfield and former Louisville mayor Wilson Wyatt in the field along with Combs. Since Wyatt and Combs appealed to the same kind of support—anti-Chandler sentiment—it became apparent that neither could win as long as both remained in the race.

As a result, four months before primary election day, Combs and Wyatt joined forces with the latter running for lieutenant governor. The combination proved attractive to voters. Combs and Wyatt won the primary in May and decisively defeated Republican opposition the following November.

As governor of Kentucky Combs quickly established an effec-

Introduction

tive liaison with the General Assembly leading to an elaborate program consistent with pledges made during the campaign. Road construction, significant increases in funds to education, park system enhancement, tourism, statewide educational television, airport development, and a state merit system were among the big-ticket items. A state sales tax helped finance a number of the projects and an elaborate public relations program promoting the tax and its benefits helped to overcome initial resentment. In fact, public relations was a key to much of the success of all programs and to the popularity of Combs throughout his term and beyond.

All was not positive, however. A potential scandal relative to some dump trucks the state had contracted to buy led to a break between Combs and Earle Clements. In the 1960 national election, despite John F. Kennedy's success elsewhere, Kentucky cast a majority of votes for Richard Nixon. In 1962 Wilson Wyatt lost to incumbent Thruston Morton when he tried to win a seat in the United States Senate. With "ABC in '63" signs appearing everywhere it looked as if the Combs era would not live past his term as governor.

But Combs and his selected successor, Ned Breathitt, rose to the occasion and in a campaign that emphasized television as never before in Kentucky politics, Chandler was defeated by a decisive margin. Breathitt was the first selected successor to win election in Kentucky in the twentieth century—graphic testimonial to the strong Combs's appeal as well as to Breathitt's attraction.

Though out of office and practicing law privately again, this time in Lexington, Combs was not out of politics. Many Frankfort officials and political leaders across the state continued to regard him as their leader. Ned Breathitt, in fact, sought his advice frequently and considered him to be the logical candidate for governor in 1967.

Combs apparently gave that possibility some consideration but eventually decided to remove himself from the field by soliciting and securing appointment to the Sixth Circuit Court of Appeals in 1967. Federal regulations required that he remove himself completely from politics, thus presumably ending the tendency of organization people to look to him for guidance.

But it did not work out that way. Democrat Henry Ward lost the gubernatorial election in 1967 to Republican Louie Nunn, and Wendell Ford, whom Combs had not supported in the primary, won election as lieutenant governor. The Republican victory threw the Democratic party into confusion and uncertainty. Some regarded

Ford as the man to rebuild the party. Others felt newly elected Speaker of the House Julian Carroll was the hope of the future. Veteran party leaders felt that both were too young and inexperienced to pursue politics any further. That left Combs as the only seasoned political figure capable of uniting the divergent elements.

While this was developing Combs discovered that he had embarked upon a life drastically different from that he had enjoyed previously. Not only did he have to liquidate all his business ventures and investments, but he was restricted socially as well. Close associations with legal acquaintances might jeopardize objectivity in forthcoming court decisions. Endless numbers of briefs had to be studied and decisions rendered in the close confinement of a dreary office. Decisions often went on to the Supreme Court where that body accorded little if any attention to appeals court reasoning because basic case work occurred at the district court level.

At the same time an increasing number of Kentucky political leaders and former associates came to him to beseech his assistance with regard to party problems. In short, as Combs became more and more disturbed by his lifestyle on the court, visitor after visitor urged him to resign and take charge of the foundering Kentucky Democratic party. Whether or not this was the reason, Combs made up his mind to leave the court and join a law firm in Louisville. It was a decision he made before he announced his candidacy for governor. In the meantime, Wendell Ford, uncertain about Combs's plans, formally declared himself a candidate. In all probability he had no choice if he wished to continue in public life because Julian Carroll, already a candidate for lieutenant governor, had tied himself to Combs. A Combs victory, therefore, would undoubtedly lead to a Carroll candidacy in 1975, leaving nothing politically available for Ford.

Nearly all political analysts viewed the Combs candidacy as a sure victory. How could such a popular figure be defeated? But he was, and for the first time since 1955, Democrats no longer regarded him as a potential candidate. Combs went on to practice law on a private basis.

Yet he never isolated himself from the political realm completely. He continued to endorse candidates for public office if they suited him and to participate in political campaigns. In 1981 he actively opposed passage of a constitutional amendment that would have allowed an incumbent governor to succeed himself in office. Shortly thereafter he assumed a more active stand for education when he became a member of the State Council on Higher Education. But perhaps Combs's most notable progressive effort came in 1988 when, acting without pay as lead attorney for sixty-six poor school districts, he won court approval of his contention that inadequate funding made the state's education system unconstitutional.

At this writing Bert Combs is seventy-nine years old. He is married (as of December 1988) to his third wife. He resides and works in Lexington though he also has a home in Cane Creek, Kentucky. He continues to function actively in the law firm Wyatt Tarrant and Combs, with which he has been identified since 1971.

Different from some lawyers who utilized their legal activities to establish political careers, Combs always remained essentially law-oriented. Politics offered an opportunity to accomplish objectives he believed to be necessary, but never appealed to him as a lifetime career. Combs always viewed public service—whether he was judge, governor, or city attorney—as means to an end, and that end was never further public service. It was always a series of specific goals that the public service would help him to accomplish. What follows is his story—the story of an exemplary political leader.

Chapter 1

The Preparation: 1911–1954

The Road to Law

Bert Combs spent the first eighteen years of his life in Clay County, either on a farm near Manchester or in the town itself. In January 1929 he enrolled at Cumberland College in Williamsburg and completed three semesters. It was his first experience away from home.

During the summer of 1930 he secured employment with the state Highway Department in Frankfort, where he earned enough money to pay some college debts. It was a political job made possible by ripper legislation that stripped from Republican Governor Flem Sampson the normal gubernatorial authority over highway administration. Combs's father was the leading Democrat in Republican-oriented Clay County and this, with Combs's college training, enabled him to obtain the position and perform his duties well. At a time when jobs were scarce and the Great Depression was deepening, it was a fortunate happening.

Combs remained in Frankfort for the next four years and experienced a new stage in his development. For the first time in his life he had some money to live on. He was single; he liked to play tennis; he went to dances; and he made new friends. Yet in 1934 he gave up the Highway Department job and Frankfort to return to college, determined to earn a law degree. This required completion of an undergraduate semester and then three years at the University of Kentucky law school. After graduating second in his class in 1937, Combs had an opportunity to return to state government if he wished, but he decided instead to go back to Manchester with his new bride, Mabel Hall, to set up practice in his home town.

The Preparation

Bert Combs (Interview 1)   I was born in Manchester, on what they call Town Branch, August 13, 1911. My father was a sawmill operator. He owned a sawmill and he would bring that sawmill to a tract of timber and cut that timber and then move it to another tract. In the meantime, he was a farmer, a small farmer. About everybody was in Clay County at that time. . . . My mother had been a school teacher, but I don't recall that she ever taught after she was married. She taught for several years before she was married. Her name was Jones, Martha Jones. She had been raised on Beech Creek, which is about three miles from Manchester.

My father had been born and raised at Oneida, the location of Oneida Baptist Institute where I later went to school some. I believe at the time they located in Manchester my father was working as a clerk in a general store. My father had not completed much formal education. I think he had gone through the sixth or seventh grade. My mother, of course, had more schooling—had received a teaching certificate. She had a first-class certificate. She had gone to school in Clay County and later to the Normal School at London, which was twenty-five miles away. . . .

We lived on Beech Creek when I started going to school. I went to the elementary school in Beech Creek, not a one-room school, but a two-room school. It was about a mile and a half, perhaps two miles from where we lived. We walked to school and back and took our lunch with us and thought nothing about it. I went to school at Beech Creek until I got to the seventh grade. It was a six-month school term, sometimes only five months. My parents thought that my sister and I ought to go to Oneida after the school term was out. Oneida had an eight- or nine-month school term. It was a boarding school and we paid a little. . . .

[Next] I was enrolled in Clay County High School located at Manchester. It was on the top of the hill overlooking the little town of Manchester. We still lived on Beech Creek so my sister and I rode a pony named Turkey to school for two years. While in school we let him graze in woods near the school. He was very gentle.

Then we moved back to Manchester. We lived in Manchester until I completed high school. My sister in the meantime became ill after [her] second year in high school and was ill a year or more before she died. All the children were born by this time—three boys and four girls. My brother was only fourteen months younger than I was. Another boy was fifteen or sixteen months younger than he was and then the three girls.

While in high school I got a job working in Dr. Porter's drugstore, called the Manchester Drug Company. It was my job to open up the drugstore in the morning before he came down, before school. They had no running water at that time so I was to sweep out the store, clean out the soda fountain. By that time it was time for me to go to school. I worked on weekends as a soda jerk and during the summer. The store was the social center of the town. People would come and get a Coca Cola and drink their Coke and talk. Young people usually came late in the afternoon after school was out. It was a pleasant place to work—hard work—but I didn't feel I had an inferior position.

I finished high school in 1927. I skipped some grades along the way, so I was only fifteen. I didn't have any plans to go to college. In fact, I didn't have any way to go. My folks just didn't have any money to spend on a college education. So I worked in the drugstore off and on. Dr. Porter didn't need me all the time. He needed me during the summer when the ice cream and coca cola business was good. I did this for a year after I got out of high school. I also did odd jobs working people's gardens and that sort of thing. I contributed some money to the family and helped also by buying my own clothes. I never handed money over to them on any regular basis.

My mother had a good friend by the name of Martha Benge who had grown up with my mother. She was a rather enterprising young woman. She had left Clay County and had become an expert secretary stenographer. She could teach business school and she also was an expert cook. She was in the process at that time of writing a cookbook. She was in Manchester the summer I graduated from high school and she told my mother she was going to teach a class in shorthand and typing and I could come for free if I wanted to. So I did for about three months. She had about ten students. I learned to type and learned to take Gregg shorthand. I got good enough that I was permitted to take depositions for some of the lawyers. We were very short on court reporters. . . .

Miss Martha decided that I had to go to college. She was an enterprising lady with a lot of imagination. Many times her imagination got ahead of her practicality and her plans didn't always work out. She told me and my parents around Christmas 1928 that she would get a job for me with a coal company in Williamsburg, where Cumberland College was located. I would be a clerk typist at the coal company and go to school at Cumberland College. So I took her at her word. I had always had a restless feeling that I needed to

The Preparation

do something, though I didn't know what. I knew I didn't want to stay around Manchester and play pool all my life.

So Miss Martha and my parents put me on a Greyhound bus with a paper box full of clothes. I remember I got sick on the bus because of the curvy roads. It wasn't a very auspicious start. I was very relieved when the bus finally got to Williamsburg. So I went to Cumberland College and registered for the second semester in January 1929. I didn't have any money to pay them, but I told them I had some plans to work. I think Miss Martha had arranged for me to have a job at the college and that turned out to be sweeping classrooms and firing the dormitory furnace. . . . In a day or two I went down to this coal company she had told me about. I told them I was ready to report to work. It was very apparent that they had never heard of me and didn't want to hear about me. It wasn't easy to get in to see the boss and when I did, there just wasn't any job there. If Miss Martha had talked to them, they had forgotten, so they said. So I had no job [at the coal company].

The next day I went to see the president of the college, J.L. Creech. . . . I told him my problem. My college job did not pay enough—less than twenty dollars a month. Dr. Creech wrinkled his brow, scratched his head—he just didn't know. Then he said, "I want you to write something—two or three sentences on a piece of paper." He told me what to write and I wrote it. I've forgotten what it was. He said, "We do have a little fund here which occasionally is available as a loan to a student. I think that you are eligible for that loan." I learned later that he put great faith in handwriting. He thought handwriting revealed the personality of your character. Apparently my handwriting passed the test and he decided that I was honest and deserving. The loan was $100. I borrowed the money and finished the semester. It was understood I would pay the loan with interest after I got a paying job somewhere. I paid the loan after I began working for the Highway Department in Frankfort.

For the next year, after working that summer for Dr. Porter, I got another loan from First State Bank president Bige Hensley to return to Cumberland College. They called him Bullet Head Hensley. He loaned me $100 on the condition that my uncle, Preston J. Jones, co-sign the note. Uncle Pete was a country doctor at Oneida. He signed the note and I made that $100, with what little I had saved, stretch through the next year.

I went three semesters at Cumberland College altogether. I didn't graduate. The following summer of 1930 I worked for the

Highway Department. My father was one of the few Democrats in Clay County, but about that time, with Flem Sampson governor, the Democrats passed a ripper bill taking the Highway Department away from the governor. Mr. Ben Johnson was chairman of the Highway Department and along with Lieutenant Governor James Breathitt and Dan Talbott established a three-man Highway Commission. My father took me to Frankfort in an old Chevrolet car driven by a friend. He managed to get me a job at the Highway Department. I learned later that Zach Justice, highway commissioner from Pikeville, had gone to school at the University of Kentucky and had taken Latin under my uncle, T.T. Jones, my mother's oldest brother. Zach Justice voted to give me a . . . job at Frankfort as a clerk-typist in the equipment department of the Highway Department.

It was supposed to be a permanent job but it was generally understood between me and my parents, particularly my mother, that I would only work there long enough to get money to go back to school. That was the blackest part of the Depression and money was precious. So $125 per month wasn't the worst job in the world. I later got up to $150 a month and then they had an economy move and cut me back to $125. I stayed there. I liked it. I was young and single. Frankfort was a good place for a young fellow to have a pretty good time—nothing extravagant. . . .

I didn't have any particular ambitions but I had a nagging feeling that this was not what I wanted to do the rest of my life. I knew that I ought to do something. About that time the National Youth Administration developed. It provided small jobs for college students and my Uncle T.T. [Jones] at UK was in charge of the NYA there. Uncle T.T. told my mother to send me to the university and he would give me one of the NYA jobs so I could finish college. So in the fall of 1934 I resigned from the Highway Department. . . .

Again, my job at UK didn't quite pan out. I only made $18 a month. So I went to see Mrs. Crutcher, resident manager of Kinkead and Bradley halls. She had an apartment at Kinkead. They needed someone to sit in the office, take phone calls, and handle laundry left by students. So Mrs. Crutcher gave me this job. The two jobs allowed me to survive.

By that time I had decided I wanted to go to law school. I was always fascinated watching lawyers in the courtrooms. Practically everybody said, "You're making a mistake. You're not cut out for a lawyer. You're not flamboyant enough." . . .

The Preparation

I had to make up a semester because at that time it took two years of college to get into law school. The first semester I was in the arts and science college and then began law school at midterm—early 1935. Very often when on duty at the dormitory I could study in between phone calls and laundry calls. I did well in the first semester of law school. Later, I got a job in the law library returning books to shelves.

The next summer I worked for the Highway Department again during the Tom Rhea-A.B. Chandler conflict. I worked on highway construction between Manchester and Hyden. I lived in a construction dormitory at Big Creek. Then I went back to UK and graduated in 1937 in the same class with Garvice Kincaid and Bob Hensley. Jobs were hard to come by. There wasn't any great demand for young lawyers. I probably could have gotten some kind of job with state government, but I went back to Manchester and got married about the same time.

Robert Lee "Slick" Combs Since our mother was a school teacher she made available reading material and we always had newspapers. . . . She read to us. Most all other families didn't have that opportunity. . . . We had to study some, not a great deal, because they didn't give much homework at that time. There was general reading and mother was a reader herself. She subscribed to the *Ladies' Home Journal*. She enjoyed reading.

We were very much a political minority in Clay County. I'd say about one hundred to one, maybe not quite that much. You didn't have to register then. . . . The hottest political races we had then were school board elections. Dad was in state politics. . . . Bert didn't seem to be interested whatsoever. He was more interested in school, reading. . . . He read more than the rest of us. He was just, especially back then, more serious-minded than I was and less interested in athletics. I played baseball and basketball. He went in for tennis. He was high school champion in his senior year and I was champion in my senior year.

Sara Combs Kaufman Mother had been a school teacher and we always read and were interested in books and magazines and that sort of thing. I recall that Bobby, the youngest sister, learned to read before she went to school and I believe went to school when she was five. . . .

We always had books to read. I can't recall where mother would get them. She subscribed to the better magazines and I'm sure that they were exchanged among friends and the family. There were always books. She would read to us as I remember—*Uncle Tom's Cabin*. We were always anticipating what was going to happen in the next chapter.

We had a radio early, I suppose, for that section. I remember at one time when we didn't have a radio a friend of daddy's had one and it might be on the weekend he'd take us over to listen. . . . I would say radio was big in that I always remember my father listening to the news. One of the first things I remember was Nashville music, which I didn't care for especially. But then after that I think the news was always time for listening at home. And the newspaper was most important in our house—the *Courier-Journal*. I recall mother telling me that her father—they lived at Beech Creek in a remote section—received the *Courier-Journal* once a week. It was her job to read it to them. She could still recall speeches and such things that she had read. This was years later.

I really have to say that all of us thought Bert was shy and withdrawn. If anyone had ever asked us, would Bert go into politics, we would have said no. . . .

Bobby Combs Rehm All of us had a good relationship with each other and with our parents. I think what probably had the most bearing on that was that we must have had an exceptionally intelligent, well-adjusted mother. Whatever that I thought was irresponsible was in our father. He was really one who made a lot of money but he was always giving it to someone else all the time rather than his own family. We really thought we could rely on our mother.

At the dinner table there was never small talk or petty talk. It was always world events or some international events. To this day if I don't read the *Courier* and listen to the news I feel like I haven't lived.

Polly Gorman (Interview 1) I worked for the Highway Department in Frankfort in June of 1933 and Bert was in the office. He and I were on the same assignment. We tabulated bids for heavy equipment for the Highway Department. Being new in town, I didn't know anybody and a very few days after that he introduced me to . . . Bob Gorman, who became my husband later. . . . Bob and Bert were great tennis players and I guess I watched more tennis that summer than I had ever watched before in my life.

The Preparation

Another thing we did a great deal was—Bob had a canoe and we ate more hot dogs on the Kentucky River bank than I cared to eat. I almost died of malnutrition. Canoeing was a popular recreation in Frankfort and if you had a canoe it was almost . . . . Bob also had a car, and Bert didn't have a car at the time. So Bob supplied the transportation to and from places and we remained very close friends.

Bert was going with one of my best friends at that time . . . Helena Levins from Williamsburg. . . . Bert and Helena went together all that year or year and a half. There was *The Summer Girl*, a riverboat that plied the Kentucky River. It was quite large and they brought musicians and there was dancing on *The Summer Girl* and that's something else that we did for recreation during those times. It was really a pretty happy time.

Law Practice and War

Bert Combs began his law practice in the midst of the Great Depression, and Clay County, where he had not lived for nearly ten years, offered little opportunity and less challenge than he may have anticipated. It also might have seemed less exciting to someone who had been out in the world of Frankfort and Lexington.

Consequently, an offer to join a firm in Prestonsburg was appealing. It enabled Mabel to be closer to her original home in Knott County and it provided Bert with a chance to work with leading Eastern Kentucky attorneys. There he gained practical experience with coal mine injury cases, established himself in community circles, and began to build a practice. He was not wealthy, but for the first time was in a position to save some money and look to a more prosperous future. In addition, he found himself more and more assured that law was an appropriate career for him.

Like many people in America at that time he was not disturbed mightily by the onrush of war in Europe. Eastern Kentucky was not a region where the "Great Debate" between isolationists and internationalists stirred strident controversy. Yet when war came to the United States, Combs, who was thirty years old, decided to forego selective service and to volunteer for service in the army. Eventually his educational background enabled him to earn a commission in the Judge Advocate General Branch and after a stint at Fort Knox, Kentucky, he journeyed to the Far East where he helped prepare evidence for the trials of Japanese war criminals.

Bert Combs (Interview 2) I had two possible courses of action when I graduated from law school in 1937. I could have come to Frankfort with some sort of a clerical attorney position. Dr. James Martin was revenue commissioner at the time. He had undertaken to bring some young people into state government, presumably young people with some potential. . . . The other opportunity I had was to go back to Clay County because I wanted to see what the law practice was like. In law school you had a difficult time visualizing what a young lawyer would do on his own in a small town, or a larger town for that matter. My father and mother and most of my brothers and sisters were still in Manchester. So I went back and started to practice law. . . .

After about a year I was invited to come to Prestonsburg to practice law with LeRoy Combs—no relation, but I had known him in law school. His father and his uncle had a partnership in Prestonsburg—Combs and Combs. I would say they were the two leading civil lawyers in Prestonsburg. They represented a number of corporations. I had the opportunity to go there and practice with LeRoy Combs. We had offices adjoining the two elder Combses'. We were not strictly partners with them. LeRoy and I were partners. We got the things that they really didn't want to handle or couldn't handle for one reason or another.

My wife wanted to go to Prestonsburg because that was close to Knott County where she had been born and raised. That was a little like going home to her. So we moved to Prestonsburg in 1938. We rented a house. Rent was pretty cheap. We were saving a nest egg to buy a house later, which we did. We bought a lot and built a house.

After Pearl Harbor I started thinking about going to the army. I was married, of course, but we had no children. I had made up my mind that I would feel better if I went ahead. I don't know if I would ever have been drafted. It was a possibility. I believe the fall of 1942 I went into the army in a program called the Volunteer Officer Candidate Program. The theory was that we would go into the army as a private, would be treated as a private, but after you had your basic training you would have an opportunity to go to Officer Candidate School. If you didn't go to Officer Candidate School, you could come back home and take your chances on being drafted. So I went into the army under that program and I was sent to Aberdeen, Maryland, for basic training. It was the biggest ordnance camp in the country. Actually I had no talent for ordnance. I still have no mechanical talents. Why they sent me there, I don't know. I guess they just needed some bodies in that department. . . .

I did not want to go to ordnance OCS. I had serious doubt I could pass, having no ability in that field and no interest. I did not come back home either, as I could have. I stayed on and later—1943—I had the opportunity to go to OCS at Ann Arbor, Michigan, for the Judge Advocate General [Branch]. I appeared before that board, filled out some forms, and was admitted. I was in that school about three months and graduated a second lieutenant and was assigned to Fort Knox, which was my first choice. It was a convenient place for me because my wife was then in Lexington.

Polly Gorman (Interview 1) Both Bob and Bert were in World War II and it so happened that although Bob was just an enlisted man and Bert was in the adjutant general's office they were both stationed at Fort Knox. . . . So Bert was living in Lexington with Mabel and [their daughter] Lois. I really don't know if they owned a house over there at the time or not. He came home every weekend from Fort Knox. At the time, Bob didn't have a car so [Bert] stopped off every Sunday night and picked him up, after he had left him off on Friday night, to take him back to Fort Knox. That went on the whole spring of that year. I can remember very well that Bert had gotten his assignment overseas and he was going to leave in May 1945. Mabel was quite upset that he'd gotten assigned overseas. He said, "Well, to tell you the truth, I think she wishes I'd gotten out three months ago because she just found out that she's pregnant." It turned out Bob also got assigned overseas. I believe he went before Bert did. Bob went to England. So they parted ways at that time.

Bert Combs (Interview 2) I stayed at Fort Knox as a JAG officer until 1945. By that time I was a first lieutenant. I was sent to the Philippine Islands as part of a war crimes team. When we got to the Philippines, MacArthur had returned and had landed at Leyte. There was still fighting in P.I. but not in Manila where I was sent. I was one of a team of eight lawyers. MacArthur had set up a War Crimes Department already. It was our task to go out in the field to the prison camps. There were some infamous prison camps in and around Manila.

We interviewed ex-prisoners, Filipinos, Chinese—anyone we heard about having any knowledge of Japanese war crimes. By use of an interpreter we would take statements from these witnesses and make a file. This material was later used for trial of Japanese war criminals.

Judge

Discharged in 1946, Combs returned to Prestonsburg to resume his law practice. He not only continued coal mine company litigation, but became moderately active in politics, particularly at the local level. He and Mabel built their long saved-for dream home, large enough to accommodate their two small children, Lois and Tommy. Combs's work required considerable travel, not only to Eastern Kentucky communities, but also to Frankfort, Lexington, and Huntington, West Virginia. His contacts in the legal profession broadened to include more and more people outside the confines of Prestonsburg.

Among these contacts were members of the Kentucky Court of Appeals, especially chief judge J.W. Cammack. Thus when Court of appeals judge Roy Helm of Hazard died in 1950, Cammack urged Combs to accept appointment as his replacement. Governor Lawrence Wetherby had indicated he would appoint to the court whomever members of the court desired, so Combs had to make a decision that clearly would change his life. Not only would it require him to accept a salary far smaller than his income at the time, it would necessitate moving from Prestonsburg to the Frankfort area. It was not an easy decision. Once made, however, Combs gave himself fully to the job, gaining additional respect from his judicial colleagues and added recognition from others in Frankfort. He and his family eventually settled in Lexington, after Combs won election to the position in 1951.

Bert Combs (Interview 2)   In the spring of 1946 I was discharged from the army and I came back to Lexington where my wife was. I was discharged at Camp Atterbury, Indiana. In the meantime, we had a family of two. While I was at Aberdeen my wife came there and stayed for several months. The oldest child was conceived there and born in 1943. We had a little girl and a little boy and so I went back, after a few weeks' looking around and trying to get my feet on the ground, to Prestonsburg. . . .

About the time I went into the army J. Woodford Howard [a civil lawyer in Prestonsburg] had said to me that when I came back from the army he would like to talk to me about coming in with

The Preparation

him. So when I got back to Prestonsburg I formed a limited partnership with him. It was a limited partnership—I didn't make as much money as he did. He had two good clients—two big coal companies that he treated as his personal clients. We split everything else, as I recall.

In his younger days Howard was in the state Senate and lost the lieutenant governor nomination to A.B. Chandler in 1931. Howard was the clear favorite when the Lexington convention started but something happened to keep him from getting it. Howard got out of politics and came to Prestonsburg to practice law.

In 1948 Jack [Howard] and I became full partners. Our offices were on Main Street about two blocks from the courthouse. I practiced all kinds of law. I chased around, took the depositions, really just did much of the leg work. I enjoyed the law practice. Jack was older, pretty much of a home body, did not like to travel much. He did the briefing and the pleading. I traveled to Lexington frequently, Louisville occasionally, Huntington, West Virginia.

Carl Perkins was practicing law in Knott County. His main practice was workmen's compensation. He was catering to the miners and I was lawyer for the coal companies. We were adversaries but good friends. Carl would get a man who claimed he was injured. He had a favorite doctor in Huntington, Dr. Henry D. Hatfield, former governor of West Virginia and former United States senator. Carl always wanted to take Dr. Hatfield's deposition. I used to kid him about having Dr. Hatfield on a contingent-fee basis. He was paid depending on how much disability he gave a man. That was, of course, a bit facetious. [Carl] had [another] one in Hazard by the name of Dr. Coldiron. I remember Dr. Coldiron had a stock phrase for patients. They were usually coal miners with back injuries. It so happened that a back injury is the hardest to diagnose and certainly to evaluate. Dr. Coldiron would end up by saying his patient had a "great limitation of his active and passive motions."

The city of Prestonsburg wanted to extend its boundaries so as to bring in more property for taxation to have enough for a fire department and a police department. I had purchased a lot right by the bridge as you come out of Prestonsburg going north, so I was the last house on that end of town. They persuaded me to be city attorney to handle annexation proceedings. Since I was the last house and I was willing to come in, it gave us a little argument to say the city attorney is bringing himself in. I didn't receive any compensation for that important assignment.

Then there was a vacancy in the commonwealth attorney's office in 1950. The Democrats couldn't agree on who ought to be commonwealth attorney. Somebody suggested me as a compromise. I said I would accept the appointment but I would also announce I would not run for election. Those who had an ambition to be commonwealth attorney could get squared away and run for it. I became commonwealth attorney. Governor Wetherby appointed me.

I had a little bit of closeness to politics prior to that time. Earle Clements and Jack Howard were good personal friends. They had played football at UK back in the 1920s. So when Earle Clements got ready to run for governor he came to see Jack Howard. I remember Jack had Clements to his house for lunch and invited me. We talked politics, mostly about what could happen in Floyd County. Then, too, I still had family and friends in Clay County and Earle was a meticulous fellow who found out I had those connections. He asked me to help him in Clay County. Clements then later appointed me to the Judicial Council, a group of about eight or ten prominent lawyers, to advise about amending or rewriting the Constitution, plus what could be done about the court system.

Lois Combs Weinberg I guess one of the first things I remember about my dad was when I was around five years old my dog got run over and the next morning before I got out of bed there was a new puppy in a box set beside the bed just waiting for me and my brother to get up. He's always been a very busy man, very work-oriented so that like a lot of other fathers he's an absentee father . . . in many respects. He was always there for the important times, like when it was time to get up in his lap and learn how to read the funny papers. Those are pretty important things. He was gone a lot of the time. There were a lot of family outings, going with him to visit older people, particularly at Christmas and on Sundays.

Bert Combs (Interview 2) Judge Roy Helm died in 1951. He was Court of Appeals judge from the Seventh Judicial District. He lived in Hazard. He was a very high-class individual, a very learned judge who had been at Oxford on a Rhodes scholarship. He was not the most practical fellow in the world. I admired him and I think he liked me.

The funeral was in Frankfort. I came to the funeral. Judge James Cammack, chief judge, asked me to come by his office after the funeral. So I went. He said to me, "I have talked with Governor

Wetherby and he has said he will appoint to succeed Judge Helm the person that the Court of Appeals wants appointed. I think that you ought to succeed Judge Helm and I think that I could get the court to go along. I just want your permission."

It really came as a surprise. I was making a fair living and had some prospects in the law business at that time. I was making about $20,000 or $25,000 a year. We had just finished building a house. My children were young. I told him I didn't think I could afford to take it financially. It only paid $5,000. I always remember what he said to me—"Well, you've been chasing around here saying that Eastern Kentucky hasn't received enough attention. State government ought to be better to Eastern Kentucky. Now is the time to put up or shut up. If you take this appointment you might be able to help those people in Eastern Kentucky. You say you can't afford it. But I say to you, you can't afford not to." I said, "Well, I'll let you know," and I went back home. I had never even thought about public office. I was more interested in trying to get established to make a living. I had never had any money. I hadn't made any money in the army or before I went to the army. So that was all I had in mind at the time.

I went back to Prestonsburg. In the meantime I learned that many people had thought that Jack Howard would be offered this appointment and conceivably he might take it because Jack was in much better financial condition than I was. I talked to Jack and asked him if he had heard anything about him becoming judge of the Court of Appeals. He said there had been a little talk about it, but he said, "I wouldn't have it. I can't live on $5,000 a year. I'd have to go to Frankfort. I'd have to run again." Jack assured me he had no intention of considering it if it were offered. Then I told him about the conversation with Judge Cammack. I guess the same day I called Judge Cammack and told him about rumors concerning Howard. Cammack said Jack was a good fellow, but the court needed a younger fellow who would do some work.

So I thought about it some more. I talked to my wife about it. I would say she was rather noncommittal. I had no preconceived notions about running for the position. I had an open mind about that. I told Judge Cammack I would run for reelection if it looked like I could win. I didn't want to be committed to running unless I thought it was feasible. Jack Howard started arguing that I shouldn't take it either when he saw I might be offered the job. He offered a lot of reasons why I shouldn't take it. I agonized over it a little but I kept thinking about what Jim Cammack had said. I had with Clements, with Perkins, and with Wetherby complained about the neglect of Eastern Kentucky. Eastern Kentuckians have almost a phobia—did in those days—about being completely overlooked and not considered as part of the commonwealth. Thus I decided to take it if it was offered.

I went to the court and came back to Prestonsburg on weekends for several months. It took five hours to get from Frankfort to Prestonsburg. Then we moved to Lexington and rented a house in Lexington. We rented the home in Prestonsburg for several years. We rented a house in Lexington on Louisiana Street. I drove to and from Frankfort every day.

Within a year Simeon Willis announced for the unexpired term of Judge Helm on both tickets. This shocked me because his prominence as a Republican would make this a partisan issue. The Wetherby people and some of the court said, "You'll just have to run," and I did.

The election was at the same time Wetherby was running for governor. In the primary I won the Democratic nomination and Willis won the Republican. I wasn't on the Republican ticket, but he was on both. He got a substantial number of Democratic votes but I won by a comfortable margin on the Democratic ticket. I really worked hard in the campaign. I'm sure I saw a lot more people and got on more radio stations and appeared at more Kiwanis Clubs than did Willis. Then, too, some members of the court preferred me because Judge Willis at that time was sixty-eight and they calculated out that with an eight-year term he would have been seventy-six by the time his term expired. Although they considered him an able man, a good judge, they wanted a younger fellow. He was not a wealthy man, and his family wanted him to come back to Frankfort. . . .

Willis may have been a little complacent about the election. He had been judge and he had been governor and I had been nothing except city attorney. I had a little advantage in that I had formerly lived in Clay County—a big Republican county—and had a lot of kinfolks. My mother was a Jones and there were a lot of Joneses in Clay County. Not many people thought I would win. They just assumed that a former governor and a former judge would win. People get that fixation. It's wrong. . . .

The election attracted some attention statewide because a former governor had been defeated by a young nobody. So I acquired an undeserved reputation for being a good candidate. My father was never too enthused about my political career. He always took it with a grain of salt. He couldn't understand it. He didn't consider me as any kind of politician. In his book I wasn't. He was Democratic county chairman of Clay County for a long time. He would help election officers and I never had the slightest interest in that sort of thing.

Lawrence Wetherby   I met Bert Combs when I was running for lieutenant governor in 1947. I visited in . . . Prestonsburg where he was then living and I met Bert at that time and he helped me in my campaign. I think shortly after that he became city attorney and then subsequent to that I appointed him commonwealth attorney. He was very much interested in all the political campaigns. He helped me in my fall campaign when I was running for lieutenant governor in that part of the state. Later I appointed him to fill out an unexpired term on the court and then he ran for a full term. That's when he ran against Simeon Willis. These campaigns required quite a bit of electioneering. As a matter of fact, I remember his campaign for the Court of Appeals very well because it got to be quite a rigorous campaign. I was running for governor at the time and we were appearing together all through that district. That was the regular election in 1951. At that time the judges ran on a partisan ticket. Bert was running as a Democrat on the same ticket I was running for governor.

Lois Combs Weinberg   After he was on the court he lived in Frankfort for a year before we moved down as a family. That was mainly due to the fact that he and Mother had just finished building *the* house they had saved for fifteen years for. . . . As I sort of remember it, that was the reason Mother and we children stayed in Prestonsburg for that year. The next summer we moved to Lexington. But he commuted on weekends. There was a tremendous amount of work on the court. In those days the backlog was just astounding and they worked long hours. There was very little social activity.

Robert Lee "Slick" Combs   Bert didn't know much about politics and politicians. Uncle Herb Smith was the political boss in his district at that time. Of course, I'd known Uncle Herb; he owned a third interest in the coal company I worked for in Harlan. He and I were in politics and business, very close. Governor Wetherby called Uncle Herb in and [said], "Uncle Herb, I'd like to talk to you about appointing a young lawyer named Combs over at Prestonsburg to the Court of Appeals." Uncle Herb [said], "Well, Governor, give me a few days to think about that because most of the Combses over at Prestonsburg are Republicans." Wetherby had Captain Preston of the state police with him and Uncle Herb still had his hand on the knob of the door when Captain Preston said, "Uncle Herb, don't you know who Bert Combs is?" "No, I never heard of him," he said. "Why, he's Slick's brother." He never did turn the door knob loose. He just opened the door and said, "Governor, I've already completed my investigation. I'm for him 100 percent." That's to show you how much Bert was known. He was known in Clay County but not well. He ran later and beat ex-Governor Willis.

John Y. Brown, Sr. If it hadn't been for me you'd probably never [have] heard of Bert Combs because the first job he ever held was the Court of Appeals of Kentucky and I was attorney for the mineworkers. I organized that district for him. I had the miners' money and I believe he's the first Democrat [who] ever carried the district. The reason he carried it was not because of the overwhelming popularity of Bert [but] because I was the attorney for the mineworkers and I picked . . . one miner in every mining camp [who] was a member of a big Republican family and I put him on the miners' payroll for maybe a week or maybe a month before the election. It depended on how big the local was. And all he had to do was go ask the members of his family to vote the straight Republican ticket except the union wanted Bert Combs. He carried Johnson County and it had never gone Democratic up to then. We carried Letcher and Perry [counties, which] had rarely ever gone Democratic—and carried them by big majorities because all the miners scratched for Bert.

Arthur Lloyd My first real association with Bert Combs came from the standpoint of seeing him rather frequently when he came down to Frankfort after the war as a judge on the appellate court. . . . He was a very good judge—good judicial temperament, very calm, very intelligent in his approach to judicial cases. I always felt like he much preferred being a judge. I got to know him fairly well on the court because at that time I was the first director of the

The Preparation

Legislative Research Commission. Our offices were on the same floor of the capitol—the second floor. . . .

I believe Bert lived in Lexington when he was on the court. His daughter Lois and my daughter Libby were about the same age. They were enrolled in the same dancing class in Lexington. I'd come over and pick up my daughter and I usually found Bert there waiting for his daughter. Frequently we sat up in the balcony and talked about government, politics, and things like that. If you brought [the girls to class], there was no point in going back home again. You might as well sit there and wait until they were through. That's where I got to know Bert better than any other place.

Jo Ferguson I had known Bert Combs from my school days. He probably wouldn't have remembered me. I was a first-year man in law school when he was a third-year man. I remember him as being one of the two top men in the class then. As usual, you remember the fellows above you and they don't always remember you. . . . [H]e and John L. Davis had been the two leading students in that . . . class. Then in 1948 when I went to Frankfort as an assistant attorney general . . . my wife . . . became very friendly with Bert Combs's youngest sister . . . Bobby. . . . [S]he was married to a young lawyer named Paul Rehm and he was assistant treasurer at the time. So my wife and Bobby became very good friends and we got to know all the Combs family then. We would see them and we knew Bert's mother, who was a very beautiful and lovely woman. And I knew his father slightly. His father was kind of an old country politician. But I think the mother had been the strong factor in the family. . . .

[After Bert was on the Court of Appeals] I came to know him fairly well. I was an assistant attorney general, but I was first assistant by that time and so I had a very close relationship with the Court of Appeals. I knew all the judges very well. Combs, of course, began to develop a tremendous reputation as a judge. He was a very good lawyer, extremely intelligent man, certainly one of the best lawyers in the state now. Already he was beginning to be recognized in the early 1950s. He became a judge's judge. The other judges admired him.

Polly Gorman (Interview 1) While on the court Bert stayed in Frankfort. He just had a room—a place on Shelby Street. He would come over and have dinner with us and that kind of thing. I remember my son, Chris, who was a very small boy at the time and is now a lawyer in Louisville. Bert has always been his idol. But it began when he was a Cub Scout and Bert was living on Shelby Street and Chris went over there and timidly knocked on Judge Combs's door and asked him to buy something the Scouts were selling. Chris came home and said, "You know he bought everything I had to sell." So that endeared him for life.

[Bert] liked being on the Court of Appeals very much. But he said he had a really hard time making up his mind to run after his appointment was over. He said, "Well, there's one thing for sure. If I run and get beat, then I'll know it's not for me." He had a dry sense of humor. I really think the original appointment came as a surprise to him. But he really enjoyed being on the court. I know that.

Cattie Lou Miller I came to know Judge Combs while he was a judge on the Court of Appeals. He and Governor Wetherby had a very high regard for each other. . . . Wetherby was and is a man of very high morals, tremendous integrity, and his appointments were people of very excellent caliber. So the mere fact that he appointed Judge Combs said a lot to me about Judge Combs. While [members of] the court then operated in a somewhat inaccessible fashion in that they did not mix and mingle with Frankfort in any political sense publicly, we still were in the same building . . . and we . . . were aware of his good work on the court.

June Taylor I believe I knew Judge Combs first around 1954 when he became a judge on the Court of Appeals. I recall thinking that he was a very deep thinker and really a little difficult to know at first except on a one-to-one basis. In a small crowd he really did outshine everyone, but when he was in a large crowd sometimes he was more hesitant to talk. If he were in a room with several who might be working at the capitol then he seemed to come forth as a shining person with a good personality. When he would get with a larger crowd, maybe a dinner crowd, he seemed to be shy.

Earl Powell I really got to know him personally and individually when he came to the Kentucky Court of Appeals. He was . . . in the same building . . . [and] I got to see him just daily whether at a coffee stand, at lunch, or just encountering him in the corridors. . . .

He struck me as what a judge ought to be. Some judges would ask more questions maybe than he did. Judges are just like people. Some people ask questions but really don't want an answer. They don't really care. They just want everybody to know they're there, that they are participating. I get the feeling that he didn't do that. If he asked something he was trying to draw them out, trying to find out something—not just wanting to be seen or heard.

Chapter 2

The 1955 Gubernatorial Primary: Political Baptism

The Selection

Whether Combs was content to pursue a judicial career for the rest of his life is not clear. He probably did not know, himself. Once again, however, circumstances outside his control provided him with an unsolicited opportunity that would change his life more profoundly than anything before.

Following the end of World War II Kentucky's Democratic party resumed its dominance in state politics. Deep divisions in the Democratic party had helped propel Republicans led by Governor Simeon Willis into leadership during the war period. But the Republicans themselves, once in authority, suffered from the same malady. At the same time the Democrats recognized the serious consequences of their division and worked to reestablish unity.

In 1947 two relatively new leaders emerged and competed for the Democratic gubernatorial nomination. Harry Lee Waterfield had been in the legislature since 1937 and was Speaker of the Kentucky House of Representatives. Earle Clements had been the state Senate leader during the early Willis administration and had gone to the U.S. Congress in 1944. Clements won the nomination in 1947, but the important thing about the primary was the relative absence of vituperative divisiveness on the part of either candidate. The factionalism of the past was apparently at an end. Earle Clements was in control of a united Democratic party.

When Clements went to the United States Senate in 1950 to occupy the seat long held by Alben Barkley, Lieutenant Governor

The 1955 Gubernatorial Primary

Lawrence Wetherby moved up to assume command of Clements's state organization. Wetherby's election in his own right a year later seemed to confirm continued party solidarity, but there was a dark cloud on the horizon. A.B. "Happy" Chandler was back in town. Chandler, who had resigned his United States Senate seat in 1945 to become National Commissioner of Baseball, failed to win reappointment by team owners in mid-1951. Always confident he possessed presidential potential, Chandler turned his attention to the rebuilding of a political base in Kentucky. The Clements-Wetherby organization, however, was already organized for 1951, so Chandler shifted his focus to 1955.

In effect, he started campaigning immediately after Wetherby's term began. To win he had to break up the existing organization. Hence factional division reasserted itself, highlighted by the incomparable personable charm and vote-getting power that Chandler could provide. Everyone knew that the Wetherby administration would support someone other than Chandler, but no one knew who it would be for a very long time.

Complicating the process was the importance attached to the 1954 senatorial race in Kentucky. At stake was control of the United States Senate by one party or the other in the midst of the first Dwight Eisenhower administration. Extremely popular John Sherman Cooper was the Republican candidate for reelection to a full term. Without too much difficulty the Wetherby administration persuaded Alben Barkley to come out of retirement to challenge. But Wetherby determined that a unified Democratic effort would be necessary to success. Hence, no administration candidate received the governor's endorsement prior to the end of the election. As a result the party was unified and Barkley won by a substantial margin.

That was the situation in late 1954 when Governor Wetherby, Lieutenant Governor Emerson "Doc" Beauchamp, and Senator Earle Clements, by that time assistant majority leader, met at the governor's mansion to determine who would be most capable of confronting Chandler's challenge. After a long discussion they decided upon Bert Combs. Once again Combs had a momentous decision to make.

Bert Combs (Interview 2)   I stayed on the court until the next governor's race. Wetherby was looking for someone to run against Happy Chandler. Happy was already an announced candidate. They

[Democratic party leaders] talked Chandler out of running against Wetherby in 1951 so it was apparent they would not be for Chandler in 1955. . . .

I was at my home in Lexington one evening, I believe it was [a] Friday night in December. I was reading a book or working on a lawsuit or something. I got this call from Governor Wetherby. He said Senator Clements, Doc Beauchamp, and he were at the [governor's] mansion. "Could you come over and talk with us?" Naturally I said yes. . . . This would have been eight or nine o'clock in the evening. So I get on to Frankfort and I go to the mansion. Wetherby and Clements and Beauchamp were sitting at a temporary table, probably a card table. . . . They said they wanted to talk to me about the governor's race. "We've talked about a lot of people. There are a lot of good people, but the main thing is to win. We've decided we would be for you. Will you run?"

I really was flabbergasted. Everybody says that but it happened to be true. I had assumed it would be one of the people [within the administration]. The only person who had ever mentioned it to me was Acree Austin, clerk of the Court of Appeals. Acree was a western Kentuckian, likable, active fellow. We had got to be pretty good friends. Acree had said to me somewhere along the line, "These fellows might just pick you." I sort of brushed it off. I had not thought there was any possibility. I thought there was a possibility that they might suggest that I run for lieutenant governor. And I thought about that going over there. I knew that the time was ripe for them to make a decision. I knew Earle Clements was in Frankfort because I had seen him in the cafeteria. So I tried to conjure up alternatives. I finally decided they might want me to run for lieutenant governor.

I said, "I just can't see myself as governor." Clements said, "I'll say to you my friend"—that was one of his favorite expressions—"nobody looks like a governor until he becomes a governor." Then I pointed out that I did have a handicapped child, Tommy, and I would not want to do anything that would interfere with his happiness and well-being. I remember Lawrence saying, "You can do a hell of a lot more for him as governor than you can not being governor."

I told them, too, that I was about ready to go to Florida. We usually visited my sister and her husband once a year in the winter— Louise Marcum, who is now back in Manchester. They said, "How long will it take you to make up your mind?" I said, "Will you give me three days?" They said all right. "You can go back and talk to Mabel about it and anyone else you want to. Then call Lawrence [Wetherby]." Clements said later, "We didn't have any doubt about it. We knew you would take it." But I didn't know for certain that I would want to run, mainly because I didn't think I could win. I didn't think anybody could beat Happy. That was a big deterrent.

But I went back and talked to my wife about it. I talked to my uncle at the university about it, T.T. Jones. Uncle T.T. said, "Why would those people be for you?" He really didn't quite believe it. I said that I didn't know but "they are, and will be. If they are, what do you think I ought to do?" I talked to a few other people. I don't recall talking to my father. I guess I did. He was always very noncommittal. In fact, he was that way about most things with his children. I remember after I got to be governor I was having problems with the sales tax and the soldiers' bonus. . . . Somebody asked him about me, "Don't you sympathize with your son with all these problems?" He supposedly said, "Well, hell, he wouldn't have it any other way. He broke his neck trying to get there so now he'll have to live with it."

Within the time frame I called Lawrence Wetherby back and told him that I would run. In the meantime I had told him that I wouldn't feel like running unless Beauchamp assured me that it was all right with him. Beauchamp said "It's all right with me" during the meeting [the one at the governor's mansion in December]. After the meeting was over, Beauchamp and I went out together and we talked some more about it. I said, "Are you sure this is satisfactory with you?" I remember tears came into his eyes. He said, "I'm not going to run." I told them also I had a half-commitment to Louis Cox, and . . . I was also concerned about Jess Lindsay. They said, "We will arrange for that. We will have them tell you that you should run." They did. Each of them called me.

So we went on to Florida and stayed a few days. I came back sometime around the first of the year and I started running as fast as I could.

Lawrence Wetherby There were three of us that worked rather closely in the Democratic party at that time and more or less they called us the kingmakers. Of course we weren't, but we were right close to the organization. That was Senator Clements, Emerson "Doc" Beauchamp, and myself. We all decided that we should get together and support one candidate for governor.

Each of us made a list of the people in the state that we could support. I called a meeting for the three of us at the executive mansion one evening. Beauchamp and Clements and myself were the only people there. We went over our lists and I had Bert at the top of my list. Doc Beauchamp had kind of wanted to run. He was my lieutenant governor. But Clements at that meeting said, "Now, Doc, you have no business running. You've been in too many scraps to run for governor. We just better forget you." I had Beauchamp on my list. But, as I say, I had Bert at the top of it.

We discussed it until late in the evening. We had eaten dinner together and we had discussed it—went over the various names we had on the list. . . . We wrestled around with it until late in the evening. I was plugging for Bert in a big way because I thought he would make an excellent governor. They asked me, "Can he make a speech?" I said, "Well, he made a real good speech when he was campaigning with me at the big labor rally in Pikeville. That's the only speech I've heard him make"—when he was running for judge of the Court of Appeals. I said, "I think he would be all right when he got used to speaking."

We argued around about it for awhile and finally Senator Clements agreed. He said, "If you want to support Bert, do you reckon he'll run?" I said, "Well, let's find out." So I went in and put in a call. I called Bert's secretary on the court to see if she knew where he was. She said he was in Lexington and she gave me a number and I called Bert and asked him if he would come down to the mansion and talk to us. "What about?" and I said, "We have some politicians down here and we want to talk to you."

So Bert came down to the mansion that evening and we asked him if he'd be interested in running for governor. He said he did not know. He had some problems over his boy. And I said, "That's the best place on earth to solve the problem because you'll have all kinds of help taking care of him and everything. You ought to run for governor." Bert said, "Let me wait until the first of the week, and I'll let you all know." This was in December of 1954.

I had three or four people specifically who had talked to me about Bert being a candidate and urging me to get him into the race and to support him for governor. One of them was Judge [J.W.] Cammack, who was on the Court of Appeals. He said Bert Combs was one of the sharpest, smartest fellows he'd ever seen—"He'd make a crackerjack governor." He came to me day after day to talk for Bert. That's one reason I was so sold on promoting Bert for governor. I knew him much better than either Clements or Beauchamp because I had been in close contact with him when I was running for governor and he was running for the Court of Appeals. Then when he was elected and came down here I would see him quite often. I was much closer to him than Clements or Beauchamp at that time.

But after the three of us agreed on Bert and got him to come to the mansion and he agreed to let us know the following week, he was still hesitant when I called him the following week. But he reluctantly said, "Well, I guess I'll do it if you all think I can do it." I don't recall any other problem he brought up except that with his son.

I think it's probably true that he had never thought of making a statewide race and it was sort of a surprise to him when I called him to come down and visit with us. He was characteristically cautious in making up his mind. As I say, after we had all three talked to him they left it in my hands to work with him. He was to let me know, but he didn't call me. I called him. And finally I went to see him. I said, "Now, Bert, you ought to do this. We've all agreed on you. It's hard to get these three fellows to all agree on one person, but we've all agreed on you." Then he went back to his son's problem and I told him, "Over there at the mansion you'd be in better shape to do something for him than any place else in the world. You can make provision for him. Somebody will be there to take care of him." [He said], "Well, I'm just a little reluctant because of the fact you get into a campaign and people will talk about it." As I say, he was rather reluctant, and I had to use a lot of persuasion on him to get him to agree to it.

The three of us were trying to avoid just what we got into—a fight with Happy Chandler. In other words, we wanted our faction all to be together on one person when we realized that the Chandler faction would probably come out with a candidate . . . . We weren't worried about the Republican party at that time. We were worried about our opposing factions.

Robert Lee "Slick" Combs He had always been kind of a quiet lawyer and on the Court of Appeals he was just a student of law. He didn't get himself involved in politics. He told me when he went down there that all he wanted to try to do was make a good judge. He wasn't going to fool with politics. But, he said, he hadn't been there six months that he caught himself with his nose to the ground trying to find out what was going on, with whom, and how, and this and that and the other. I guess it was just in his blood to start with. That was the first time he got involved. This was the time that Governor Wetherby decided that he would support him for governor. I wasn't surprised. A lot of people were.

Ed Farris It's impossible to pinpoint the basic reasons for anything in politics—it's almost impossible. It may be just an old cliché to say that even in those days in the old politics you still wanted intelligent, clean-cut, fresh, appealing candidates. Judge Combs seemed to meet many of those essentials. Also, Kentucky generally, I think on a historical perspective, has some sort of special trust and respect and confidence in people bearing the title "judge." I don't think he was overwhelmingly ambitious at that time to be governor. I certainly think it grew on him. My analysis would be that when it was determined through somewhat of a consensus mechanism that Judge Combs was available [and] would be a good candidate, I think he soon got in harness, so to speak.

Sara Combs Kaufman I was surprised when he ran for governor. I think that perhaps Bert felt that there were lots of things that needed to be done, and that he could be instrumental in at least starting some of those things. I think what surprised me was that he was the person chosen to be the candidate. I would have thought someone who had been active in statewide politics would have been chosen. Governor Wetherby liked Bert and he and Doc Beauchamp were close friends. They had a great affection for one another. Bert called me one day and said to me, "I have been chosen to run," and he said, "Do you know of any reason why I shouldn't?" So I think he felt that the family might be affected. I think he was really sincere in his questions, and I'm sure he was giving it great thought.

Arthur Lloyd I can't answer the question of whether Bert had said anything to anybody about wanting to be governor or not. He never did to me. But I know that the judiciary, particularly the senior members, were highly in favor of it and I think maybe they may have suggested to him that they'd like to see him run and [would support] him. Actually it [his appeal] was from the standpoint of being a young candidate, a young man who had made a quiet but distinguished career in law in Eastern Kentucky. He had good connections. So I think it was a matter of appealing to Democratic votes in Eastern Kentucky. . . . It was Eastern Kentucky's time.

John Ed Pearce I think Bert wanted to run. I don't think there was ever even any doubt in Bert's mind. As Bert said to me years later when I asked him, why did you want to be governor, "I think all of us would like to leave a few tracks around to let people know we've been here." He meant it. He always wanted Kentuckians to know he'd been here.

Ed Prichard I think that he was chosen partly because of the geographical situation. I think that the Clements organization believed that he would hold the line in Eastern Kentucky where Chandler was naturally strong. And I think they felt that he had the sort of reputation for integrity and ability, but not a wide political reputation. The alternatives all involved problems. Doc Beauchamp, who was then lieutenant governor under Wetherby, had some ambitions to run and I think there was a feeling that he would not be as strong a candidate as they would hope for. He had the image of a small-town politician. Some of that might have been an unjust image, but he had it. . . . [T]hey wanted an alternative.

June Taylor I was definitely surprised when he was selected. I had no idea that he would be the candidate. . . . I felt that he had the ability to be governor, but I was surprised that he had quit the judgeship to run. I think his hardest [problem], from my observation, [was that] it was very difficult for him to be a candidate, to really make himself go out and mix with all the people. I know when we had the headquarters at the hotel he would be interested in his research papers or his mail and when we had people come in it was a little difficult for him to say, "Would you vote for me?" He didn't like to tout himself.

The Campaigner

Bert Combs had campaigned for public office only one time prior to 1955—when he defeated former Governor Simeon Willis and won his seat on the Court of Appeals in 1951. Not only was it not a statewide race, it was a judicial contest in which bread and butter issues were nonexistent. Because a former governor had faced off against a rela-

tively unknown lawyer, more than average interest had accompanied the 1951 election, but still its intensity paled before the parallel gubernatorial race.

Combs did, however, achieve a measure of applause from Democrats because he had defeated a former governor. That, plus his excellent record as a prudent, objective, and scholarly judge, suggested to many that he possessed political promise. He was handsome, eloquent in small group conversations, perceptive and incisive. Yet most Frankfort observers were surprised at his selection by Governor Wetherby to run for governor. Democrats outside Eastern Kentucky and Frankfort hardly knew he existed, and Combs, in turn, knew little if anything about western Kentucky and much less about basic problems the commonwealth faced at the time.

Why did Clements, Wetherby, and Beauchamp select him? Simply stated, they did so because they believed he could win. Other possible candidates were so closely tied to the "in" faction that the scars of past political wars made them vulnerable to a challenger with A.B. Chandler's campaign skills.

Combs was a relative newcomer to politics. They reasoned that this could be turned to advantage against the better-known Chandler. Like most personally popular political figures, the former governor–former senator–former baseball commissioner had been involved in a fair share of controversial situations during his career. To be sure, he had a large body of loyal admirers. But a sizable number of people distrusted and disliked him, too. On the other hand, Combs faced no built-in personal animosity. He was popular among his fellow judges on the Court of Appeals and among lawyers in general. He was intelligent, attractive, and respected. In political terminology, he was "clean."

With eight months remaining prior to the primary, Wetherby, Clements, and Beauchamp felt confident they could mold him into a viable political force despite his inexperience. Administration support unquestionably would be a factor in his favor. Not only did Wetherby's backing insure adequate financing for the campaign, but it guaranteed access to key Democratic leaders in the counties and cities of the commonwealth. Equally important, Clements, recognized as the most efficient political organizer of his lifetime, was eager to devote his skills to the cause. Even the regional setup looked good: Beauchamp's political strength lay in southwest Kentucky, Clements hailed from western Kentucky, and Wetherby's base was the metropolitan Louisville-Jefferson County area. Combs, of course, represented Eastern Kentucky.

It would be wrong, however, to assume that only political organization and personalities were important. Economic conditions affecting postwar Kentucky were also vital. The ten years following the end of World War II had produced changes in the attitudes of Kentuckians toward what constituted the good life. Influenced by progressive citizen groups, efforts to improve the health, education, and welfare of people had produced increased government services and prompted hope for more. How to finance these services had become the underlying issue in a state where the tax base had always been low. Not surprisingly, this was a major issue in 1955.

Combs's lack of specific knowledge about Kentucky's problems led to his initial hesitancy to accept the opportunity to run for governor. He discussed the question with Mabel and sought the advice of a long-time confidant, his uncle T.T. Jones of the University of Kentucky. He consulted with other relatives as well, analyzing at every turn the possible consequences of whatever decision he made. Finally, after reassurances from Wetherby that Beauchamp and several other administration Democrats were definitely not interested, he made the commitment. Combs may have appeared reluctant as well as unsure while he pondered his options, but once he decided to go forward he never again equivocated.

What followed was a typical Combs approach to any job or problem. Mindful of his less than prominent image in western and northern Kentucky and his only casual awareness of Kentucky's needs, he set about to overcome these deficiencies. For the first three months of 1955 he talked with many people and read everything he could find about Kentucky, paying particular heed to studies dealing with the state's financial conditions. He traveled to nearly every county and made informal talks to civic organizations and courthouse groups. He also did a lot of listening. He absorbed much about Kentucky and what he discovered eventually formed the basis for carefully reasoned campaign objectives that were revealed in succeeding months. Unfortunately, he did not pick up the techniques of politicking as quickly. By nature not a glad-handing, backslapping, effervescent type, Combs did not seem sufficiently forceful to many of his new acquaintances. Local residents of Paducah, Henderson, Owensboro, Covington, and Newport, hearing for the first time a full-blown mountain twang, were uneasy.

Kentuckians in the 1950s were not adverse to consideration of issues during election campaigns, but they also expected to be entertained and inspired by a candidate's personality and presence. Eight months was a short time in which to develop those skills. Combs did improve, but not enough to be successful.

Bert Combs (Interview 3) I really was not informed about the problems that would face the incoming governor. Particularly, I just knew in a very general way about the financial conditions of the state. Of course, I had seen many of the people who ran state government in the Wetherby administration since my office as a judge was at the state capitol. But I saw them more or less casually, perhaps as a social friend. I thought the first thing I needed to do was to become informed about some of the problems that would face the next governor. I started trying to learn about the condition of the state. I had some general notions about where the state ought to go in things like education, highways and parks, and airports. I had very few specifics. So from January for the next two months I talked with people who I thought were knowledgable about state government [and] read the things that I could lay my hands on that would give me some idea particularly of the financial condition of the state and what it would be during the next governor's term.

Also, I was traveling around the state in different counties. I made most of the counties more or less on an informal basis. I would go into a county and of course somebody from the governor's office, from the Highway Department, whatever, would notify those leaders in the county—political leaders who were favorable to the Wetherby administration—that I would be there on such and such a date. So I made those kinds of visits during early 1955.

I made informal speeches, usually to a small group. They would invite me to a Kiwanis Club, Rotary Club, or maybe just get all the officials [and] assistants in the courthouse together. I would talk to them more or less informally. I was not making speeches as such. I was trying to find out from them what the problems were in that particular area, specifically in that particular county. Usually they didn't have much interest beyond their own county. As you know, one of the problems that Kentucky has, and certainly in my lifetime, is that we have too darn many counties—one hundred and twenty, as you know. I think that's about third in the nation. I would get information from county officials, political officials, as to a particular county. Then, of course, I would attempt to organize that as to a region, particularly to a congressional district. Then, too, I would be telling them something about what I thought the next governor ought to do. I thought I should tell them the kind of governor I wanted to be and what they could expect if I were elected.

I was much more idealistic in those days, if that's the word. I had the belief, and I still have the belief, that anyone running for governor of Kentucky, or any policy-making office for that matter, ought to be intellectually honest enough to tell people what they could expect. It was very apparent that the state was in a precarious financial condition. . . .

I was looking for sources of revenue. Obviously that was perhaps our biggest problem. I made no secret of the fact that I didn't care about being governor unless I could be a progressive governor. I talked to people like Lawrence Wetherby, Earle Clements, Henry Ward, those others who were identified with me in the campaign [and] in my administration. I had no problem about that. Nobody ever said you ought not think about progressive reforms in Kentucky. I think many of them took it with a grain of salt. I think they probably thought, "Well, that's good talk, and that's a good objective and you ought to work toward it, but as you go along practical problems will cause you to rationalize your objectives and you'll get maybe a little something done but not much." I sort of had that impression.

I reminded people in various counties of an old saying in Kentucky—"We're too poor to paint and too proud to whitewash." I would say, "I don't think we're too poor to paint some." Maybe we can't paint everything like we would want to. Kentucky has good people and people who wanted their children to have a better opportunity than they had had. Kentucky ought to go first class. We were not too poor to go first class in many fields—not every field, but certainly some.

I thought that Governor Chandler was not a progressive governor. I didn't mean that as personal criticism of him, but it was a matter of record that Happy Chandler was a great admirer of Harry Byrd. Harry Byrd in Virginia had the slogan "Pay As You Go" and consequently Virginia didn't build highways unless they had the money to build them. They didn't do much about education unless they had the money to do it.

I thought that particularly in the matter of highways that we could afford to borrow money and build a proper highway system and pay for it as we used it. I guess that's when the toll road program emerged in Kentucky. I would talk to them about those kinds of things in a general way. I never did say we will have to have a sales tax. But I did say to them that we have to have new sources of revenue.

Albert B. Chandler If Clements hadn't chosen Combs he couldn't have run. He had no chance to run against me because we had our ducks in a row. I would have won that thing by one hundred thousand or two hundred thousand if he hadn't run. He [Clements] was smart. He picked this boy [Combs]. Nobody knew about him. He was a brand new judge of the Court of Appeals. He was a very personable young fellow. He had that mountain connection. He took thousands of votes away from me. I damn near beat him in Floyd County. I carried four of the five magisterial districts up there. I guarantee I'd have gotten them all if he hadn't been running.

Harry Davis Combs was a controlled candidate in that campaign. He was selected by Wetherby and, I guess, by Clements. . . . He wasn't a well-known man at the time. I've always liked Bert Combs because I went to school with him. He was in law school when I was in commerce college at UK. I'd known him over a period of time. . . . Bert Combs's defeat in 1955 was not Bert Combs's defeat. It was Wetherby's administration's defeat. Nobody ran against Bert as a candidate. We ran against Wetherby's administration, and then tied Bert very tightly to them.

Ed Farris In 1955 he was a salable candidate, but he was not a great candidate. His techniques, the way I remember them—and I had a good deal of opportunity to observe—were of the low-key variety and certainly as compared to his adversary, Happy, it almost made Bert a shrinking violet. So I think where Combs is contrasted to Happy maybe we give undue emphasis to Combs's timidity and lack of gusto.

Jo Ferguson Bert was very much of a mountaineer back in the times when the mountains were not as opened up as they are now. My wife tells the story of standing in line with him, probably at some occasion in the inauguration of Wetherby, and she said, "He would talk to you, but he never would say a word to me." Here she was, a good friend of his sister's [Bobby], but a mountaineer in those days didn't speak to another man's wife. He was [a] very reserved sort of fellow, although handsome and certainly attractive to the women, but he didn't know how to talk to them. I always remember my wife complaining to . . . Bobby that her brother looked away from her. So that was the type of fellow he was. He got out to start to campaign and he was incapable of campaigning at that time. They used to tell stories that you'd be in a big room and he was supposed to be campaigning and you'd find him over in a corner some place.

J. David Francis Judge Combs approached the campaign in a quiet, dignified sort of way and . . . a spellbinding, table-beating orator Judge Combs still is not, but he has improved his delivery and his speaking ability immensely. But he still speaks quietly and has developed what I've heard people refer to as "the Combs method of speaking," which is more recognized as being effective now. But in the race against Chandler I would say that Judge Combs was somewhat ineffective as a speaker.

Polly Gorman (Interview 1) He was not the greatest political campaigner. Of course, there are those of us who thought so much of him we could excuse all the things that we thought he could have done better, particularly in 1955 when he was not a natural-born politician. He found it difficult in a crowd to just shake hands and say, "I'm Bert Combs, vote for me." You just about had to push on him to do it. He definitely was not the greatest campaigner in the world.

Robert R. Martin The thing I recall most about him [as a campaigner] was he was a highly intelligent man. He apparently just had very little experience at public speaking and he was not a forceful speaker and was not a competent speaker, either, and was not a successful candidate. I think the speaking was part of his problem, but he was running against an old pro—Happy Chandler. [Chandler] had been in Kentucky politics [and he] took advantage of every opportunity and ran a very strong campaign—not against Combs so much as he did against the incumbent governor, Governor Wetherby.

Cattie Lou Miller I recall that Combs was somewhat at a disadvantage in several respects. He'd had a recent illness with surgery and was not totally up to energetic par. He had been on the court and of necessity judges on the court in Kentucky didn't circulate too much out in the state. Thereby his public recognition factor was nowhere near that of Chandler. . . . He did not decide to get into the race until rather late. It was my impression at least that maybe the desire didn't originate with him, himself, to run for the office. . . . Instead, I think that he was somewhat persuaded to run, not necessarily by the public at large but by thinkers and planners within the Democratic party. So what I recall of that race is that Combs went in at a disadvantage.

Harry B. Miller The 1955 primary wasn't very pleasant as far as I was concerned, mainly because we lost Fayette County by about five thousand votes. Happy was very popular in Fayette County and Bert really had an unknown name. The real problem in the campaign was name identity. Nobody really knew Bert. Truthfully, he was not a forceful speaker. He was a very clever, witty speaker, but he didn't have the fire and brimstone type speech that Happy could make.

J.R. Miller In all due respect to Bert the fellow couldn't talk. He came to western Kentucky with his mountain twang and he had one joke to tell. As I recall it was the story of the cowboy who came out of the saloon and pulled his six gun and started shooting at the feet of the prospector who had just come up on his burro. He asked the prospector if he knew how to dance and the prospector told him no, and he started shooting at his feet and said, "Learn." So the prospector did dance, dodging the bullets as much as he could, and he counted to six and when he counted his last shot, he pulled his gun and he asked the cowboy if he had ever kissed a burro's butt. And he said, "No, but I always wanted to try." This is all Combs had. He had nothing else.

Ruth Murphy I had been impressed with his integrity, his interest in government, and I had thought that he was gubernatorial material from the time that I got to know him. I realized that he had a handicap in his manner of speech, but everybody has handicaps some way or other. In a room, one-on-one, he was very effective. He was reluctant to be involved in publicity. I remember . . . the opening of the 1955 headquarters when photographers were all there in the front room of the Seelbach [Hotel] headquarters suite, waiting and waiting and waiting, and he never did show up. I went into the back room where he was sitting and I got him by the hand and said, "Come on, they want to make pictures." But he pretty soon got over that, too. He had just not been involved in a statewide campaign prior to that time. He was more of the judicial nature.

Foster Ockerman Bert was not the most effervescent sort of a fellow in the world. He was quiet, reserved. To compare him to some of the young people nowadays that run for office, there was quite a bit of difference. He was much more effective with a small group of people than a large one. I think it was easier for him to project himself in a small group. His sincerity came through much better. In a large group I think that people tended to measure him by his delivery of his words and his appearance more than what he had to say.

John Palmore I remember when he made a speech in the park at Henderson. He was the worst speaker I believe I've ever heard. But there was one thing that impressed me very favorably about Bert at that time. . . . We were trying to get Bert to say that he would not support a sales tax because this was what was being used against him and this was what was really hurting him. I'll never forget. He said, "John, if I have to go anywhere with strings on me, I don't want to go. I can't make a commitment like that because I don't know." I liked that. I thought that was the way a statesman ought to feel. He didn't want to tell anybody any lies. I've been his friend ever since.

John Ed Pearce He was a bad campaigner. My God, he was a bad campaigner. I remember him coming into the headquarters over at the Seelbach and there were quite a few flowers around. It was just after opening day. When Happy would come into a room, you could hear him for half an hour away, and he was laughing and hollering, slapping and hugging [and] talking. Combs sneaked into a room. We were all standing around and all of a sudden there he was sidling into the room. Somebody said, "He looks like he's coming to a funeral with all these flowers." He came in and gave you a sort of lukewarm handshake, said, "Howdy." His . . . mountain accent in those days was very strong. He had a very hesitant way of speaking. If you listened to what Bert said, it made an awful lot of sense, but he said it in such a way with that heavy accent. One-on-one he was persuasive, impressive. Furthermore, you got the idea he was very bright.

James C. Ware He came on visits to Kenton County at that time. I saw him campaign and he was a very poor campaigner. At one time he came up to Kenton County and we went to the Kenton County circuit court and all of the lawyers were here. He came in and it was very difficult for him to meet people. I would say he was more indifferent than shy. I think he wanted to run, but he didn't really know how to be a politician.

Dix Winston Everybody had a feeling, at least I did, that the man was basically honest, basically down-to-earth, brutally frank, and everybody felt that this was contrary to the opposition and would come through. . . . I remember when he came to Paducah and Judge Brady Stewart, a very close friend of Judge Combs, and he were staying at the Ervin S. Cobb Hotel. There were several ladies there—very influential in the community—for dinner. We were trying to get exposure for Combs in west Kentucky, which is about as far from Prestonsburg and Clay County as you could be. We wanted him to meet everybody possible. Combs had a phone call at the desk and he turned around and we were trying to introduce him and engage him in conversation, and Judge Stewart was doing all the talking and Combs was looking at his watch. He wasn't shaking hands so there wasn't anything else to do. He was terribly, terribly shy.

Shelbyville

Bert Combs formally opened his 1955 gubernatorial campaign on June 2 at Shelbyville, Kentucky. It was an ideal location since Frankfort state office workers and an abundance of Jefferson County Democrats could easily participate. Accordingly, a crowd of approximately nine thousand gathered inside and outside the Shelby County fairgrounds to hear Combs outline his goals for Kentucky.

It was the candidate's first major address and a kind of keynote for the campaign to follow. It was a good speech; the organization and structure were excellent. The points made concerning progress, natural resources, tourism, education, highways, and industrial development were carefully conceived, with promise of more specific details to follow. Two things, however, seriously dampened the ardor of the multitude. First, Combs read the speech in its entirety with little humor and a monotonous lack of inflection that only heightened the intensity of his mountain twang. Second, he recognized candidly that what he proposed would cost more money than the state at that time received from existing revenue laws and that, as governor, he would recommend that "sufficient funds be provided in the year 1956"[1] to insure adequate financing.

None of this was news to those with whom he consulted. Securing enough funds to support desirable programs had been particularly hard during the administrations of both Clements and Wetherby. Neither, however, discussed the problem publicly prior to an election. But Combs believed that candidates for public office were obligated to reveal their objectives, or at least spell out major problems as they envisioned them. For him, the basic problem was inadequate revenue—specifically $25 million less than needed.

To say the least, his supporters felt he had been unnecessarily frank about a touchy subject. Though he did not propose any method by which the additional funds might be accumulated, Combs laid himself open to the charge that he favored a general sales tax—a charge he was never able to refute effectively. One reason for this was that he refused to state categorically that he would not consider such a tax. Never did he endorse a sales tax, but never did he denounce one either.

Bert Combs (Interview 3) I knew in 1955 that somewhere along the line I would have to make some sort of statement as to tax revenue. I had been talking to people about these things throughout— Dr. James Martin, Henry Ward, Earle Clements. I never said I wouldn't have a sales tax, and that had the effect of raising the question in a lot of people's minds that if he won't deny that he will have it, chances are he will. At my Shelbyville opening I said the state had to have more revenue and that was the headline in the *Courier-Journal*.

I don't recall that anybody made any serious objection to the Shelbyville statement. The speech was my speech. . . .

Very few people ever talk to a candidate about policy things— what he believes and what he's going to say, how he's going to say it. Nobody did talk to me at that time that I have any recollection of. A lot of this is hindsight. True, the next day a great many people said to me. "That was a great mistake." The saying got going around, "Combs opened and closed on the same night." I wouldn't have changed my mind . . . because I thought that in honesty and fairness to the people . . . I had an obligation to give them some notion of the kind of governor I would be. I just think that is basic honesty.

I knew that it would cause some discussion, some argument. I visualized the type of headline that might be in the paper the next day. I thought the *Courier* was not as objective about the headline as it should have been. I didn't think that was the important part of the speech. But Hugh Morris, who was reporting it, knew that the matter of new taxes would be the big issue in the campaign, because Happy had historically always run against any new taxes and did this time—particularly a sales tax. Most candidates oppose taxes if [the issue is] brought up. But most candidates will evade it if they can. Happy's policy was to jump up the rabbit and then shoot it down. He was a little different from most candidates in that respect—a great part of his success, no doubt.

What I'm saying is not a criticism of Happy. I'm saying it as a historical fact. I didn't want to say I was going to have a sales tax, but I didn't want to put myself in a position where I couldn't if I thought it was best. I didn't know what form it would take. I knew that we would have to have more revenue. I think that's about the substance of the Shelbyville speech. Certainly, at that point of time in Kentucky, we just didn't have enough revenue. Kentucky has been unfortunate in that it has three very glamorous industries—whiskey, tobacco, and horses—but none of them have ever been big revenue producers like the oil industry or shipping or cotton—that sort of thing.

Lawrence Wetherby Bert was sincerely honest in his approach to the campaign. He realized we needed more money for education and on his opening speech, as Hugh Morris of the *Courier-Journal* wrote the next morning, Bert opened and closed his campaign at Shelbyville. . . . [Bert] said that we needed $25 million additional money for educational purposes. Morris headlined that and said that meant a sales tax. Of course, that was the one thing that Chandler wanted. He wanted to get us in the position that we were supporting a sales tax and he could run against it, which he had done before and been successful. He figured he could defeat us on that basis. Everybody believed we needed more money, but they were all reluctant to support a tax program to produce the money. . . .

The need was primarily in education. We had passed an amendment to the Constitution in 1953 in the fall so that the state money for educational purposes could be distributed on the basis other than a per capita basis. So we repealed the section of the Constitution that provided for that and then in the 1954 session of the legislature we passed the minimum foundation program which meant that you were going to need, to finance it, a whole lot more money. That, of course, was the basis for Combs saying we needed $25 million more money. The question was, where are you going to get it?

Phil Ardery I remember very well being at Shelbyville at the opening of that campaign. . . . [Bert] said that the people of Kentucky are entitled to better schools and better roads, and this and that and the other, and he said, "But you must remember that it takes revenue to bring these things and we've got to raise the revenue to pay for these privileges." And Hugh Morris, who was a political writer for the *Courier-Journal* at the time, was seated right beside me and he threw his pencil down and said, "That's all she wrote."

Barry Bingham, Sr. It was not a popular thing to say and he didn't say it very appealingly. He had a direct honesty which always came through in his speeches and which was a part of his nature, it seems to me. But perhaps just to say it so flatly as he did was not politically expedient. I hate to think that people are just going to be against any candidate who talks about taxes. Bert Combs, being an honest man, knew that he was going to have more taxes in this state and wasn't willing to say that he would never do it.

John Crimmins It so happened that we had a pretty good delegation to go from Jefferson County for the opening of Bert's campaign. . . . That's the night that Bert was trying to tell the public the truth about the fact that they couldn't continue operating the state on the present income. . . . That's what got him in trouble that particular year . . . because Happy came out and said that the state could be operated on its present income—that they didn't have to have any more money. I think definitely that was the reason that Bert lost that particular race.

Robert Lee "Slick" Combs We had a hard time, when he'd go to a rally or something, to get him to mix with the people. We finally got him to take his coat off—get in shirt sleeves and sweat a little. His first speech at Shelbyville, he had a bigger crowd than Senator Barkley ever had—twenty thousand people at his opener. When he made his speech, he said he was going to try to make a good governor and do some things such as have the best park system, best roads, and so on, but it was going to take money and he probably was going to have to have a tax. Now, Herb [Smith] and [I] decided he beat himself that night. I had no idea he was going to do that. I'd [have] choked if you [had] mentioned [more taxes]. I don't think anybody knew about it. I asked him about it later, and he said he thought the people would understand that it did take money to do the things that they wanted done, but that's not the way it works in politics.

Arthur Lloyd Bert was rather shy—almost to the extent that he did not want to ask somebody to vote for him. I thought he was a very shy, somewhat low-key kind of candidate. I did admire his honesty. He didn't evade issues. I actually cringed at his opening campaign speech when he said that we had to have more taxes to run the government. I knew it was honest and I knew what he meant and I even knew why he said it. But for a governor candidate to open his campaign before all the people and the media, to say it was bad.

William May We were not really prepared to back him as we should. I think we had adequate financing in that race, but true to his integrity and his desire to let the public know what he really believed in he advocated a tax raise right off. All of us accused him of opening and closing his campaign the same day. I rode to and from Shelbyville with him and I left there—he did too—with my head hanging pretty deliberately. He got a poor response to a proposal to levy an additional tax.

Cattie Lou Miller He made an unfortunate opening speech at Shelbyville and part of the speech included an open statement that really was presented pretty much as a pledge that he planned to increase taxes by some specific number of millions of dollars, if he were elected governor. While idealism would have led one to say that frankly and openly in a first speech, the plain truth of the matter is that an opponent like Chandler could work on him for that. From the moment he stated that sentence he probably never had a chance at any time in the rest of the campaign.

Harry B. Miller I was at Shelbyville and I would say that that came about as close to losing as you can. . . . The crowd went away dead, with no real enthusiasm. That probably more than any one thing contributed to his defeat. He never could generate the popular appeal after that speech. There was another issue, too, though.

Combs would not come out and say positively that he would not go to a sales tax. He never said he would, but Happy ran on the platform that he'd removed the sales tax and he was going to keep it off. At least he attributed to Combs an affinity for the sales tax.

Ruth Murphy I took the speech and reached over and got a pencil after I read the first three lines and started to mark through. And he said, "What are you doing?" I said, "You can't say this." It was that line about Kentucky is going to have to have more revenue. I don't remember the exact wording. Anyway he stopped me. He said, "You leave that like it is." I said, "Bert, can't you see the headlines in the *Courier-Journal* if you say it this way? It's going to come out, 'Combs advocates more taxes.'" And he said, "Well, it is the truth. As I understand the situation, Kentucky cannot function unless we have some additional revenue. And if I can't be elected telling the truth then I don't want to be elected. I'm not going to lie to people." So that impressed me that much more. But he's a very headstrong man and you can't bulldoze him into anything. You may coax and cajole and get a little cooperation but once he has his mind made up you might just as well leave it alone, which I did.

Ed Prichard He was committed in 1955, but he was ill at ease in the statewide political arena without any doubt. He was not a handshaker. He was not a formidable stump speaker at that time—rather retiring in a lot of ways. I'm sure he felt ill at ease in that campaign, but I think he was committed. For example, when he went over to Shelbyville in his opening speech and said that we were going to have to raise additional revenue to finance the educational program for education and some other programs, that was certainly not what a typical candidate would have done. It unquestionably hurt him in the campaign. His election campaign techniques were very poor.

June Taylor I went to the Shelbyville opening. I remember that very well. I had taken the speech at the headquarters. We worked on that for quite some time. He did most of it but there were others in there advising him. I remember people trying to persuade him not to mention taxes, but he would not do anything other than what was his conviction. He knew what he was doing. He felt that the taxes were needed and he felt that he had to tell the people. It was a mistake, but I feel that he felt he had to tell the people the truth. When it was over, everybody was drooping.

Dix Winston That speech was worked on [for] a week. There was a lot of controversy and Combs versus the world regarding one word, and that was *"tax"*. Combs said we needed a new tax and everybody else said that's what will kill the campaign. This speech was written and rewritten and rewritten. When we got to Shelbyville it was not in the speech, but Combs put it in off the cuff and of course it hit the papers and we lived with it the entire campaign. . . . Combs was his own man when you got down to his personal, philosophical honesty. If he thought something needed to be said, he said it regardless of the advice, if you couldn't show him where he was wrong. He had a basic honesty that nobody could close down.

Chandler v. Combs

Bert Combs neither endorsed nor condemned a sales tax, but his opponent made his position eminently clear on the subject. Chandler had risen to political prominence in Kentucky on the wave of anti-sales tax hysteria in the middle 1930s. Thereafter, he never missed an opportunity to remind anyone willing to listen that general sales taxes were not only unsound but unnecessary.

While an increasing number of states (twenty-six by 1950) had adopted a form of sales tax to finance government services, Kentucky remained outside that pattern. In fact, aspirants for public office at nearly all levels shied away from sales tax terminology even as they elaborated upon the need for more state aid to education or welfare or anything else. Thus Chandler pounced like a hungry tiger upon Combs's Shelbyville statement. Skillfully and repeatedly, the former governor tied the sales tax to the Combs campaign in a manner reminiscent of his 1935 victory over Tom Rhea and Ruby Laffoon. He ridiculed Wetherby's alleged extravagance. He denounced Clements as a would-be dictator. And he pledged again and again that he could provide all the services Kentuckians craved and needed without any additional taxes.

Kentuckians had a choice. They could vote for a man from Eastern Kentucky who had no experience as an administrator in government, and who believed that more revenue was imperative, or they could vote for a veteran political leader who had been governor and who saw no need for more public monies.

Other factors influenced Chandler's victory. First, Harry Lee Waterfield, traditionally opposed politically to Chandler, spurned of-

fers by Wetherby and Clements to join forces with Combs and opted to run for lieutenant governor on the same slate with Chandler. The loser to Clements in the 1947 gubernatorial primary, Waterfield continued to be active politically and still retained a power base in western Kentucky. Second, Earle Clements was unable to bring his full attention to the struggle because unexpected duties in Washington kept him away during most of the campaign. Lyndon Johnson's heart attack in 1955 made it imperative that Clements attend to the job of acting majority leader [of the U.S. Senate], allowing him no time for state politics. Third, Alben Barkley did not campaign actively against Chandler until the very end. Perhaps the most popular Democrat in Kentucky at that time, the former vice-president had never been on good terms with Chandler. Yet he had always scrupulously avoided trying to influence the results of a Democratic primary other than those in which he was a candidate, and he hesitated to do so in 1955. Only incessant pressure from Clements, Wetherby, and others brought Barkley into the fray, but not until the final week when he presented several statewide radio and television broadcasts critical of Chandler.

The contrasting personalities of the two candidates was an additional factor. Combs was just not entertaining while Chandler was a personable, accomplished, spellbinding campaigner. Ben Reeves of the Courier-Journal contrasted the styles of each candidate on the eve of the election. According to the journalist, a sound truck heralding his imminent arrival always preceded Chandler's speaking engagements. Then in the midst of the ensuing excitement the former governor appeared, smiling broadly as he wended his way through the multitude, pausing here and there to clap a back, grasp a hand, or kiss a baby. Once upon the platform Chandler removed his coat, loosened his tie, and began the stage portion of his performance. Frequent references to the Bible and more greetings to his friends in the audience, whom he called by name, established the desired "home folks" image. Then, after lambasting the incompetencies of his opponents, Chandler concluded most rallies by singing a song. This revivalist atmosphere had everything but a solicitation to sinners to come forth for confession and was clearly an entertaining spectacle.[2]

By contrast a Combs rally resembled more the executive session of a group of elders in the Presbyterian church. Combs usually got out of his car and walked several blocks to a meeting site, shaking hands and exchanging quiet comments with well-wishers. Once on *the platform, he stated the points of his program without humor, shouting, or exhortation, affecting a delivery described by one observer as "conversational."*[3]

Bert Combs (Interview 3)   I recall that Lawrence [Wetherby] had a meeting with Harry Lee [Waterfield] and Harry Lee decided to go with Happy [Chandler]. I don't recall that I ever talked to Harry Lee. I hardly knew him at the time. If I ever talked with him it was more or less casually, but I do remember that Lawrence made a special effort to get him to be for me.

Happy had been running for two or three years and he had been in every nook and corner of this state and he had made a lot of alignments, obtained a lot of support before I ever got in the race. It was recognized at the time that Happy had a head start. He already had labor's support before I even announced. By the time the primary rolled around, the Chandler people were sending out postcards with a bright new penny taped on the postcard saying, "If you don't want a sales tax, vote for Chandler."

Shortly before the primary we had some defections from the Wetherby administration which we thought at the time—I still think—psychologically were very damaging to me—Vego Barnes, commissioner of Economic Security. I doubt if there was any preconceived plan. I would guess that Barnes knew that there was a possibility he might do it. My thinking is that he waited up until ten days before the election because he decided his influence and the timing of it would tip the scales. I'm sure that if Barnes thought I was far ahead at the time he would have stayed. But he was an astute politician. So he defected. I would say he was conservative fiscally.

But the programs that Chandler was so critical of, Barnes had initiated. Barnes was a very influential member of the Wetherby administration. His department was becoming very important because of the federal programs—old age pensions, all of that business. One of the issues in the campaign, and perhaps one that tipped the scale, was that at that time if a person who was eligible for an old age pension owned any kind of property they had to put a mortgage on that and give that mortgage to the state so that after their death the state could recoup the pension money. That was Barnes's program. Some of us attempted to get that changed because Happy was killing us in the rural parts of the state. But Barnes convinced Wetherby

The 1955 Gubernatorial Primary

that it was irresponsible fiscal government not to have that and Wetherby refused to change it. We took a lot of punishment supporting Barnes's program and when we lost him, we lost both sides of that.

The issue boiled down to Chandler saying that he had been there before [and] knew what he was talking about. He wouldn't have to impose any new taxes. I think he said it across the board—no new taxes. Combs was saying we have to have new revenues—not certain where it would come from, but we have to have it. So Chandler won by eighteen thousand or nineteen thousand [votes].

I hadn't been in the executive or legislative branches of government. People thought, "Combs doesn't know," and I thought I didn't know—"Chandler perhaps knows more about this than I do." I couldn't believe that Happy would be saying that [he wouldn't need to raise taxes] unless he knew pretty well that he could do it. . . .

I wasn't a very good candidate. I had been in the judiciary all my life, first as a lawyer and then as a judge. I wasn't a very good speech maker. I guess I was adequate shaking hands one-on-one, but not overwhelming.

You have a great deal of trepidation starting out, but after a very few days you are so busy trying to make certain that you don't goof off that you don't have time to worry about the impression you are going to make. Of course, you try to have something with a little substance to say. And you try not to make the same speech over and over. But that wasn't much of a problem. I think I had more of a problem going to the courthouses early on than I did later making speeches.

I went to Paducah the first trip I made as a candidate. Brady Stewart went with me. Paducah is close to five hundred miles from Prestonsburg and about all I knew about Paducah was it was the home of Alben Barkley and Irvin Cobb. You just don't talk to people much about the Barkleys and the Cobbs in their own neighborhood. They think they know so much more about it than you do that there's no reason to talk about that sort of thing. Many of them sort of resent being identified with somebody like Barkley or Cobb because every man considers himself important. Most of the people in Paducah didn't consider them much more important than they were. That's just a fact of life.

I'm not a self-starter anyway so it was a problem what I would talk about. I don't think I set the woods on fire with small talk. The courthouse people obviously would be comparing me with people like Happy Chandler and Alben Barkley as a campaigner, or Wetherby or Clements. I think it was several months before I really started coming through to people.

Bert Combs (Interview 4)   I think [the absence of Clements] had a very decisive effect. As I recall, he was present in Kentucky practically full-time until Lyndon Johnson had his heart attack. That was four or five weeks before the primary and Earle was assistant majority leader of the [U.S.] Senate. With Senator Johnson completely out of the picture temporarily, it was thought necessary for Earle to be in Washington. So he did go to Washington. He may have returned to Kentucky on weekends, maybe on a one-day basis, but he was out of Kentucky for all practical purposes from the time he went to Washington until the primary. Although he was not designated as the campaign manager . . . for all practical purposes he was the campaign manager.

He was perhaps the most knowledgable person in Kentucky in the political field at that time. He had many contacts. He knew everybody in the political field in the state. Too, he was a superb organizer, administrator, and that becomes very important particularly in the final days of any campaign. Poeple generally don't recognize this, but without a good campaign manager there aren't many political races won. It's just that important. So I think it was rather decisive in the 1955 campaign. I've always thought that if Earle hadn't been required to leave Kentucky and go to Washington at that time that the race would have been closer than it was. Perhaps it could have made the difference.

I don't know that I thought much about whether I would win or lose. I'm certain that I had doubts about my ability to win going in. I think as we got closer to the primary that I became more optimistic. I would say that I thought there was a definite possibility that I could win. But I was never overconfident about that race.

We were having good crowds at our meetings. There was a great deal of enthusiasm for my candidacy in the later weeks of the campaign. You know Governor Chandler doesn't have many neutral people as regards their sympathy for him or lack of it. The people that were for me were very much for me, which can cause a candidate to get a false sense of his strength. I know now that many of those people were for me because they were so much opposed to Governor Chandler. . . . They were not just a little for me or a little for Chandler. They were very strong one way or the other. That makes it difficult to gauge the strength of a candidacy. . . .

I would say the most disappointing thing to me was I didn't think I had been a very good candidate. I thought that if I had been a better candidate perhaps I could have made up that eighteen-thousand-vote [difference]. Of course, I rationalized it this way and I think, properly so, that if I had known even a few weeks in advance that I would be a candidate I could have been better prepared. I could have started out in the campaign as a more mature candidate.

I had run for judge of the Court of Appeals, but you don't make a political campaign. There's no way that you can do that running for judge. All you can tell people when you're running for judge is that you'll be fair and impartial. Most people don't want that if it's going to interfere with what they want to accomplish. There's no glamor in just saying I'll be fair and be a good judge. You don't make political speeches as such. You have to stick to law and justice and impartiality. You can tell a few jokes. Actually you usually don't have much of an audience unless somebody else makes the crowd. Nobody is going to come out to listen to some judge talk about why he should be elected.

So I had really not made any political speeches as such. Of course, I was pitted against a master—one of the better courthouse stump speakers that the state has had recently. There isn't any question that he outcampaigned me. Of course, he was reckless. I think that's a safe word to use. Happy was always a great promiser. I was very careful in that campaign not to overpromise. You know I still was a judge. Then, too, I didn't think a candidate ought to overpromise. I still don't, for that matter. There are many ways of getting the point across—letting people believe what they want to believe without overpromising. I think that if we'd had a month to go I would probably have won.

Lawrence Wetherby Chandler pulled the big lie technique and ran against me on the basis that I had wasted the state's money, that I had redone the capitol building, put in air conditioning, that I spent $20,000 for a rug for the governor's office. I got the invoices, put them in the paper, put them on television, put them on the radio, put them all over the state as to what the rug cost. It cost $2,400 for all of the offices in the governor's suite instead of a $20,000 rug. . . . And even after I put the invoices in the papers, he'd go around over the state and get a crowd and say Wetherby spent $20,000 for a rug in his office. . . . He was a great entertainer. He consistently lied. Most people, when you catch them, stop, but he wouldn't. He'd keep rolling it around.

John Y. Brown, Sr. Happy was so much better at the ancient art of campaigning in a sordid sort of way—that facts have no meaning. It's what will go over with the public. An illustration of that—one time before I decided to take any part Happy honked his horn at me coming out of Louisville and I stopped. He got out and came up and talked to me in my car. I said to him, "Happy, you know that statement of yours about Wetherby's rug costing $20,000 is not true. That rug cost $2,000." "Oh," he said, "they love it the way I say it." It never made any difference to Happy whether he told the truth or not. It didn't bother him a bit.

Harry Davis I don't think Combs was a good campaigner. I don't think Bert had the charisma to attract voters. In the campaign he was too much of a lawyer, too much of a judge, and I don't think he was able to sell, and politics is strictly selling. . . . I don't think he had much to do with handling his campaign. I don't know that, but our intelligence was that he wasn't running the campaign. . . .

Chandler is more open and more aggressive. Combs is more subtle. Both of them are smart men. I would say that Chandler would shoot from the hip more. Combs would plod a little bit more. Sometimes one is good and sometimes the other one is good. It depends on what answer comes out.

Arthur Lloyd In 1955 I worked for Combs because I was part of the organization team there in Frankfort. Even though I worked for the legislature rather than the governor, I was part of the team. Happy assumed that since I'd been for him in 1935 and been part of his first administration that I would be for him the second time. There was a fellow I won't name, a friend of Governor Chandler's, also my friend, who assumed I would be for Chandler in the 1955 campaign. He wanted me, however, to stay in my job until ten days before the primary and to resign my position and come out for Chandler. I couldn't do that because I couldn't be a spy in the ranks—because he wanted to be informed about the strategy in the campaign and tell who was for him, and who was against him, who contributed money, and all that sort of thing. I told this fellow I couldn't do that because I had to shave every morning and if I did that I couldn't look at myself in the mirror, and I didn't think I'd look well with a beard. So I refused to do that.

J.R. Miller That was my first real bloodbath in politics—managing Bert Combs's campaign in 1955 [in Daviess County]. Combs visited Daviess County on at least three or four occasions. We simply couldn't sell him. Bert would come down and [he] had this mountain twang. His humor—he was introduced as a judge of the Court of Appeals in spite of the fact Chandler had ridiculed this quite effectively. We just didn't have anything to go with except that Lawrence Wetherby and Earle Clements and Louis Cox, to some extent, talked Bert Combs into running.

Ed Prichard Everyone recognized that increased services required increased revenue. Some recognized it and lied about it. Combs recognized it and was perhaps too candid. All the states were increasing services. All were raising taxes because they needed more money. Massive federal assistance was not available.

Even Chandler promised increased services. His principal pledge was to finance the foundation program for education which had been developed in the Clements and Wetherby administrations but hadn't been financed. It was on the statute books. Neither candidate at that time really said they shouldn't finance it. Chandler said he could finance it without increasing taxes. Combs said you couldn't. The general public, whatever their views may be over the long run, tend in the short run to be opposed to tax increases. The public is never very enthusiastic about tax increase. In the campaign you often get the short-run view on the part of the voter. Chandler took advantage of that and Combs got the disadvantage. I really don't think anybody really preached in 1955 that you shouldn't finance the foundation program, shouldn't finance some of the other services, although Chandler never went to the extent Combs did in other things.

Dix Winston I actually felt we would win up until the last month of the campaign. The last month every courthouse it seemed like you'd walk in, even in Eastern Kentucky, you'd see a penny stuck on the bulletin board of the courthouse which was tying back to the sales tax. Of course, that was Happy's whole attack from the time Combs opened the campaign in Shelbyville and you could just feel that last month, at least I could, death hanging over us and the campaign.

The Agony of Defeat

Chandler defeated Combs in the 1955 primary 259,875 to 241,754 and went on to crush Republican Edwin Denny by nearly 130,000 votes in November. Combs did not participate in the general election, nor did Wetherby. Apparently the Chandler faction did not solicit their support. Such was the nature of renewed factionalism in Kentucky politics.

Combs and his family returned to Prestonsburg after five years of living in Lexington and Frankfort. Combs resumed his law practice with J.W. Howard, handling personal injury litigation, for some coal companies and against others. He also organized a Federal Savings and Loan Association in Floyd County. His income while on the court had been minimal and even less than that during the campaign. Supporting his family and making a living were vital concerns. But, he was not the same person he had been. Politics had become part of his life, and the turmoil and intensity of a campaign such as 1955's could not be easily forgotten. Moreover, he was now a statewide figure as he had not been before. Even if he never ran for an office again, his interest and involvement in politics were now assured.

Bert Combs (Interview 4)   You have to get unwound when the campaign is over. But anyone with any judgment realizes when he starts a campaign . . . that it's not a lifetime job. The campaign will last six months or so, or if you hold an office it will be for two years or four years. Anybody with any foresight prepares for that. I think the average person doesn't realize that the person in the public eye knows better than anybody else that it's a temporary thing. People seem to think that when a man is elected governor for a four-year term that he thinks he is going to be there forever. He would have to be very, very stupid not to know that this is just an interim period—a four-year period—and that you'll be carrying your own luggage and you'll be driving your own car and lighting your own cigarettes [when it's over]. Most of us did that before we got there and it's really not hard to readjust. I have seen a few people that I thought had severe withdrawal pains, but not many.

Part of the reason you don't like to lose is because you do know that many of your friends who have gone beyond the call of duty and have made personal and financial sacrifices will be subject to punitive action. That's true with the Chandler philosophy of politics. It was that way because Governor Chandler believes it ought to be that way. I think that he would be the first to admit that when he is elected, say as governor, that he ought to bring all of his friends in and push out those who are there if it's necessary to push someone out. That's a philosophy of government. I don't subscribe to it that much. I believe in being good to your friends and in a case of doubt that you ought to appoint your friends rather than your enemies. But Happy believed that more than most. So I knew my friends would be subject to punitive action and they were. I wasn't surprised by the Christmas Massacre. I clearly expected that to happen. From the time of the primary almost everybody who could find [another job] did so.

I continued to live at the same house in Lexington for two or three months until I got my ducks lined up and then I went back to Prestonsburg to practice law until I started the race for governor. I was in Prestonsburg for more than two years, although for much of the last year . . . I was traveling. I went back to Prestonsburg and I formed a law partnership with J.W. Howard and W.P. Mayo.

Lois Combs Weinberg At twelve you're pretty philosophical and . . . I hadn't been intricately involved in the campaign. . . . It was a disappointment, but ours was a . . . stable family . . . and life went on. . . . I remember [my mother] saying—the only time I remember her making this kind of comment—that he just nearly drove her crazy because he was depressed. . . .

I don't think [the decision to run again] was an overt decision. He just kind of moved into that and I guess Mother knew it. But more than anything I think he was just regrouping. . . . [H]e may have decided the day after he lost that he was going to run again, for all I know, but he was not one to announce his intentions about anything until it was time to do something. He is cautious, perhaps careful.

Fontaine Banks Combs put up a real good front. I think he was like a few of the rest of us. He suspected that we were going to have problems. But any time you spend that much time campaigning for the high office of governor you have to feel down, and I'm sure he was. But he did a good job of keeping the rest of us up. That very night I felt we had . . . a candidate [for] four years later. It was probably the last thing he wanted to hear of, another governor's race. We felt that we had gotten a feel of the pulse of the people and that he would be the most logical and a successful candidate next time.

Ed Farris Combs is not a fellow whose personality and feelings are obvious to the point that an outsider could read very well. . . . I'm sure he felt the sting of defeat because anybody that's ambitious enough to run for governor doesn't like to lose. On the other hand, things were in pretty much a disarray with the Clements-Beauchamp-Wetherby-Combs faction of the Democratic party and Happy's crowd took over with vengeance. I would say that it would [have been] premature for Combs or anybody else to have much knowledge or foresight as to exactly what they should do personally, or what the faction of the party could do, until things fell into place a little bit.

Polly Gorman (Interview 1) The times that I saw him, and I saw him fairly soon after the election—I was working for the Department of Education at the time—and I recall I was walking to work at the State Office Building and he came by in his car and picked me up. He said, "Are you afraid to ride with me, or have I done enough to you already?" I said, "Of course not, how are you?" And he said, "Well, the only thing I think about is how I have let my friends down." He was afraid that anyone who worked for state government, that he had put their jobs in jeopardy. . . . The possibility that there would be wholesale firings was far more feared then. It was one of the things that people in state government expected.

Sara Combs Kaufman We had all gone to Louisville as a family to hear the returns. Really, when we walked into the hotel we knew what was happening. We felt so badly having worked for him. Judge Brady Stewart came down and he said to me, "The world hasn't come to an end, and Bert can run again." And I thought there's just no way that anyone would want to go through this again. First of all, I thought, how would you raise the money to finance another campaign? I really in my wildest dreams didn't think he'd be a candidate again. Brady Stewart, who was wiser, predicted what would happen.

Robert R. Martin Judge Combs, I think, took that defeat rather bitterly. He did not participate in the fall campaign. I have the personal feeling—I can't really document it—that he had a high resolve for a second chance at running for governor and a sharp determination to remove any deficiencies that appeared in the first campaign. . . . I mean lack of experience in speaking particularly.

June Taylor Judge Combs's [concern] was what he had done to his friends when he lost. So many of his loyal followers would probably lose their jobs and he was very depressed about that. He wrote a number of personal letters himself. I typed them for him, and he wrote individual notes on many of them. He did take his personal time to write a number of people and thank them. He felt a deep personal responsibility for what was going to happen to them.

Chapter 3

The 1959 Gubernatorial Primary: Political Maturity

The Decision to Run

While Bert Combs was attempting to recoup some of the income lost while he was on the Court of Appeals and during the 1955 primary, Happy Chandler's faction continued to spar with the organization headed by Senator Earle Clements. Clements was not only a United States Senator but he was intimately identified with Lyndon Johnson who, in turn, had presidential ambitions. Concurrently, Chandler viewed the nation's highest office as a post for which he was eminently qualified. Hence, the struggle for control of the Kentucky Democratic party had national as well as local significance.

During the first stage of Chandler's administration this inherent conflict remained muted—Chandler and Clements at least refrained from open combat. But there were indications of what was coming. Chandler promoted passage of a new law that moved primary elections from August to May. Then he endorsed the candidacy of another Democrat for the May primary and Clements had to interrupt his Senate service to campaign, albeit successfully, for the party nomination.

When Alben Barkley died unexpectedly on April 30, 1956, Chandler appointed Joe Leary, his 1955 campaign manager, to the position for the four-month interim until the November election. However, members of Clements's organization, who were still in control of the Democratic State Central Committee, voted to support Lawrence Wetherby for the senate seat in the election. By the end of June, when county meetings would elect delegates to the state convention, a major factional war was inevitable. Indicative of the in-fighting to come was Chandler's statement that he would give full support to Clements's reelection but do no more than vote for Wetherby.[1] Even that turned out to be an overstatement, for the results of the county conventions were more than Chandler had hoped for. The governor won 1337 uncontested delegates out of 2484 possible while Clements secured only 431.[2] That translated into majorities for Chandler in all the congressional districts except Louisville and Jefferson County. Clearly, the Democrats would now have a state central committee sympathetic to the governor, not Clements and Wetherby.

Initially there were no outright indications of reprisal because Chandler believed himself to be a genuine darkhorse possibility for president at the Chicago National Convention. Only after mid-August, when that eventuality failed to materialize, did the full force of administration animosity toward Clements and Wetherby unfold. In fact, Chandler was so determined to avoid supporting Clements and Wetherby that he side-stepped many Democratic party obligations, including failing to host presidential candidate Adlai Stevenson when he visited Kentucky in October. As a result, not only did Dwight Eisenhower sweep Kentucky by nearly 100,000 votes, but both Wetherby and Clements lost as well. Within one year Happy Chandler had won the governorship, seized control of the state Democratic party, and helped drive from the field all major Democratic political opponents. He now had the necessary political base he needed to make a serious presidential bid.[3]

What transpired during the next three years ultimately subverted that bid, and Bert Combs played an important part in the process, although not immediately. Once Chandler's victory over his Kentucky opposition was complete there was no more need for Clements, who genuinely disliked factionalism, to work for unity. He was now in a position where the only hope for a resurgence of his political strength lay in undermining Chandler's power.

The first indication that Clements still had some bullets in his gun came with the announcement by Lyndon Johnson that the Kentuckian would be appointed executive director of the Democratic Senatorial Campaign Committee. Chandler was appalled. "I don't understand," he complained, "how this fellow's Texas buddy has the right to make appointments for the Democratic party." No one in Kentucky was consulted, he added, and therefore not "one cent from Kentucky" would go to the Democratic National Committee as long as Clements was on the payroll.[4]

Concurrently, Chandler suffered a mild setback at home that heartened opposition to his control. When Charles O'Connell, clerk of the Court of Appeals, died suddenly, the governor challenged the court's assumed right to name a successor. When the court selected Doris Owens, deputy clerk for twenty-three years, for the post, Chandler threatened to use force to keep her from being paid.[5] The court promptly ordered state treasurer Henry Carter to pay her. Eventually Owens ran for the unexpired term and defeated a candidate backed by the governor in the primary. In the same primary a number of Chandler's key legislative supporters were defeated while equally important critics survived.[6]

By the time the next legislative session convened in 1958 it was obvious that anti-Chandler forces had been strengthened and would challenge the governor. The situation in 1958 was even more intense because Chandler planned to run for president in 1960 and that depended in part upon the nomination and election of his political ally, Lieutenant Governor Harry Lee Waterfield, in 1959. The 1958 general assembly, therefore, operated more like a political nominating convention than a legislative session. Chandler's opponents gathered momentum when they rejected the governor's choice for president pro tem of the Kentucky Senate and followed that by opening up the administration budget to amendment.[7] Outgunned by Democrats, Chandler turned to the Republican minority for help and fashioned a coalition between Chandler Democrats and Republicans to retain control over most issues. But as the legislative session drew to a close, one last battle solidified the opposing faction.

State treasurer Henry Carter had been openly friendly to the anti-Chandler group, known by this time as the "rebels." As a result, the governor determined to strip Carter of some of his powers through ripper legislation. A week before the end of the session the state Senate voted twenty to fourteen in favor of the governor's plan—the six-vote margin provided by half a dozen Republicans in that body. When the contest shifted to the House it was clear that it was more than a question of Carter's prerogatives: it was a test of strength between the administration and the rebels. The final vote that rejected the bill by seventy-five to fifteen was not the real story. Supporters of Chandler actually managed forty-four votes but could secure no more. Significantly, sixteen Republicans joined twenty-eight Democrats to comprise the forty-four.[8]

Regarded by anti-Chandlerites as a victory, the defeat of the ripper legislation highlighted the rebel impact as the session ended.

Intertwined with that victory was Bert Combs's announcement in Frankfort that he was "sharply interested" in running for governor. "We, the people," he went on to explain, "have a big house-cleaning job to do in Frankfort. I want to talk about how to do that job. If somebody else can do it better than I can, then I'm for him. Otherwise, I'm for Combs."[9] Shortly after that Wilson Wyatt of Louisville revealed that he was "seriously considering" the possibility he might run, and this was followed by news that Earle Clements had arrived in Louisville.[10] The stage was set for further factional conflict. Only completion of the cast selection remained.

Bert Combs (Interview 4)   As time passed more opposition developed in the legislature to Governor Chandler—the so-called rebels came along. . . . I don't know if they were even called that in the first session of his administration, but by the time the second session came around he had a rather formidable opposition, a strong nucleus of opposition.

They were in contact with me on a very informal basis, a very casual basis. They contacted me during the second session of Governor Chandler's term. Actually, I had almost forgotten about politics, intentionally dismissed it from my mind. It would have been that way whether it was a matter of choice or not. I had no desire to lead any one-man crusade against Happy Chandler. I realized that people had elected him governor. I thought he was entitled to serve his term out. I was rather nonplussed when at the first session of his legislature he did exactly the opposite of what he had said he would do in regard to taxes. True, he didn't impose a sales tax as such, but he imposed taxes that were just as regressive as the sales tax. . . .

The rebels called me during the second session, I would guess about midway of the term—that would have been 1958. They asked me to come to Frankfort and to meet with them and I did. I was trying a lawsuit in Pikeville. Judge Mac Swinford was the federal judge there. I think I told Judge Swinford when I received the call that I needed to go to Frankfort. . . . He used to kid about it later that he helped me to become governor.

They admittedly were talking about who should run for governor. They didn't want to be for Governor Chandler's selection. Everybody knew that he would have a selection. Everybody expected it to be Lieutenant Governor Waterfield. We discussed it at I think maybe two meetings. I didn't know they wanted me. I knew they wanted to talk to me about the political situation. Of course, I could visualize that at least some of them would think that perhaps I should run. It was not unanimous among the rebels. I think it was almost unanimous. They were unanimous in their opposition to Chandler.

Some of them were not convinced that I would be the best candidate. We talked about that. I don't recall anybody in those meetings that [was] not [a] member of the legislature. The person that called me was Paul Huddleston, the lawyer from Bowling Green. He . . . was one of the leaders. Hoppy Hopkins was pretty active at that time. Foster Ockerman—as I recall, he was one of the rebels, along with [John] Breckinridge. I would say that Ockerman, Huddleston, and Breckinridge are the ones I remember as being most vocal. Jim Ware in the [Kentucky] Senate, although not known as a rebel, was sympathetic and was considered one of them. In the [Kentucky] Senate we had Gates Young from Louisville, who was a leader in opposition to the governor. . . .

I remember a meeting at DuPont Lodge at Cumberland Falls. There was talk about Earle [Clements] running for governor. The news media had more or less anointed him as the candidate to run against Happy's selection. As the last candidate for governor on our side I was invited to that meeting at Cumberland Falls. I was asked to make some remarks. I teed off on the fact that Happy had betrayed the people and also had betrayed me because he had convinced me that he could run the state without new taxes. I really was just sort of pouring out my irritation at how dumb I had been in believing Happy. I guess the sincerity of it and the fact I had done some homework—spelled out in detail the promises he had broken—[were impressive]. There were a few remarks after that—"Well, we didn't think that you could ever get that enthusiastic—bitter—so maybe you do have a little more fire than we thought you had"—something like that. It was generally admitted that I hadn't been a very good candidate, which I admitted myself. They thought I had been too judicial about the whole thing, I think—too objective, that sort of thing, which I guess was natural because my background and my experience had been as a lawyer and as a judge.

I didn't decide to run, I'm certain, until after the end of Happy's second session. I would not have seriously thought about running except that the rebels gave me the notion, although there were some doubters in the group. It was very clear to me that a big majority of the so-called rebels thought I ought to be the candidate. . . . Their reasoning was that I had told the truth about the financial situation in the state and that Happy had not. Now, that was their version. In any event, Happy had run against me as an advocate of a sales tax. They thought that because I had told the truth in the previous campaign that I would have some sympathy and a backlog of support from the people.

I talked to Clements about it several times and I . . . said to Earle, "If you want to run I will not." He knew that and I told the rebels that. But the rebels wanted me to run rather than Earle. Many people thought Earle should run and that I shouldn't. I realized that. But the rebels were the vocal group. So Earle and I talked about it.

About that time there was talk that Wilson Wyatt wanted to run. I recall that Wilson called me at my home in Prestonsburg in the spring of 1958, probably after the legislature adjourned. . . . Wilson said he would like to run for governor and I think I told him I didn't have to run, that I just wanted the strongest candidate to beat Chandler. I [told] Wilson . . . that if he wanted to run and that if he had the support of those people who were in opposition to Happy that I would not run. I don't know what I said to him exactly, but I'm sure he got the impression that if he should run, I would not.

Then there was very strong talk that Wilson was getting ready to announce. So the rebels came back to me. Earle got into it. Earle was not for Wilson. I came to Louisville and I told Wilson that if I gave the impression that I didn't want to run that I wanted to clarify it. I had taken a second look—had been in touch with people for whom I had respect—and I did intend to run.

Then there was a tug of war while Wilson and I both were jockeying for position. We were trying, Doc Beauchamp and Earle Clements and I, . . . to put together a ticket with me as the gubernatorial candidate and a strong man from western Kentucky for lieutenant governor. We thought Smith Broadbent would be the best man for lieutenant governor. Smith was probably about my age—a very successful farmer, a good Methodist, [a] highly respected businessman. He had never run for office. Earle knew him well and Doc Beauchamp knew him well. I didn't know him that well. We met with Smith and I met with him here in Louisville. I tried to persuade Smith to run for lieutenant governor with me for governor. He made the argument that he should run for governor and I should run for lieutenant governor. I had no intention of running for lieutenant governor. I didn't have to run for governor, but I didn't intend to run for lieutenant governor.

Then, two or three days later, Earle went to western Kentucky and met with me at Doc Beauchamp's home. We were talking with

Broadbent and we were trying to convince Smith that he ought to run for lieutenant governor. We got a telephone call. This person said, "Have you heard that Wilson Wyatt just announced for governor?" That broke up our meeting.

Earle arranged for a meeting in Louisville of all rebels. . . . We kicked it around. It was an open discussion. What should we do that we could have as much assurance as possible that we could beat Harry Waterfield? Out of that meeting it was generally agreed that I should go ahead and run, that Wilson couldn't win—being from Louisville, identified with the *Courier-Journal,* and so on. . . . I got the strong feeling that it was the consensus of that group that I should run. Then, too, I thought that Wilson had jumped the gun. . . . I think the following day . . . I got on the radio in Louisville and announced that I would be running.

Lawrence Wetherby Combs indicated to me [after his defeat] that he would be interested in running again. We had several rallies in the succeeding years and in each and every one of them we'd try to get Bert in and get him before the people. I recall one specifically up at Cumberland Falls and he made a speech that just rattled the rafters. At that time, I said, and Earle Clements was right next to me, "It looks like Bert is ready to be a candidate again." There was some feeling that he was not forceful enough in 1955. But . . . [in] the next race he was outgoing and did a tremendous job. . . .

I was supporting Wyatt. . . . I talked to Combs at my home below Middletown and asked him if he was going to run. He said, "No, I'm not." This was two or three months before the primary. . . . Subsequent to that a great bunch of our people got after Combs and talked him into running. I, in the meantime, having come from Jefferson County and Wyatt having contacted me, had agreed to be for Wyatt.

Lois Combs Weinberg I remember he took a trip to Lexington and Louisville and we all knew that it would be the deciding point as to whether he would run. I guess he was talking to some of the politicos and whether or not they would support him. He called back home. Apparently they had given him the necessary word and he said, "What shall I do? Shall I run or just let it go?" I remember I said in my youthful enthusiasm, "Fire away, Daddy."

Ed Fossett At that time the Legislative Research Commission was not developed as it is today and it was difficult for particular anti-

members of the House to get the necessary typing done and research done that they needed. The LRC was more controlled by the administration at that time and they did not have the support that individual members, even mavericks, get now. Certainly the young turks, as they were called, Foster Ockerman, John Breckinridge and others received support from our office [of the attorney general] in research and in typing bills and amendments. At that time I couldn't say that they were in contact with Judge Combs or being led by him. I'm sure that you know Jo Ferguson was a very close friend of Combs. They really weren't rebels. They had their own things going. I would say they were united in their opposition to the governor.

Gil Kingsbury (Interview 1) We didn't really know [if Combs would try again]. I was anti-Chandler and I ran for the General Assembly along with Jim Ware, a lifelong friend of mine. He ran for the [Kentucky] Senate and I ran for the [Kentucky] House in 1957. We both won and went down there and we were part of the anti-Chandler faction in the General Assembly. We were the rebels. . . . The majority of the Democrats were rebels but there was cooperation between the Republicans and the remaining Democrats to give Chandler control of the General Assembly. At that time we were in touch with Ned Breathitt and Bert Combs, asking them for advice, and they called us and wanted to know what we were doing. There was a general exchange not so much in person as by telephone and by letter.

As the next election approached and Chandler's administration was coming to an end and Waterfield was the leading contender for the nomination, the group got together in Louisville . . . and decided who we were going to support. . . . On April 13 Combs announced for office . . . and we opened headquarters in the Seelbach Hotel. . . . [T]here were just two people on the staff at that particular time. There was Ruth Murphy from Pike County and myself. All we had was one room in the hotel. I stayed a lot in the headquarters.

Ruth Murphy It was the last part of the session . . . and the rebel group was trying to get a candidate out of their group. . . . One day Paul Huddleston, two or three days before the session was over, came in my office in the press room and asked me . . . to call [Bert] and ask him to meet with the rebels on Saturday. I told him that Bert would not come if they wanted him to run for governor. He said, "We've got to some way get him to announce." So I gave him the number an told him to call and tell him that they wanted his advice and wanted him to come down to Frankfort and meet with several of them—advise them on who he thinks would be the best candidate out of the group. Paul did this and when Bert walked in they all unanimously said, "You are the one. We have decided on you." But if [Paul] had called him to come down and talk about running for governor, he would not have come. He was almost adamant against saying that he would run, and got into a little trouble later on by putting it off too long.

James C. Ware   Gil Kingsbury and I ran together in the 1957 election. We went to Frankfort and we rented an apartment and we held all of the meetings of the rebels in our apartment. It was at that time when we were visited on several occasions by Bert. He would come in and counsel with us so far as what we were doing in the [Kentucky] House and in the [Kentucky] Senate. . . . We were setting the stage for Combs to run again. I don't think there was ever any question about his running. There was no question in my mind and certainly none in Gil Kingsbury's. We were absolutely sure that he was our candidate.

Tommy Carroll   Clements really, beginning around 1957 and 1958, led me to Combs because Clements had picked up a candidate in his mind he was determined he could defeat Chandler with. By the summer of 1958, as I now recall, I was working for Combs and by the fall of 1958 was in close contact with Clements and had begun to take trips out into the state. Those preliminary trips were for the purpose of contacting people in various counties and trying to commence a Combs's organization. That was back in the days when politics were a whole lot rougher than they are today. You had the 2 percent assessment on state employees. You had the so-called black-bag man [who] went through the various highway districts and collected and brought the money to Frankfort. You had to fight fire with fire.

Robert R. Martin   I was in on some of the initial work in which they were planning for the campaign. [Bert] asked me to serve as campaign chairman . . . on an occasion when he and I were guests in the home of Senator Clements in Morganfield. There were lengthy discussions and the next morning he . . . told me he wanted me to manage the campaign because he wanted to emphasize education and he wanted to do whatever was necessary to advance education. That was the reason why I was interested. . . . I had to make a decision whether I wanted to stay in politics. There was nothing that opened up for me so this was the best opportunity I had. But I would not have done it except . . . that he emphasized that he really wanted to do something for education.

John Palmore Clements called around on the telephone and asked various people what they thought. I remember very clearly that he asked me what I thought about Combs. I was in favor of his running again if he wanted to run. Senator Clements was very careful about things like that. He would consult people at listening posts or whose opinions he valued as to local feeling. He'd call people all over the state and ask them things. There hasn't been anyone else in Kentucky politics with as much horsepower as he had. Clements never asked me about Wilson Wyatt. We all thought that two candidates would insure the election of Governor Waterfield. We didn't think there was a chance with Wyatt and Combs both in the race.

William Scent He had during the four-year interim kept up his contacts. Chandler was a political leader and a politician that nobody was ever fainthearted about. I mean you either liked him or you didn't like him. There were a lot of people that didn't like Chandler, didn't like his administration, and Combs represented to them the epitome of anti-Chandler forces. So I think they just naturally gathered around him as the anti-Chandler candidate. Waterfield had to carry the reputation of Chandler, and Chandler did not get along with the media representatives. He never got along, for example, with the people who ran the Louisville papers, although it seemed like many times he'd win anyway, even when they were against him.

Dix Winston There was a change—a tremendous change [from 1955 to 1959]. He was still the same Combs to me, but, of course, we had grown to be very close friends. His attitude and approach changed. In 1955 . . . [j]ust to go through the routine of introducing himself and speaking to someone new, he almost dodged people. . . . He had met a lot of new friends and between 1955 and 1959 he had refreshed—and these friends lasted. People he'd met for the first time in the 1955 campaign grew to know him even better. . . . [T]hey didn't abandon him as a friend but they stayed in contact for four years and I think this had a lot to do with . . .

breaking him out of the shell or the ice cube. . . . Combs, to my knowledge, never did abandon any friend. If there was a break between Combs and another person that break had to be instituted by the other person. Combs would not turn anyone down that I ever knew of.

Wilson Wyatt When I decided to run for governor in 1959 I really thought that Bert was not going to run. I don't mean by this to make any accusations against him but I had talked with him and I interpreted him to mean that he was not going to run. I think if he had told me positively he was going to run I would never have entered the race. I would have simply returned to the law practice and would never have entered it, and, therefore, never have served in office. On the other hand, I don't think he meant to deceive me. I just think that he wasn't categorically positive and maybe I didn't ask as positively as I should. But I had the impression that he was not going to run and therefore I entered, really anticipating his support. If so, I thought that I could win.

Robert Bell I think that Wyatt had started being active, at least in terms of traveling across the state to see what support he could muster. An interesting aside—I believe that at some point in this period Wilson Wyatt went to Washington and had a visit with Earle Clements and I think Earle Clements advised Wyatt to go back and talk to a lot of the courthouse-types of people that had been very close to Doc Beauchamp. I think that probably Clements gave him that advice knowing that he would receive a somewhat negative reception. I think Wyatt instead of following that advice went back to Louisville and submitted his obviously strong position in Louisville and Jefferson County . . . where he . . . in essence locked up the Louisville political situation in behalf of his own candidacy. From that point on he was a force that had to be reckoned with in the primary of 1959.

Combs v. Wyatt

Wilson Wyatt formally announced for governor on April 9, 1958, with the strong endorsement of the Louisville-Jefferson County political organization. Four days later Bert Combs officially threw his hat into the ring, and on April 21, Earle Clements publicly endorsed him. Harry Lee Waterfield did not make his official announcement

The 1959 Gubernatorial Primary 73

until late June, but everyone knew he would be Chandler's candidate.[11] For the remainder of 1958 there were three active candidates in the field. Waterfield could expect the support of his own loyal western Kentucky followers as well as that of administration adherents. Combs was the choice of the rebels and what remained of Clements's statewide faction. Wyatt, the former mayor of Louisville, had the solid backing of Jefferson County and Louisville, including people like Lawrence Wetherby. Though Wyatt tried to project an image of being above factions, and therefore an alternative to both Combs and Waterfield, his strongest endorsers in Jefferson County were among the most hostile to Chandler. Thus it became increasingly evident as the three-cornered race progressed that Combs and Wyatt would split the anti-administration forces, enabling Waterfield to win the nomination. Even local officials prone to be anti-Chandler were wary of supporting either Combs or Wyatt if victory seemed impossible.

Consequently, it became a matter of determining which anti-Chandler candidate had the better chance. For the most part Wyatt and Combs campaigned against what they regarded as the irregularities and broken promises that characterized the current administration. Each pointed to Chandler's 1955 pledge that he could run the state without additional taxes, which was followed by higher income-tax levies. They criticized his widespread replacement of state employees with unqualified cronies and condemned his highway construction procedures. Combs and Wyatt rarely talked about each other. At the same time, the positive sides of their campaigns were strikingly similar. Each favored clean government, a merit system, industrial development, aid to education, and state park improvement, among other things.

Bert Combs (Interview 4)   Wilson and I continued to be friends. We both campaigned hard from that time until we finally merged. [There was] no campaign fund set up. In those days it was thought that you needed to get in all the counties and see the so-called political leaders. If you could get enough people to make a speech, do that, but mainly . . . visit the courthouse and all the important business establishments. Someone had always given you the names of important people that you needed to see in the county. That's what Wilson and I did primarily from the time we both announced until we effected the merger.

Clements was in Washington a good part of the time with the Tobacco Institute. But he was in Kentucky quite a bit. He was doing those things that he knew how to do better than most people. He was saying to people, "Combs can win, Wyatt can't win." "You ought to get for Combs." "Everybody ought to be for Combs." Wilson had a good send-off. He didn't lack for publicity. He is a dynamic, energetic, capable individual. But I think that I did have residual support from the last campaign because Happy had become very unpopular and I was more the symbol of opposition to Happy than was Wilson. Wilson talked about factionalism, that we ought to eliminate factionalism. But that didn't go over as good as my saying, "I'm against Happy Chandler." We still liked our politics straight in Kentucky in those days and every person felt we ought to be on one side or the other. We also knew that Harry Lee Waterfield was ahead of us. By that time polls were being talked about and used. It got to the point where a lot of people would have liked to be for one of us [but] didn't want to take that gamble because Waterfield was ahead.

Wilson and I were both campaigning hard. A lot of people who wanted our side to win talked to me. "You and Wilson ought to get together. A lot of good people are in [an] uncomfortable situation," and . . . "If you both run Waterfield will win." There was considerable talk and I'm sure Wilson had heard a great deal. At one time he and I met in Cincinnati. We met there to keep it a secret. We didn't publicize it. Not many people knew we had met. We talked about our problems a couple of hours. But there was no room for agreement. He was adamant about running for governor and I was adamant. I thought he ought to run for lieutenant governor and he thought I should. That kind of talk had persisted—that we ought to get together.

Tommy Carroll   In the fall of 1958 you also had the situation of Wyatt and Combs running against each other as well as against Waterfield and anybody with any political know-how or feeling could tell that there's no way in the world you could beat an incumbent state administration with two candidates running against it—at least at that time.

A lot of the local leaders were holding back. This was back in the days when the courthouse crowd was much more important than it is today . . . and a lot of the county judges, the magistrates, the sheriff—they weren't going to jump until they felt like they had a reasonable chance. A lot of them very frankly said, "If you can't get these two fellows together we're going to go with Harry Lee—even though they didn't particularly like Happy. They wanted a winner.

Ed Farris That was a rather difficult situation for me personally. I was strong for Combs in 1955 and was closer to Combs and the people that were for him than I was to Wyatt. I would have to say, though, that I was younger then and more impatient and I think that Combs delayed his entry. I think an early entry into the race and a more obvious show of intent to run for governor would have probably precluded Wyatt from running. . . .

I don't think that Clements could ever be described as a supporter of Wyatt—not at that time for governor. They were different personalities. Wilson and Clements were not close. Clements was best in dealing with people in situations that he felt comfortable with and [had] intimate knowledge of—and he and Wyatt had never been particularly close. Wilson was a national figure. Wilson did not have any bedrock support in Kentucky, as Clements would put it. Wyatt and the *Courier-Journal* were never favorable to Clements and vice versa. The *Courier-Journal* hierarchy was definitely for Wyatt—no question about that. But they did not turn their newspaper over to Wyatt and his campaign as they had turned their newspaper against Happy.

Cattie Lou Miller It was obvious that Combs wanted to run and was going to run long before the actual filing occurred. About a year before the primary election Combs had opened a headquarters at the seventh floor of the Seelbach. I had been working at the Louisville Chamber of Commerce. It was kind of a poor man's campaign at that time. I think there were only three or four at headquarters—maybe only three rooms. It was almost an unfinanced effort. But I had and have always gone on the theory that you don't pick who you want to be for on the basis of what their prospects seem to be. You pick them on the basis that you want to be for them and would like for them to win. So I went over to his headquarters one day on the lunch hour and he was in room 743 and we spoke and I voluntarily said to him without any pressure on his or anybody else's part that I was glad to get over to his headquarters, that I was glad that he was running, that I was for him, and that if he would have any interest in my working for his campaign I would be willing to quit working at the Chamber of Commerce and come to work full-time in his campaign. He said yes, so that afternoon I gave my notice at the Louisville Chamber where I had a very pleasant and interesting job, very good relations with the folks at the Chamber. . . . I operated in the headquarters at the Seelbach for a year before the main primary. The staff built up very slowly because there was as slender a financing from the outset as any that I'd ever known.

J.R. Miller Clements came to Owensboro and talked to me. . . . [We] sat on a concrete wall around the corner of St. Anne and Fourth streets in Owensboro. We left the hotel where we had a meeting when it dawned on Clements that I was not committed. So he decided to give me an attitude talk. He pulled from his pocket a poll he'd had made. He convinced me that neither Combs nor Wyatt could beat Waterfield in the primary—that they were going to have to join and the logical candidate for governor was Combs, and Wyatt should be the lieutenant governor. Clements was a master at justifying his opinion and he convinced me. I told him I would like to get active if such a merger took place but I didn't want another bloodbath like I'd had in 1955. I knew Chandler was going to put his entire administration behind Waterfield and I felt that the same people I'd done battle with in 1955 would probably leave Clements and Combs and perhaps go with Waterfield based on what I'd learned. I was being very careful, if not cagey.

John Ed Pearce Bert came back this time an older man who had been defeated and . . . gotten better organized. . . . He had a lot more friends this time. He had his mountain counties better organized. Whereas Happy had been able to organize some of the mountain counties, Waterfield couldn't.

Wilson Wyatt helped, too, in a strange way. Wilson was not terribly well known in the state, but usually where he was known he was fairly prominent. I'm not saying he was terribly popular. He was known as a New Dealer and something of a left-winger in some quarters. But he was a prominent man on the national scene. He knew famous people. He operated on a high level. When Bert and Wilson started running against each other they sort of publicized each other and they fought along for a long time and as a result they had picked up quite a bit of support when Clements finally was able to bring about the coalition.

The Merger

When an impartial poll at the end of 1958 revealed that Bert Combs had more statewide support than Wilson Wyatt, the latter, though disappointed, consoled himself with the fact that Combs and he sought similar objectives for the commonwealth. By no means was it easy, but Wyatt decided finally that the only way to oust the incumbent administration and secure the goals he wanted was for him to join with Combs.

The meeting between Combs and Wyatt at the Standiford Motel in January 1959 was the turning point in the race. From that time forward the reconstruction of the old Clements-Wetherby faction became a reality.

Bert Combs (Interview 4) Earle [Clements] decided to have a poll made. Earle didn't talk to me about that, although I suspected that he was. But I didn't know and I never asked him. I was campaigning in Mount Sterling in January 1959. I got this telephone call because Earle knew generally where I was. He had a schedule out of headquarters and he knew who I would be talking to in Mount Sterling either at nine o'clock or ten o'clock. He knew I would be talking to Jack Reynolds and his brother Bob.

I had this call at Reynolds's office and Earle said, "I know you have some appointments over there, but I think it would be much more important if you came up to Louisville. I have arranged for a meeting at the Standiford Motel with Wilson Wyatt and one of Wilson's friends." So I came back to Louisville.

I got there in the middle of the afternooon and then Earle told me about this poll and that he had talked with Wilson. He had conveyed to one of Wilson's friends—Dick Moloney—that he had this poll. . . . Bob Burke had checked the poll, and the work sheet, and talked to the pollster, and Burke was convinced that it was a bona fide poll. How much communication there had been directly between Earle and Wilson I don't know. . . . Wilson came to the Standiford Motel around 7:00 P.M. He told me very frankly that he knew about the poll and he was willing to run for lieutenant governor providing we could have a statement of principles. I knew without asking him that there would be nothing in the statement I couldn't subscribe to. So we got the statement of principles written up. We got a couple of young fellows who knew how to write. They prepared the statement and we initialed it. So then it was just a formality to announce the merger.

The question of Wyatt's political future was never mentioned. Wyatt and I both were rather dedicated people at that time. We wanted, number one, to win, and number two, to do some things and initiate some programs, and I believe that we both thought that if we were successful the future would take care of itself.

The programs as they evolved were more specific but they implemented what we thought were in the statement of principles. Then we campaigned together for the most part for the first two or three weeks. We had separate schedules after that, but frequently we would have joint meetings.

Wilson Wyatt I called Earle Clements in Washington and . . . asked him to come to Louisville. I said that I thought there was a matter that could be of interest to him if he would fly to Louisville that evening. . . . He didn't say, "What is up?" or anything else. I think his intuition must have told him something, but he knew it wasn't just to sit down and have a hamburger. So he flew to Louisville that evening. . . .

I told him I [had] reached the conclusion . . . that there was a real danger that neither Bert nor I would win it. On the other hand, I [felt] that if we merged forces we [were] bound to win it, and that if we could merge forces on the basis of accepting everything in the platform that I had announced up to then and—which wasn't a problem because most of it was in line with what Bert had also announced—that then I thought we would be willing to go on and do it. If I did it I would expect as lieutenant governor to take an active hand in the administration, but I would only expect there to be one governor—I remember mentioning that specifically to him and to Bert. . . . I would be in office and would have a significant position and could see that my followers and friends were not left out in the cold as an afterthought. . . . I felt in fairness I owed it to them. You've got to make these decisions in light of where you are and what the reality is, and I felt it would be letting them down and it would be failing to accomplish for the commonwealth things that I'd hoped to get done and that with Bert running this was an offer that could not be refused, would be immediately accepted. It was immediately accepted and within less than twenty-four hours the merger was on, the programs were announced, the problems were fused, and we started going down the campaign to what then became the largest majority in the history of Kentucky.

J. David Francis They met on Monday night. Wilson Wyatt called me at my residence on Sunday night. There had been a meeting during the day Sunday [January 19]. I'm advised that Governor Wetherby, Mr. Moloney, Miss Lennie McLaughlin, Ed Farris, some others [were there]—for some reason I wasn't there, I don't right now recall why. Anyway Mr. Wyatt came on the phone and told me they'd had this conference and had decided that the [most important thing was] to accomplish the program . . . and the best way to insure that was that they join together and that Combs run for governor and that he run for lieutenant governor. . . . [H]e said he wanted me to be there to attend the meeting that they'd probably have that night, at which this would be put together.

I went into Louisville [the next morning] and I remember meeting with Mr. Wyatt in his office in the Marion Taylor Building. We spent quite some time together. I believe we sent out for some lunch and went on through to the afternoon. We worked most of the day. There were certain things we were going to require as part of going together.

[That night] we went to a room at the Standiford Motel. . . . [W]hen we first got there I don't believe anybody was there except Senator Earle Clements. This was Senator Clements's room. We had only been there getting our hats and coats off when Judge Combs and Robert R. Martin arrived. I had met Judge Combs before but I had never met Dr. Martin. We met there for a good part of the evening. There were certain things that Mr. Wyatt wanted agreement on. Number one was that the campaign and the administration would be carried on more or less as a team effort. Not as co-governors—we all understood one would have to be governor and one lieutenant governor, of course. But that Mr. Wyatt would have the primary responsibility of industrial development and development of job opportunities and things of that kind. There was another thing or two. One was the attorney general—Mr. Wyatt very much wanted John Breckinridge to be the attorney general. . . .

Senator Clements I don't believe ever sat down. . . . He just walked around. If he ever said anything, it was when he was asked. . . . If someone would have the idea that he sat down and dictated this whole thing, that would not be fair to Senator Clements at all. . . . I was glad he was there. I didn't feel I had been made to do anything on his account. . . .

I think [Combs and Wyatt] respected each other highly. Both recognized each to be an outstanding lawyer and an outstanding statesman, which they are and which they were. Dr. Martin and myself each became co-chairmen—he was chairman for Combs, I was chairman for Wyatt. . . .

Just like Dr. Martin and myself, Combs's people certainly recognized that in Ed Farris we had the one best man to organize the counties in the state. . . . Farris went in there the next day and went to work on that thing. He had the telephone going with both hands and never let up. I would say that all our people were the same people. We just came together in a family reunion. I think a lot of them were just really relieved that we had gone together. We were very lucky. I don't think any of this had ever been planned. It came to me as a big surprise the night he called me on the phone but we knew in the Wyatt camp that the real enemy was not Combs. The enemy was Governor Chandler. We talked a whole lot about the idea that we wished the Combs crowd would come with us.

Robert R. Martin At that time we had a situation in which the anti-administration, anti-Chandler group was divided between Judge Combs on one hand and Wilson Wyatt on the other. We did a lot of spinning of wheels, so to speak. People constantly said to us in many counties, "We're not going to make up our minds until you fellows get together." Then I remember quite well I was called around the 20th of January 1959 and was asked to meet with Governor Combs by Senator Clements. When I got there Judge Combs was already there. He and Senator Clements had already had some lengthy discussion. I would have been . . . in on all of it except that it was a matter that he got there first.

Then we were told about the conversation that had been held between Senator Clements and Wyatt. A poll had been taken by Lou Harris. The Harris poll showed that Combs was a far stronger candidate than Wyatt. There had been an informal agreement between Senator Clements and Mr. Wyatt that, everything being worked out satisfactorily, Mr. Wyatt would be willing to run for lieutenant governor.

The three of us talked and I believe the time was 8:30 P.M. when three people came in—Wilson Wyatt, Richard Moloney, and David Francis from Bowling Green, Wyatt's campaign chairman. We then went into further discussion and reached agreement and understanding. At that point, a great many people were called by telephone and were told about it.

J.R. Miller I got a phone call on a weekend and Clements asked me to come to Louisville and I did. I met him and some other fellows at the Seelbach Hotel and he suggested that I drive him to Standiford Field, which I did. I was at Standiford Field when the trade was made. I had no idea what was going on, though I suspected. Clements never came back out. I guess he spent the night there and I got tired of waiting for him so I went back to the Seelbach Hotel and parked the car we had there and got my car and went back to Owensboro. So then the next day it broke that Clements had brought the coalition about. I don't know whether he sat up all night. I just got tired of waiting when he went in and decided he was going to spend the night there. I didn't see them come out. I just assumed they all spent the night there.

Gil Kingsbury (Interview 1) The way the campaign moved along, Wilson Wyatt was running, too, and we knew that in order to beat Waterfield we couldn't have a divided faction in the party. So we were careful, and I did the publicity for Bert Combs, not to say anything mean about Wilson Wyatt. We confined our bolts to Lieutenant Governor Waterfield. I remember as the primary election was approaching I had a call at home about three o'clock in the morning that the matter had been solved and Wyatt was to run for lieutenant governor and Bert Combs was to run for governor.

Ruth Murphy I think Ed Farris was the next most important thing [to Clements] in that he was the one that convinced Wilson to come out. The meeting was initiated, I'm sure, by Clements, who had the poll. Clements was smart enough. They didn't want to insult Wilson and, of course, Clements didn't have any love for Wyatt and the *Courier* anyway. He got a copy of the poll in to Ed Farris—Farris and Clements were close—before the meeting and this is why Wilson even agreed to come to the meeting. Ed did not let Wilson know how he came to have a copy of the poll but when Wilson saw that he did not have any more strength than he had, Ed was able to make his point that it would be better for Kentucky if he would come out and insure that Combs would be elected rather than perpetuation of the Chandler regime, so to speak. Then I guess Combs got back to the hotel—I don't know what time it was—sometime in the early hours of the morning because he telephoned me and said, "I have a running mate for lieutenant governor." The next day we had to start the merger of the staffs and all that goes along with the campaign and it became quite a hectic pace. There were no problems in merging.

John Palmore When the news came out that they had merged and that Wyatt was going to run with Combs, I'll never forget my partner, Leonard Mitchell, walking up and down the street and when he would see somebody strong on the other side he would say, "Ain't the candidates sweet?" and he'd laugh. We felt then that it was a lead pipe cinch that Combs would win, and he did win.

Fontaine Banks I think from the very beginning it was the feeling of most people that I knew that something had to happen—that the two forces, the Wilson Wyatt campaign and the Bert Combs campaign, had to get together to do something. If both ran for governor then the Chandler candidate . . . would be elected. So I think from the very beginning we felt that something had to happen although at the time we didn't know what it would be.

Robert Bell I think in the fall of 1958 the Wyatt polls began to tell the organization that not only was it impossible for them to win the primary but as long as he and Combs were both in the race, it was almost certain that Waterfield would win. I'm sure that this influenced the merger.

Wilson Wyatt was considered to be a liberal from Louisville with a liberal Democratic background having problems projecting himself to the other sections of the state, although he had scattered support and some very strong support [from people] like Dick Moloney. . . . He was very much in the Wyatt camp. I think subsequent events tend to confirm that Earle Clements and Dick Moloney were the conduit through which the merger of the Combs-Wyatt forces occurred in the primary of 1959.

Tommy Carroll I was not at the merger meeting. They called me at three o'clock in the morning. I got the impression that the relationship between Combs and Wyatt was excellent but there might have been some strain between Wyatt and Clements, perhaps by Clements putting a little bit too much pressure, which he was adroit at doing, on Wyatt, and Wyatt feeling it and resenting it.

It was my understanding that in addition to running for lieutenant governor . . . Wyatt got a commitment that the administration would support him for the United States Senate in 1962. I got this from Earle Clements himself. Clements felt that this was an unwise commitment on Wyatt's part—that Morton would be extremely difficult to defeat and that Wyatt should actually have asked for a commitment for the governorship in 1963, which he would have been given. But he wanted the United States Senate.

Ed Farris Clements played an important role. The prelude to the meeting was that Wyatt himself had to be sold that he was not going to win the primary. That was the key thing. . . . There was a poll that indicated that. I don't think even the poll was the compelling thing. I think it was that Wilson's campaign was not well organized or as strong on the county level as Combs. He did not have the grass-roots political strength and organization that Combs had, or certainly that Combs would have very easily if Wyatt were not running.

Ed Prichard I think this was orchestrated primarily by Senator Clements whose absence in 1955 was probably the crucial factor in Combs's defeat. . . . Now Wyatt says that he originated that meeting [at the Standiford Motel]. He says he called Earle Clements. But anyway Clements got the polls and Clements brought them together and that was the foundation of "The Team You Can Trust."

Jay Spurrier I think Wyatt's withdrawal solidified Combs's campaign a little because Wyatt was a very highly thought-of fellow who had gotten out and done pretty well in the campaign. It was probably the key factor in the race, but I think if Waterfield had denied that he was Happy's friend the race might have been closer. . . . [T]here were times that he could have broken with Happy, which would have been the politically expedient thing to do. There was a time that the *Courier-Journal* said that if he had broken with Happy they would have given him their support.

The Team You Can Trust

Immediately following the merger, "The Team You Can Trust"—as they now described themselves—embarked on a series of regional meetings, first in Paducah and then successively at Hopkinsville,

Bowling Green, Somerset, Elizabethtown, Williamstown, and Pikeville. They stressed their dedication to responsible government and scored the Chandler administration for its policies of revenge and reprisal. "Kentuckians," Combs said at Somerset, "are proud people and . . . are tired of temporary measures taken for political advantage. They are tired of the patronizing attitude of this administration. They want to work and we shall labor with them to establish new jobs with permanent incomes."[12] Just as Chandler had attacked the Wetherby administration during the 1955 primary, Combs and Wyatt now concentrated their assaults upon Chandler rather than Waterfield.

The only danger came from possible overconfidence once Combs and Wyatt joined forces. Sensitive to that liklihood, Earle Clements worked hard to counteract that tendency. In fact, though Robert Martin and David Francis were official co-chairmen for the campaign, no one doubted that Clements was in charge. He did not make speeches, but he maintained a constant liaison with local leaders by telephone and, if necessary, in person, and he influenced many of them to regard him as the real leader of the Combs-Wyatt campaign. In addition, he effectively ran the headquarters operation in Louisville and participated on all the committees active there. It is not surprising, therefore, that many Kentuckians anticipated that he would be a prominent force in the new administration.

Bert Combs (Interview 4) I think most of the people who voted for me in 1955 did so in opposition to Chandler. But I do think that Wilson and I had built up a lot of good will by 1959. Harry Lee Waterfield has never been a very controversial individual. People like[d] him personally and consider[ed] him an honorable, decent individual. If he hadn't had the Chandler burden, things might have been different. But of course, we ran against Happy. Waterfield was a man caught in the middle—Chandler's net—couldn't escape. People assumed that Waterfield would be obligated to Chandler if he were elected, regardless. . . .

It's hard to tell what was administration strength and what was Waterfield's personal strength. He had been popular in western Kentucky. He had been a popular member of the legislature. He hadn't antagonized anybody personally as lieutenant governor. A lot of people like[d] Harry Lee Waterfield. He stayed out as much as he could from controversy in the Chandler administration. Nobody had any particular criticism of him. Wilson and I managed to sell our program. We had a good program and we convinced thinking people of the state that we had a platform that would be good for Kentucky. Waterfield was not strong on programs in the campaign.

Harry Lee Waterfield Bert got the upper hand on me in that campaign as Happy got one over him in the 1955 campaign about little things that didn't amount to anything. The small things in a political campaign that people can get their teeth in are really what are effective. Happy, in the 1955 campaign talked about the $20,000 rug. He didn't lie about that. He stretched it a little. . . .

The thing that hurt me more than anything in 1959 was the crippled goose. Earl Wallace had completed this Ballard County reservation for ducks and geese down in western Kentucky. He wanted Chandler to go down and see it. So he finally consented to go and spend the night. They were going to take him out into a blind and shoot some ducks or geese or whatever. My judgment is that Chandler had not shot a gun in twenty-five years, but he went and some of the game wardens on the other side had it set up. They shot at some geese and the game wardens immediately appeared and said that they were two or three minutes before twelve o'clock. The federal law is that you can't shoot until high noon. They put that charge against them and then they said he'd crippled a goose, and produced it, I think.

The thing got in the newspapers and got fanned around pretty good, you know. They filed charges . . . and Happy wouldn't pay his fine. Everywhere I'd go to make a speech I'd get these duck [and] geese calls. It was terribly annoying. There would be a big crowd and especially if it was . . . out . . . in the open, somebody would turn an old goose loose and put a hot stick to her and she'd squawk and you might just as well go home, you know.

Chandler wouldn't agree to go in and pay his fine. It didn't cost more than $22.50. I said to him I'd be glad to pay his fine for him because there are 400,000 people who have to buy a license to fish or hunt in Kentucky. At one time or another most of them have violated the law and most of them paid fines. I said, "I believe those people would be on your side." He said, "No, I never have paid a fine, and I'm not going to pay one now. I've never even had to pay a parking fine in my life."

They built little wire cages and had a little gosling in the cage and they set them around either in the hallway of the courthouse or the entrance or on the steps or out in the yard or wherever the people sat around, and they would have a big red sign up on this cage—"Happy Killed My Pappy." Then I would start making a speech and some of the boys would do these goose calls. People got on to that. They got their teeth into it. That was worse than the $20,000 rug. It was little things like that in the speaking days that really [were] effective. That wouldn't work on television today. It wouldn't amount to anything. When you have four hundred to five hundred people and you get a mass reaction then you can take a thing like that and magnify it and really do the job. Happy was a past master at that. I think it hurt me as much as any one thing in the campaign. I always had the feeling the same thing Happy did to Combs in 1955 they did to me in 1959.

J. David Francis [After the merger] the first thing we did—somewhere I've got a picture of Judge Combs, Mr. Wyatt, Bob Martin, and myself and this new banner [that said] "The Team You Can Trust"—the four of us standing there together, and I think we've got our hands together, something like that. Anyway, we set up immediately a series of meetings across the state that were called "Meet the Team" meetings. We went to Paducah, Pikeville, and had regional meetings. . . . We had any number of them and you see this was the real unification of all the people that were for both of them.

I want to tell you now—they were all there. These were big crowd meetings. Then we had little meetings with them, the leadership, before and after, to work out these little rough spots in the counties where two fellows wanted to name the Highway Department representative. They were good meetings and we had fun. Everybody at those meetings kind of developed the victory spirit. You could feel it.

Robert R. Martin There was never any problem about working out organization anywhere immediately after the merger. Campaign headquarters gets to be a sizable staff and there was someone in charge of speaking engagements, people who gave attention to organization—there was the constant arranging of meetings and that kind of thing. It's one thing to have an organization. It's another thing to generate enough enthusiasm to get them to work—[to] organize and get out the vote. There's a tremendous amount of work that goes on. . . .

Sometime in June I had a chat with Governor Combs and we had very carefully gone through the primary without committing ourselves or discussing taxes. He told me in June that he wanted to leave some tracks and he realized that if he did anything he was going to have to have additional revenue. I never did repeat it. We'd been very careful about that through the primary because once burned you dread the fire. They had pinned the tax thing on him in 1955.

However, we discussed it because John Robsion opened the fall campaign at Bardstown with [a] big emphasis on taxes. We had a discussion on Sunday afternoon. I know that Mr. John Watts and some others there said that's a very simple matter. You just say that you are opposed to any additional taxes. . . . The next day the Chamber of Commerce was meeting and Combs was busy on some matter and John Watts spoke and he made just about such a statement about any additional taxes. The next day Combs repudiated the statement, which was a pretty bold thing to do. But he did it. Fortunately, however . . . the soldiers' bonus passed overwhelmingly, which called for a sales tax. So he just secured additional money which went for education.

Gil Kingsbury (Interview 1) Every Sunday morning at headquarters we had a strategy meeting. Earle Clements presided and sometimes Combs was there, and Wyatt, and sometimes neither attended the meeting. Earle Clements, being a masterful leader and a strong man, didn't care whether they were around or not. As a matter of fact, if they weren't around it was probably better because we could go ahead and do things that they might object to. So at that meeting were people like Ed Prichard, myself, Bill Young, Doc Beauchamp, and maybe one or two others. Clements would get up and tell us what we were going to do that week. If [Combs] was to visit Clinton County we would find out what their interests were down there. We wrote speeches. I wrote some of his speeches, Prichard wrote some of his speeches. When Combs had a chance to read over the speeches prior to delivery he did a good job. He had a photographic mind. But when he read the things cold he was horrible. I'd listened to him on the radio when he was reading some of my stuff and you're proud of what you write, but I just dreaded when I'd hear him read it. But when he read it in advance he was all right. He discarded the written stuff and made the talk off the top of his head.

Tommy Carroll I became convinced around the first of April that we were on the verge of throwing it away. Clements, because of

1956 and because of his background going clear back to the double primary of 1935 and even further than that, had a deep, deep suspicion and fear of the power of the state administration to manipulate the election machinery. If you will recall, that was at a point when Louisville was one of the few areas in the commonwealth that had voting machines. There were voting machines scattered around the commonwealth but there were a lot of places that still used the paper ballot.

I was put in charge of the legal phase of the campaign and the principal task I had, which ended up taking all of my time up until the primary, was to make certain that our side was protected both at the polls and at the count. It was something I don't think had ever been done in Kentucky politics before. It involved methods and procedures for making sure that we got the challengers on election day, that the voting machines where they were used were inspected properly before they were opened election morning, that there was no skulduggery with paper ballots. . . .

I think that probably had a great deal to do with Combs winning the primary because we were protected all over the state. I made with Earle Clements two swings of the state and we would have regional meetings. One time I remember we started from here one day—from Louisville—and we headed west. We stopped at Elizabethtown and he bought a bushel of mixed fruit and I didn't have anything but fruit to eat for two days. He lived on fruit, but I was weak from hunger after two days. We would hold these meetings and we'd have three or four hundred people that would come in. What they were was they were instruction courses on how to keep them from stealing the election. It was just that simple. . . .

I don't think Combs really comprehended what we were doing. This is not meant as a reflection on him because he simply was running an eighteen-hour day every day. He was making a tremendously better candidate than he had been in 1955. He had gotten to the point where he could inject sarcasm and humor into his speeches and he could captivate a crowd, and once again this was when people still went to political rallies.

I can remember political rallies like in the Franklin [County] High School and down in Somerset in Pulaski County where you had literally thousands of people. You don't have that kind of thing today. And Combs, of course, had his famous Castro speech which was the play on Happy and Vego Barnes and the others sending money to Cuba and buying a casino and Castro appropriating the casino when he took over—and Happy going down to the sands of Key West and getting down on his knees and crying out, "Castro, oh Castro, send me back my money." Combs really got to where he could tell that story and play it like a master violinist. He had the crowd screeching and hollering. That was back in the days when young Bernie Crimmins, Johnny's son, dressed up like Happy Chandler with the rubber mask and would come into a rally right into the middle of Combs's speech leading on a leash a live goose and carrying a sign—"Happy Killed My Pappy." That, of course, would send the crowd roaring. Once again that sort of thing doesn't go over anymore. . . .

[The soldiers'] bonus was a beautifully contrived subterfuge to get the sales tax. State government had to have the money. I have no question in my mind but what there was a definite undercurrent organization that knew the state had to have money. They knew that the sales tax meant political death with Chandler being such a rabid opponent to it. And the soldiers' bonus was used to get the sales tax in. I've always believed that. And we worked for the soldiers' bonus, everywhere, yessir! I don't think the veterans' organizations knew they were being used. When it passed, Combs then very adroitly got the sales tax at 3 percent [and] took either 1 or less than 1 percent to pay off the bonus, and that was only over a period of a few short years. It saved state government as far as solvency was concerned. I don't think Combs knew what was going on [when the bonus was being pushed].

Cattie Lou Miller Clements was the real leader at headquarters. Clements and Combs were the two fulcrums of power in both the primary and the general election. [John] Watts was [the] most helpful, pleasant, uninsistent kind of chairman. He had good thoughts and contributed a great deal of talent to the campaign, but no one around Earle Clements in a campaign sought to unseat Clements as the manager, regardless of who bore the title. Clements and Watts were great personal friends and so Watts would have had no desire to strike off on any avenue that wasn't either originated by Clements or else thoroughly planned out with him. Combs was and is no milquetoast so he projected his own thinking and desires and beliefs and needs into the campaign strategy planning. By this time his very dogged qualities had come to the front that I, for one, had been totally unaware of in 1955. His tenacity had begun to show. It also became one of his earmarks as governor—his untiring kind of a relentless campaigning. He could go all day and all night. He was a dynamic candidate and he picked up ideas like a blotter and created his own ideas quite well and projected all of those into the campaign.

Fontaine Banks The only concern that we had in the fall election was making sure that there was not supreme overconfidence and that would be to get the vote out. We felt that if we got the vote out we'd have a record vote, and it was.

As I remember the [veterans' bonus amendment] it was the veterans and veterans' families who were all for it. Governor Combs's position was, "It's on the ballot. If people want it, fine. If they don't want it, fine. But it's up to you." There were several people on the . . . campaign staff who thought it was crucial to stay neutral but to have as much interest in that question as could be aroused. But as I remember it, [Combs] stayed aloof.

Of course, it was tied to a tax. [Combs] knew, I think, from the very beginning that he was going to have to do something with additional taxes. I think he thought there was no way he could do the things that he thought had to be done for Kentucky with the tax base that was then in effect. The sales tax came easier because of the veterans' bonus. People had voted for it. After it happened I had many, many veterans tell me that they had gone away to work in Ohio, Michigan, or other places but that summer they came back and re-registered and voted in Kentucky.

Jo Ferguson Certainly Bert had learned a lot and changed his personal style. He was much easier with everybody. He had become less parochial. I don't think there was any doubt once he got this three-way race worked out that he would win [the primary]. . . .

He had the problem then of winning in November after he got the nomination. That's when I was active for him. I made a few speeches but that wasn't what I was doing mostly. In the fall campaign and after the campaign was over and he had been elected I was one of the four men, including himself, who worked on his program for him. It was Bert Combs, Wilson Wyatt, John Breckinridge— who was to succeed me as attorney general—and me. We were the program people both during the campaign and after.

John Crimmins Bert was a lot better campaigner in 1959 than he had been in 1955. He met the people better. When I first met Bert I thought he was a rather shy person, but he was more outgoing in

1959. He was able with more ease to sit down and discuss things with people. He met with people no matter where we wanted him to go in Jefferson County. He could meet with people, talk with them. He was very outward about how he felt about things.

Robert Matthews I was in the campaign headquarters the last two or three months of the campaign. I was very vitally interested in the outcome of that campaign. The campaign was pitched on the idea that Combs and Wyatt as a team would run against the administration of Chandler. If they ever mentioned Waterfield's name, it was a mistake. They pitched the whole campaign against Happy and it turned out to be a very successful way.

William May In Governor Combs's successful race in 1959 we did things then that I don't hide now are against the law. . . . We got some very bad filming of Governor Chandler, and I've forgotten how we acquired it, but he came through very poorly on television. I think maybe he bought some time on one small station. So then we had access to the material or the tape and we bought time to run the thing because it was a very poor showing of him. We called up his headquarters and told everybody to watch it. He really had a very poor appearance, which supports the position that politics has changed considerably. We couldn't do that today. It wouldn't be successful and I think it's illegal too. Politics is no fun anymore.

John Palmore When Combs came to my district to campaign I always met him and would go with him. He was improving as a campaigner. I'll never forget [when] my wife and I drove up to Meade County at Muldraugh, Kentucky, not far from Fort Knox. They were going to tour through the district, winding up at Henderson that night. . . . We rode with Combs that day in my car. My wife likes to tell the story that as we were driving down the road I was doing most of the talking, which is customary, I guess. She looked over and Combs was sitting there sound asleep.

John Ed Pearce Wyatt and Bert helped each other. Once the coalition was formed, it was a rather natural one because Bert had matured a lot. He had learned how to tell the little human interest story. He had learned how to get in the knife thrust—how to make the cutting, killing remark without seeming to be nasty as Happy could always do. He'd learned how to make fun of people. He would get out and do the rough and tumble work and Wilson would come in, more or less, on clouds of joy and intellect hitting the high road. They made a rather effective team.

Lois Combs Weinberg I think by 1959 he had cultivated storytelling and joke-telling and just speaking in general. He was his own man. He wasn't the administration candidate. He was under his own steam. I think he'd gone back to Prestonsburg and he'd gotten in touch with his roots. He had a base. Coming from Lexington, that was nowheresville. . . . He'd been gone from Eastern Kentucky for five years, and [was] just naturally out of touch with friends and supporters who just added an awful lot to the 1959 campaign—the motorcades that went across the state leaving from Floyd County, the financial support from Floyd, and, I'm sure, from other Eastern Kentucky counties. He'd thought about it. He'd mapped out a tentative approach during those years. Like in poker, he knew when he could bluff and when he couldn't.

Chapter 4

The Combs Administration: Political Reality

The inauguration of Bert Combs as governor of Kentucky on December 8, 1959, began four years of labor to achieve the pledges made by "The Team You Can Trust."

In his inaugural address, he reiterated his campaign promise of reform and progress. "By reform," he elaborated, "I mean the elevation of the moral and political tone of government, the development of better methods to carry on the everyday tasks of public service. I mean an attitude of mind which views every problem of state government and every task from the standpoint of scrupulous honesty, decency, and ethics."[1] Specifically, that meant a sound statutory merit system, reform of election laws with voting machines in every county, and greater freedom for the legislative branch from executive domination.

"By progress," the governor explained further, "I mean the advancement of those programs which will stimulate the economy of our state and improve the living conditions of our people."[2] Specifically, this meant educational advancement, industrial development, improvement of parks and tourism, development of research and better marketing for agriculture, building more and better highways, conservation of forests and other natural resources, and control over water supplies.

Combs was particularly concerned at the outset to deemphasize any desire for revenge that his supporters might feel. "In politics," he warned, "generosity is often the truest wisdom. Vindictive minds have no place in a great Kentucky."[3]

Advice and Counsel

Ed Easterly I had gone down to handle public relations for the dedication of the Cumberland Gap National Historical Park at Middlesboro. In connection with the celebration some local people gave some parties . . . for the Republican nominee for governor, John Robsion, and for Judge Combs. . . .

[As I arrived at the party for Combs] my host, who was a Middlesboro attorney, met me and brought me up to Judge Combs [who] was standing there talking to a group of people. My host said, "I assume you know Judge Combs?" And I said, "Yes, it's nice to see you again, Judge, and congratulations on your victory." He said, "Thank you Ed—by the way I'd like you to go to work for me." I was still working for Chandler and Waterfield, and I was shocked. "Judge, are you kidding?" He said, "No, I'm real serious and I'll be back in touch with you." . . .

The result was that I was rather impressed by Combs—and I had almost made up my mind to get out of government and go back to weekly newspaper publishing. We had acquired the two newspapers down at Nicholasville, Kentucky. But the thought of working for Combs was so intriguing that I accepted with the understanding that I take August off and come to work for him in September.

Arthur Lloyd I saw Combs fairly soon after he won the election. He asked me to come down and talk to him. Bert and I had been friends. I lost any possibility of being any part of the administration between 1955 and 1959 by virtue of my support of him as a candidate. . . . Bert told me he wanted me to have a place in his administration . . . .

He said to me, "Is there any job that you would like to have in this administration?" I said, "If you want me to be your adjutant general, I'd be honored to accept that position." He said, "That's not important enough. It's not a very big department. It doesn't have many employees down there." I said, "Bert, I may be a little more familiar with that position than you are. To me it's a right important position. It doesn't have very many full-time state employees, but it has several hundred federal employees in the National Guard and reservists."

Dix Winston When the campaign was over I wasn't anxious about going to Frankfort. Again Combs and his usual Combs mannerisms

The Combs Administration 95

decreed that I should, so I did. But before we ever got to Frankfort for the inauguration Ned Breathitt—who had worked very hard in the campaign in western Kentucky, particularly in the first district—and I kept one small suite of rooms in the Seelbach, and opened that up about three weeks before the inauguration.

We were meeting with the various county leadership positions and delegations as to their ideas to people and replacements in state government and what they wanted done. We filled up several tablets meeting with all the 120 county delegations from time to time during that three-week period prior to the inauguration.

On inauguration day Combs moved us into the Department of Personnel and we stayed there until the merit system became effective. Ned pulled out and went to the Public Service Commission and I went to the governor's office as administrative assistant. As I recall, Combs [said] at the time, "You fellows got to get out of there. We've got to get a white horse in there now because we've got a merit system."

Wilson Wyatt I felt that Combs was always completely reasonable with me. He, of course, had problems with people who had been "his people" as I had problems with ones who had been "my people." I think he was reasonable and I think he feels I was reasonable. We would work those out and the result was that I think he and his people did respond to the fact that here was something that was offered as the chance to let him be the governor rather than me and they responded to it in a very fine way. I think people who were lined up with me were recognized and considered.

Robert Bell Wyatt phoned me [in] probably late November or early December of 1959. . . . As I mentioned earlier, I had done a few things in his interest during the campaign before the merger. I think because of that and because of my relationship to Senator [Dick] Moloney he telephoned and asked me to visit with him in Louisville.

I had no idea what was on his mind. I went up and he asked me if I would consider returning to the public service and working in his office as his executive assistant. Frankly, when I went to Louisville I had no particular interest in doing that but he painted a pretty exciting picture of what he and Governor-elect Combs planned to do, especially in the areas of economic development. . . . I decided that it seemed to be a pretty good opportunity to turn to the public service—particularly state government in an area that I had not had any previous experience in—working with the legislature. It seemed interesting to me, so I accepted.

Jo Ferguson Combs had promised me that I would be chairman of the Public Service Commission. Then when he made his deal with Wyatt, . . . Wyatt said that his campaign manager, David Francis, had to be taken care of. It turned out when Bert was sworn in, both David and I thought we were going to be chairman of the Public Service Commission.

So Combs with his usual Solomon-come-to-judgment said, "Well now, let me appoint both you boys to the commission and one of you serve as chairman for two years and the other serve as chairman for two years." I thought about that for awhile and I thought, "well, I'm going to go out in private practice anyway pretty soon, so . . . " He also didn't know who to appoint as head of the Economic Security Department and he had a program for putting in Medicaid. Medicaid didn't exist anywhere in the United States, but the federal program had just been set up to work through the states. So he offered me that position [commissioner of Economic Security] and I thought that might be interesting and I'd just stay for awhile.

Ed Fossett John Breckinridge [the attorney general] asked me to stay on, so I was happy and enjoying my job. When Jo Ferguson was appointed to the Department of Economic Security he asked me to come as his administrative assistant there and because of the close, personal friendship with Jo—and it was a raise in pay—I was pleased to go.

[Later I became legal assistant to the governor when] Bob Matthews, who had been assistant attorney general with me [and was] Combs's original administrative assistant . . . left the governor's office to take the position of commissioner of Finance. Wendell Ford was elevated to chief assistant. I suppose it was Bob Matthews who recommended me. All I know is that one day Jo Ferguson and I were asked to come to the governor's office. The governor asked me to come as legal assistant, so I just stayed. I didn't go back to the Department of Economic Security. I didn't know anything about it until we got to the governor's office. I was thrilled with the offer and Jo let me go without protest.

Polly Gorman (Interview 1) [He asked me to work for him] at a state picnic, the first time a state picnic had ever been held for employees, probably in early June. My maiden name was Preston [and] my nickname was "Presty." He said, "Hey, Presty, I've been meaning to talk to you"—if you can imagine, at a picnic with several thousand people. I said, "I've been hearing that you're going to talk to me and I can come over any time you want me to come and talk to you." He said, "Well, hey, I want you to come work for me," and I said, "That never would work out because you and I always fought like cats and dogs. You'd wring my neck every day." He said, "I know it, but I need to have somebody's neck I know I can wring and get by with it"—and so help me, that was all the discussion we had. I said, "Wait a minute, I haven't had a vacation in more than a year. I can't come to work the first of July because I'm going to take a vacation." He said, "I'll call you before then."

This was early in June. He never did call or anything. So just before I left to get on a plane to go to New York on probably June 30 I called his office and I talked to Cattie Lou Miller. She said, "Wait a minute, you had better talk to the governor before you leave." She put me on hold and I stayed on for fifteen minutes. He never did come on and I went on to New York without knowing if I had a job when I came back or not.

So on the Monday morning I came back I thought, I'll go up there and see what he's got in mind. So I did. He walked out and said, "Where in the hell have you been?" So that was our relationship with hiring.

Cattie Lou Miller Just a year from the time that he became governor he created the Department of Public Information and I then went to that department. . . . The conversation [about my appointment] was brief. It occurred when I was sitting by his desk going over some mail. . . . [There] were two letters from personal friends of mine in Louisville, both of whom had excellent backgrounds—one in an advertising agency who had been an instructor of advertising at the University of Louisville. The other was the head of advertising public relations for the largest corporation in the state. . . . I frankly said to him that I had two letters from these two good men and I thought either one of them would just be a swell person to head the new department. He said, "Cal, I'm going to appoint you." My mouth kind of dropped open because I had had no thoughts of myself going to that department or becoming the head of it and was not aware in any sense that he or anyone else was thinking in that direction. We talked about it a little bit and we decided that I would do it.

Walter Gattis I was recommended for the job of commissioner of Personnel by Felix Joyner. Mr. Joyner was commissioner of Revenue. He had been active in Governor Combs's campaign. I had worked for Mr. Joyner as budget examiner for several years in the 1950s. . . . I was awed by [Governor Combs] as almost anyone is being in the presence of the chief executive of the state. I considered him to be a man of ability and integrity. I don't remember that he gave any instructions other than I had been recommended. I remember specifically he said, "I really don't know you. I'm taking you on the recommendation of other people, in large measure Mr. Joyner and the board." That was about it. He said something to the effect that, "You're supposed to know something about the law and what it's about. You do it. I'll back you."

Jack Matlick I met Bert Combs in 1960. I got a call from the governor's office saying that the governor wanted to see me just shortly after I had sold my publishing business. Having never been active in politics, I was surprised but went over to see what he wanted. I didn't even know Governor Combs at that time.

He told me that some people that he'd been talking to thought that I would make a good commissioner of Conservation. This was so foreign to me because I guess I would have bet anybody $1,000 that I would never work for the state of Kentucky. I'd spent a number of years in the publishing business and was ready to retire. When I came home that night after talking to Governor Combs, my wife wanted to know what he wanted to talk about. So I told her he wanted me to be commissioner of Conservation. I told her I took the job. She wouldn't believe it until she heard it on the ten o'clock news that night.

Earl Powell [How I became commissioner of Economic Security] is an amazing story. . . . One day Jo Ferguson, who had gone over there and served about a year—you might say just kept the seat warm, did not want the job, wanted to go to Louisville and practice law—told me he thought the governor was going to appoint me commissioner of Economic Security. I told him I didn't want it, but Jo said he was thinking about it. A day or so later, Ed Fossett, an attorney on Combs's staff, called me over to his office and Judge

Combs told me in his mountain twang he was going to make me commissioner of Economic Security. I said, "No, you're not." He said, "Why, you mean you wouldn't take it? You're a good soldier, you're supposed to be on my team helping this administration. I'm going to appoint you." I said, "Okay." Now that's exactly how it happened. There was never any prior discussion. There wasn't anything. I walked from one side of the capitol building to the other. It was just that simple.

Harry B. Miller I had no connection to the Combs administration except to help advise him if he had any problems. By virtue of being treasurer of the state Central Executive Committee, I would meet with him probably once every two or three months to go over party finances. In the course of that he would try me with ideas that had been brought up to him—as he tried many other people . . . to see if it seemed like a good idea to you or a bad idea. He was very dogmatic in trying to get as much advice on any one subject as he possibly could before he made a decision to get the feelings throughout the state, before he made a [final] decision.

Henry Meigs, II There was interest expressed to Governor Combs and his administration by the bar here in Frankfort [to create the forty-eighth judicial district] on the ground that the volume of business in the Frankfort circuit court was increasing at such a rate that it could no longer be handled comfortably or conveniently by one judge—who had the responsibility as well for three other counties throughout the district. It was thought that it was high time a separate district should be created for taking care of the extensive business of the state which was almost all . . . exclusively within the jurisdiction of the Franklin court. . . .

After the legislation had been enacted there was a lot of speculation around Frankfort as to who might be appointed. The effective date of the act was not until June or later. All I know is I was appointed in September of 1960 and I was the most surprised member of the bar because speculation which had gone on between March and September had centered around one or two Democrats, naturally. I thought I'd be the last one in the world to be selected. There were only at that time four Republicans practicing law in Frankfort.

I met with Governor Combs at the request of a couple Democrat lawyers, who were his close associates, on the day of the appointment. I believe I drove to Lexington and met him at the airport, and we discussed the matter and he said he had been favorably disposed to appoint me on the recommendation of lawyers who were his friends in Franklin County. If I accepted, he would appoint me. I had advance word, you understand. It wasn't cold turkey that day, but that was the first time I'd had any contact with Governor Combs about it.

Julius Rather Wendell Ford had been his chief administrative assistant and Ed Fossett had been the legal assistant. There had been some illness in the family of Wendell Ford so he resigned to go back to Owensboro to take over his father's business. Ed Fossett moved up as chief administrative assistant to the governor, leaving a vacancy. . . .

Governor Combs called me down one day and I talked to him for awhile and about thirty days later he called me back and, typical of Combs, he was very kind and very nice. After all I was only twenty-five years old. I never had been in politics. I never practiced law. He looked at me and said, "Well, let's try it. If you're not happy, you let me know. And if I'm not happy, I'll let you know." So on that basis I became legal assistant to the governor and he only had one. That time forward I was the governor's legal assistant.

Lois Combs Weinberg What the governor's wife does is different for each governor. It depends on what the woman in the job brings to it in terms of her interests and her talent. I think her greatest job is that of an equalizer or a leveler of her husband. . . . I think my mother did serve that function as well as she could. Anybody that's in politics—you can look at any era of politicians and see that they begin to be carried away—all of a sudden they're in power. Things happen when they decide that they should happen and that's quite different from the rest of us. We're lucky just to keep things churning along, let alone make things happen.

I think that a governor, particularly a Kentucky governor with the power we give them, needs a kind of balancing force that a good wife can give to him. It's a difficult job and some have failed along the way, but that was an important role that my mother played.

The Sales Tax

Bert Combs (Interview 5) It was generally agreed that Kentucky was in desperate plight in the field of public education and down and across the board. But the situation was apparently more acute in elementary and secondary education. Our teachers' salary scale was very low—one of the lowest in the nation, and we were losing many if not most of our best school teachers over this. . . . So I thought that aid to education was a top priority, perhaps the highest priority in my mind. It so happened that at the November election, when I was elected governor, the people passed a constitutional amendment to pay a soldiers' bonus and the amendment specifically provided that the bonus should be paid by revenue from a sales tax. The bonus amendment passed as a surprise to most people, including me.

We were faced with the situation where in order to carry out the constitutional mandate on the soldiers' bonus the legislature needed to enact a sales tax for that purpose. It would have taken roughly one half of one cent—something like that—to pay the soldiers bonus. I decided that if we had to have a sales tax, had to set up the machinery for it, had to be subject to the annoyance of paying a sales tax, even though a small one, that it ought to be of sufficient magnitude to do some of the other things that needed to be done badly, education being perhaps the number one priority.

I had anticipated providing more money for education, but I hadn't clarified my thinking beyond that point. I didn't know whether I was going the income tax route, severance tax on coal—I had not seriously considered passing a sales tax. That fell into my lap, so I recommended to the legislature and announced through the media that since we had to have a sales tax we ought to have it big enough to do some of these things that had to be done.

Consequently, the legislature enacted a three-cent sales tax and about one half of one cent of that was used to pay the soldiers bonus. About 66 percent of the balance was allocated to public education. So, in brief, that is the reason that we had a sales tax and that is the means by which money was provided for education. Regardless of the controversy about the tax I think most people did recognize and did admit that we made very rapid strides in public education during my administration.

Many people accused me of using that bonus tax as a subterfuge to get the three-cent tax. The legislature did call it a soldiers' bonus tax. But admittedly, and I never made any statement or argument to the contrary, we didn't have more than [a] half-of-one-cent tax to finance the soldiers' bonus. I may have been for a sales tax anyway. I just had not clarified myself.

Gil Kingsbury (Interview 1) I remember the evening of the election when it was evident that the Combs–Wyatt ticket was going to win. And then we started paying attention to the bonus issue on the ballot. That had a dampening effect upon the celebration. When it appeared it would pass, there was a little bit of dismay as to how to handle it, what to do about it. It wouldn't be a popular issue, and yet it was mandated by the people. . . . We felt that the money wouldn't be sufficient to make any major changes in the economy of the state and it would go for trifling things—a used car, maybe a coat of paint on the house. The General Assembly had agreed to put it on the ballot because it was too cowardly—I was a member—to levy the tax itself. So they put it to the people. Maybe that was wise anyway. If we hadn't had the sales tax I don't know where Kentucky would have been today.

James C. Ware I remember the whole thing very well. I was in the [Kentucky] Senate, of course, when they passed [the bonus referendum]. I was amazed that Happy supported it but at that time I hadn't had the experience some of the others had. Ever since World War II was over, every succeeding session of the legislature, somebody wanted the bonus. It just seemed to snowball. Each time there would be half a dozen bills with different ways to provide payment. I don't think there was a great clamor for the payment of the bonus, but it was a popular issue with people. . . . I was amazed that the people approved it. I don't think Happy expected it to be passed either.

Lambert Hehl The year he was elected governor the people voted for the veterans' bonus. On his inaugural day I forgot how many high school bands participated in that parade. I sat on the sidelines and one after another was carrying a banner—"One cent for G.I. Joe, two cents for G.I. Joe's son." I knew then that we were going to have a 3 percent sales tax. The electorate had voted for a veterans' bonus to be financed by a retail sales tax. The bonus cost about $100 million, if I'm not mistaken, and in the first year of the sales tax the revenue derived from it was well over $100 million. So we could have paid it off instead of paying off a thirty-year bond issue.

Robert R. Martin I don't know that Combs [ever talked about the soldiers' bonus] but as he was out in the field campaigning he realized it was going to pass because the sentiment was overwhelming. . . .

Combs never questioned extensive support for education. Quite the contrary. He said repeatedly when we were preparing the budget for [the] 1960 legislature over a six-week period . . . that he wanted every dime that could go to education to go to education. The bonus had been developed and they were working on the budget within the framework of the then revenue. He wanted it left that way because even the budget analysts didn't realize that he was going to get this additional source of money. Practically all of it went to education.

Cattie Lou Miller   The [bonus referendum] was a problem for the campaign. We had no burning desire that I personally recall for it to either pass or not pass. We looked on it as most things were considered in the context of that campaign. It was no surprise when it passed because the polls showed it would pass. The veterans were vigorous for it and many veterans living in Ohio came back home to ride the trails to get votes for it. I never heard of the possibility that the referendum tax might be used for increased state income until later.

Samuel Van Curon   I've always said it was fortunate for Bert [that] during Happy's term we had the big push for the soldiers' bonus. There was no way to finance it unless you put on a sales tax or something. Happy just wouldn't do that. The legislature could have voted a sales tax in Kentucky any time they wanted to. In fact, I ran a poll and the people overwhelmingly were for the sales tax. Even John Y. Brown [Sr.] introduced one, but the bill didn't get out of committee. The pressure from the bonus forced Happy to figure out some way to pay it. So he conceived the idea of placing the soldiers' bonus on the ballot and the sales tax on the ballot to finance it because Happy didn't think it would pass because of the sales tax. I always said after that that the sales tax was conceived in deceit and born in subterfuge. But the thing did pass.

Harry Lee Waterfield   In the 1958 legislature I personally picked the constitution amendment for the veterans' bonus and I had it in my speech before Combs opened his campaign. The night before I was to speak some of my advisors by telephone—I was in Paducah—finally about three o'clock in the morning got me to take a pencil and mark it out. I still have the original copy. . . . Bert picked it up and he ran with it. . . . I can't blame anybody about that except myself. I was for some reason persuaded that I shouldn't do it.

Phil Ardery It seems to me that the veterans' bonus was set up to implement a sales tax. I think really the strategy was not to have a bonus but to figure out a way to get a sales tax. I accepted my bonus but in my heart I didn't think it was a good thing except to the extent that it did make palatable a sales tax, which I thought we needed.

Barry Bingham, Sr. Chandler, of course, made the sales tax anathema in Kentucky. I think that it was absolutely necessary. If we had not had the sales tax for a good many years in this state, I just don't know where we would be. We never would have had any progress on building highways or any of the other things that we've been able to do through the years. Always it's possible to demagogue against a sales tax and when Combs put the sales tax in, he certainly, I'm sure, was not eager to do it because he knew it would be politically difficult.

Albert B. Chandler [The sales tax] is the worst tax on earth. . . . That's an income tax turned upside down. It makes it more difficult for the average fellow who has to spend 75 to 80 percent of his money and maybe more to live. It's a total tax on the total income of the average fellow. Now, if you had a national wholesale tax for everybody and repealed some of the other taxes I might not mind that. . . . This is a tax on necessities, on the things people have to have in order to live. It's wrong. I never agreed to it and I never quit my opposition to it and I would never quit. All they were looking for was a way to pick the goose to get the most feathers with the least squawking. That will get you the most feathers. It is just a tax collector's boondoggle.

Robert Bell Of course, the sales tax, being so broad-based at that point . . . in our political and governmental history, probably offered the best possibility of adequate financing of a lot of needed services and programs. There were concessions made in the way of certain exemptions at the time the sales tax was enacted that would make it more attractive to heavy industry.

Lieutenant Governor Wyatt was very interested in the way that the sales tax would be—the actual statute, the language, and, maybe even more important, the administrative regulations that followed. As I recall, Henry Ward was the chairman of an advisory committee. He was then connected with the Louisville Chamber of Commerce and he worked very closely with then–revenue commissioner William Scent in order to provide a statutory and regulatory basis for state sales tax that would not discourage investment in plant[s] and equipment on the part of industry.

Arthur Lloyd I didn't know until after a bill had been introduced in the General Assembly in regard to the veterans' bonus that it was going to be administered by the Department of Military Affairs, and that the adjutant general would be ex-officio administrator of the veterans' bonus. I was real upset about that because I felt Bert should have talked to me about it. I wouldn't have up and resigned . . . but I could have helped write the bill so it could have been administered more easily than it was under the law that was written. I think I could have made several changes in the bill which would have facilitated the administration of the whole veterans' bonus thing. But I didn't have that opportunity.

Ed Easterly Everything depended upon the sales tax and I do know that under the supervision of Jack Matlick, commissioner of Conservation, we set up an intensive public relations promotion program in the governor's office and I was given *carte blanche* to go out to all the state universities and colleges and borrow the most competent public relations [people] they had and bring them in to work with me to inform the public of the things that needed to be done and how they could be accomplished with the revenue from the sales tax. . . . The Combs administration was so effective in putting into operation these programs utilizing the revenue from the sales tax [and] the public was so pleased by the results that criticism of the sales tax just faded away.

Jack Matlick At the first meeting that I ever attended Governor Combs said we've got to get busy and pass this sales tax. I was hesitant to say anything at my first meeting but finally I got up nerve enough to say in kind of a weak voice, "Governor, wouldn't it be better to try to sell the benefits of a sales tax?" He didn't pay much attention to me but when the cabinet meeting was over, he said, "Matlick, come up here. See that desk back there in the corner of the cabinet room. Now I want you to go back there and sit down at that desk as long as necessary to put down on paper all the different ideas of how we can sell the benefits of a sales tax."

They used to think that the press wouldn't use a news item if it mentioned sales tax, but we had volumes and volumes of them—scrapbooks full—because we would go out and each department was asked in state government, if we had a sales tax, how was it going to affect the people you serve? Press used that information. Radio used it. No problem getting the sales tax passed and I think it is the fairest tax that has ever been developed.

William Scent I met often with him. When we came up with the sales tax practically everybody who was in business in Kentucky was going to be affected by it. . . . [L]uckily the Revenue Department, since the time it was organized by Dr. James Martin, has in large part been run very professionally. There were a lot of minor jobs that went out for political reasons but by and large we had a great nucleus of personnel who were real good tax administrators. So there was a good base to build on for the sales tax.

John Ed Pearce After he was in office Bert showed a great deal of savvy and a great deal of courage in espousing that sales tax, and furthermore he knew exactly where he wanted to put it. He wanted to rebuild the schools of the state, modernize the highways, and establish his modern park system. And he knew what he wanted to do with that park system. I have today looked back on the Combs administration as the beginning of, if not modern government in Kentucky, [then] modern public facilities in Kentucky. He had the plan and the money.

The Merit System

Bert Combs (Interview 5) When I was running for governor and Wilson Wyatt was running, we both were in favor of a merit system for state employees. The situation really wasn't good. People think it's bad now, but they don't remember how much worse it was before we had a merit system.

After Wilson and I merged and ran as a team we had what we called a statement of principles and that was one of those principles—that we would advocate to the legislature that there be a statutory merit system approved and implemented. The legislature on our recommendation did pass that merit system and it was implemented not overnight but as reasonably soon as we thought we could without too much disruption of state government. I think the merit system has been fairly successful. It's far from perfect, but it's better than no system at all. . . .

I did have opposition—certainly grudging support by many of my political friends who really were important in electing me governor. Doc Beauchamp made no secret of the fact that he thought it was ridiculous. He used to say, "Combs is destroying the Democratic party." To some extent Beauchamp has been a good prophet because prior to the merit system a sitting governor had tremendous influence in a primary election. It was exercised in most elections but particularly in the primary to select a nominee to succeed the incumbent. I think that I see less and less control by the incumbent governors. . . .

Jo Ferguson We really had some hot fights over [the merit system]. The state had no merit system outside of the Economic Security Department at that time. It had ceased to be customary to fire engineers and people of that nature, but the average employee was subject to being discharged at any time there was a change of administration. I think everybody agreed that that situation had to change to some degree, but there was a very considerable disagreement on how far that should go.

We found . . . a rather strange alliance of viewpoints. Bert Combs and John Breckinridge took the real liberal merit system viewpoint and Wilson Wyatt, who was supposed to be the big liberal from Louisville, and I, a western Kentucky conservative, took a bit more conservative viewpoint.

The principle points of disagreement were with relationship to the Highway Department maintenance workers. They had always been the basis for any political organization in the state. Wilson and I were both anxious to keep some control over those people. If you didn't have the foreman under your thumb you didn't have much control over them. So that was the big dispute.

William May Combs was sincerely dedicated to a merit system. I, being a political animal, . . . was not. I remember a very definite meeting we had on the subject. I guess I was the only politician there. It was at the Lafayette Hotel in Lexington after he'd been elected but before he'd been inaugurated. Dr. Robert Martin, Gladys

Kammerer, and Governor Combs and I met there and talked about it and I resisted it as hard as I could. I was in favor of the spoils system.

But the merit system we now have was prepared by Kammerer, and Dr. Martin had criticized it and reedited it to where it met his needs and that is what actually is on the law books now. Those four people are the only ones I know in on the conference on the subject of merit system. Governor Combs could not be dissuaded. I had considerable influence with him. I used it all. I didn't stop him. . . .

Yet many qualified people are in state government because of the merit system. They feel protected. I guess when you reach my age you can see things you couldn't see when you were more enthusiastic as a would-be political leader. I'd have to say that the merit system as started by Governor Combs has certainly been a real benefit to the operation of state government. I do think it has encouraged a bureaucracy that's too built up in too many places. . . . Maybe that's necessary to protect the state's money. I don't know.

Robert Cornett   The merit system that he built, he intended—he was probably the one man in Frankfort that understood how to get that thing solidified—to get it in place so it would last. He knew he had to make some accommodations to the political facts of life of that day. He couldn't take patronage out of the personnel system all at one fell swoop. Yet you had to take it out enough so that you had some credibility with the general public, with the Republicans even.

I think he steered that line very carefully—drove poor old Walter Gattis absolutely crazy, but he always supported Walter when it came down to it. Poor Walter would have to threaten to resign about twice a week—would agonize horribly over what to do. This would be over what you do for somebody who comes in from Prestonsburg and wants a job, and the governor wants him to have a job, and he's not qualified. How do you stretch the rules? Poor old Walter managed. Governor Combs knew that Walter was doing really what he wanted done. Governor Combs never interfered with that basic process. He made sure it went forward. But at the same time he took care of his friends.

Walter Gattis   The idea that public jobs are not the personal property of partisan political leaders died hard. . . . There was a lot of cynicism the first year or two. My memory of that first year was a steady stream of delegations that would come and say that "We have a replacement for 'Joe' in the Revenue Department because he didn't help us out in the campaign. We got a fellow to go in his place." Finally it became almost like a broken record. I'd say, "Fine, if the commissioner of Revenue wants to fire 'Joe' and your person takes the test and places among the top three, then he can be hired. But the commissioner has to tell 'Joe'—and we're together on this, I know he will—but if he doesn't, 'Joe' will come to this department and we'll explain his rights—that he has the right to file an appeal within thirty days if he thinks he's getting unfairly treated. He has a right to a hearing and . . . if the board agrees that he was dismissed for political reasons, it's going to order reinstatement." That ended it. People would go away grumbling. That ended a great many requests to fire someone for partisan reasons.

Once in a while during the first two or three years many people would come and say, "Governor Combs wants this or that." Finally it became clear that I could not and didn't have to take instructions from third or fourth parties on what the governor said. There were seven telephone lines coming into that desk. The governor had access to every one of them. He had no hesitation about making his wishes known directly to me.

The governor of Kentucky is very personal. I guess there are hundreds of people, if not thousands, who think the only way to get a job is to get to the governor himself. Quite frequently the governor would call and say "These people are in my office. They are my friends. They have a fellow who is badly in need of a job. Do all you can for them." He meant to do all I could within the law. The cases in which the person could not qualify or could not pass the test I have never had him directly or indirectly say, "You've got to do this." I'm sure a lot of people won't believe that but the governor never asked me to do a totally wrong thing. Many times somebody else would say the governor insisted this be done or he's promised this but I'd get to him finally in an airplane or somewhere and all he would say was, "I didn't say that. All I said was, 'Do what you can for him.' I'd like to see him get a job but if he can't qualify, he can't." He told me several times, "It's your job to enforce the law."

Robert Matthews The merit system, he was in favor of that. He ran on a platform that there were too many people on the state payroll. But after coming in and looking at the payroll I don't think we ever did much about reducing the payroll. That's a hard thing to do. In state government I think you get better efficiency than you do certainly out of the federal bureaucracy. But the merit system—the trouble with the merit system is it protects the unqualified and the unproductive as well as the productive and qualified.

Tommy Carroll I didn't think it would work. It's worked better than I thought it would. I wasn't too much for it, to be perfectly frank. I'm not too much for this business of people getting on the payroll and then you can't either discipline or fire them unless you can prove they are guilty of treason.

I was in favor of the elimination of the 2 percent political assessment. I don't think a person ought to have an assessment on their salaries automatically, like a checkoff of union dues. Particularly, I don't think that your secretarial, clerical, and your ordinary state employees should. Conversely, I think that a person who seeks actively the appointment to a commission or a board from which he receives pretty good remuneration and only works a little part of the time should voluntarily contribute. I feel that way as a person.

Albert B. Chandler It makes statesmen out of everybody. I think we'd [have] been better off if we never had fooled with it. I helped with it. I'm responsible for that. I always felt that my fellows had more merit than other fellows and they felt the same way. Who's the judge of merit? Each fellow in his turn judges who's got merit and who hasn't. Qualifications are all right. A lot of fellows are just making time—drones. The government has got hundreds of drones and that's largely attributable to the merit system.

J. David Francis I'll be frank with you about it. When they first brought it up, I wasn't much for it. I think it is subject to many abuses. However, I guess as many people as it takes to run the many facets of government and the recognition that there just can't be a turnover of all those positions every four years, it's probably a pretty good thing. I believe this is one of the things that Wilson Wyatt insisted upon at the merger. But I wasn't as interested in that at the time as he was so I might be wrong about that.

Harry B. Miller I think the merit system is very good and Combs said he was going to put it in . . . and he put it in. It has worked very effectively. It has gotten stronger throughout the years because more positions have been put under it. We were supposed to have a merit system somewhat before that time, but he lived and bled and

The Combs Administration

died with the merit system. There were some people that he certainly didn't like that were in positions that he would have liked to have had other people in. I talked to him about that. Unless they violated some of the laws that would disqualify them he never tried to fire any employee that was under the merit system. He might have encouraged supervisors to look for reasons to get rid of somebody if they weren't doing their job, but he wouldn't fire a man just because of his political beliefs.

Ed Prichard I don't think there is any doubt that probably one of the most fundamental changes that the Combs period instituted was the merit system. I don't think anybody at the time realized it. But I think a combination of the merit system with the attitude that the courts took during the Nunn administration, when it was first placed under heavy assault, has made a deep change in attitude. State employees vote now as they damn please.

Lawrence Wetherby Chandler had said he had a merit system but it was his merit system. Combs adopted a merit system by statute and put it into effect. It's had a tremendous effect upon the morale of employees and on the continuity of programs. The employee now is not scared to death when a political campaign comes along. He knows if he wants to contribute to the campaign he can. If he doesn't want to, he doesn't have to. Each and every one of them, if they're interested in government, they'll go out and work just the same as they would have if their job depended on it. I think it's been a tremendous boost for the state. We've been able to keep employees year to year and through administrations. Before, . . . under some administrations, they'd walk in and sign an order firing everybody. Chandler did that on Christmas Eve in 1935.

Toll Roads, Parks, and Tourism

Bert Combs (Interview 5) I was strongly of the opinion that we needed to develop the tourist industry in Kentucky. I thought that . . . Kentucky's history and . . . the romance attached to the name Kentucky made it a natural as a tourist state. Obviously, in order to develop the state as a tourist attraction, number one, we had to have something for tourists to do and to see. So we decided to concentrate on upgrading and constructing, developing new state parks.

The other leg of that stool was we had to upgrade our highways in order to attract people into the state. Tourists like to travel on good roads, of course, and it was very apparent that the state road fund—and that's separate as you know from the general fund where the sales tax went—could not with its revenue resources build many major highways.

So we decided to concentrate on a toll road system in Kentucky. Now, Lawrence Wetherby had already built one toll road, the Kentucky Turnpike, running from Louisville to Elizabethtown and it was doing well. There was a lot of opinion, a lot of argument really, that, yes, a toll road would pay for itself in the populous area of the state like Louisville to Elizabethtown, but a toll road would not be practical say from Winchester to Campton or Hazard or Prestonsburg in underdeveloped parts of the state.

One factor in favor of a toll road system was that the interstate system then was underway, was then being developed, and our state highways were being built in Kentucky, but all of those highways ran north to south. . . . As you know Kentucky is about five hundred miles in distance from Paducah in the west and Elkhorn City on the east. So it was my thought that the toll road system ought to be built generally east to west. We started with the Mountain Parkway. As a matter of fact, the plans, the design for a mountain parkway, were largely complete by the time I was elected governor. After the primary I said to one of the highway engineering firms in Kentucky—actually it's a matter of record—Bill May's firm, Brighton Engineering. I said to Bill May, "You know the situation. I'm the Democratic nominee. I think I'll be elected in November. I want to build a toll road, . . . and if you want to gamble on this job and want to start drawing the plans and the design now so we would be ready to start shortly after I'm sworn into office, you can have the job. If we lose the election, you lose. If I win, you'll profit too." So he did start shortly after the primary, as I understand, and we were ready to start moving on the Mountain Parkway. So the Mountain Parkway was started early in my administration, and, incidentally, was dedicated months before my term expired, which is what I wanted. . . .

The bond people, the Kentucky bond people, were very dubious about being able to sell bonds for the Mountain Parkway. It was the first one, so that's symbolic. We consulted with several of the big bond firms in New York and some of those—the top ones—were reluctant to put their name behind bonds on the Mountain Parkway.

We found a bonding company, Allen and Company, which was not one of the very big financial institutions in New York. I believe I heard it was about sixth in size. I don't know how accurate that is. Allen and Company was willing to put its prestige and its credit behind bonds on the Mountain Parkway.

The phrase that came to be associated with the Mountain Parkway was that it was a "developmental highway"—not a highway designed to accommodate existing traffic [but] a highway designed to develop traffic. It was a new concept to me, and perhaps it was in the industry. So that company did handle the bond issue and we sold them at a reasonable rate of interest. I think we sold them for 4-plus percent.

The Mountain Parkway was accepted by most people. Of course, my old friend and opponent, Happy Chandler, made some little humorous remarks about it to the effect that it started nowhere and went nowhere. When you got on it, you couldn't get off. When you got off you couldn't get on. That sort of thing. But I think it was generally accepted and particularly it was accepted by the mountain people [whom] it accommodated. . . .

I would like to point out, however, the sales tax had very little to do with the financing of the toll road system and the same is true with the park system. There had been a very small bond issue, issued prior to my administration—[or] rather, authorized by the legislature and by a previous administration—but [it] had not been finalized or implemented. We needed money for the state park system. I had in my mind building ten or twelve new state parks. We ultimately did build them. I thought that was an appropriate program to be financed by a bond issue. We're not talking about money anything like the amount needed for highways. At the time state parks were built in the early 1960s prices were much lower than they are now. We had a bond issue for state parks somewhere in the neighborhood of $25 to $35 million.

To my mind the state park system is perhaps the best program for the least money that the state has or can have because these parks for the most part pay for themselves. The people who visit the parks pay their money for rooms, food and gasoline, fishing boats, and so on. So I pushed hard on getting the park system complete. We built them pretty fast.

I think we built them within the concept of what the Kentucky state park system ought to be. They're not elaborate, but they are convenient, and are comfortable enough that a family will not feel like it's roughing it even though it's in a state park. Incidentally, Kentucky is one of the very first states to have that concept. Most state park systems then or most of them now are pretty rustic. They're designed to show you nature—and nature in the rough—for the most part. So our concept [was] if you wanted to rough it, you could. You didn't have to stay in the lodge. You could have a mobile home or a trailer, or a tent, or a backpack sleeping bag. . . . We admitted that we had the finest park system in the nation and I think most people generally accepted that.

William May I had made rough projections of the Mountain Parkway that we could do it. I talked to people who financed a toll road project in another state—Oklahoma—that we had worked on. We had this novel plan of financing down there.

The Mountain Parkway could in no sense of the word be called a road to accommodate traffic. The traffic wasn't there. It was an economic road. We were trying to pierce that route up there and get people from east Kentucky to central Kentucky and vice versa.

So we had to work out a novel arrangement of financing. It's this simple. Create a toll road authority to borrow money and build the roads and [then] lease the roads to the Highway Department. . . . [T]he tolls did not cover the cost of debt service. We had a deficit right along, but not a big one [and] we had the road also. So that definitely was an issue that was a vote-getter in the Big Sandy [River] Valley and I think it worked to advantage some in the Lexington area because there was just no travel between Lexington and Eastern Kentucky.

Political leaders in the Big Sandy knew about this. I knew them and I campaigned very actively in my old home county, and even made these plans before the election—showed them the estimated cost and everything. The leadership in local government, they all knew about it. . . .

I felt then and I feel now that transportation is basic to the area. A lot of money is being spent up there now . . . on access roads. But Governor Combs gave it the impetus. He gave it the go. This has had—you might not get any business leadership in Lexington to acknowledge this—but the Mountain Parkway has had a vast impact on central Kentucky. Everything we ever did in the Big Sandy Valley we went to Huntington and to Cincinnati. There was no way to get to Lexington except the train to Ashland and then on down. So it changed the whole traffic pattern. East Kentucky finally became ac-

The Combs Administration

quainted with central Kentucky. That was an acquaintance it didn't have until we had the Mountain Parkway.

Gil Kingsbury (Interview 2)   During the campaign Bill May's engineering operation, Brighton, was doing a survey on the Mountain Parkway. Bill May's engineers drove stakes all over the mountains to show that Combs was ready to do something about roads.

Combs spent a lot of money on the Mountain Parkway, except they called them turnpikes. Combs came to me one day and wanted to know how we could merchandize these roads and get them to be used more. I thought about it awhile and during the Derby I told him "Bert, when you're in Florida would you rather drive the Florida Turnpike or the Sunshine Parkway?" I said, "That's the reason we should name these turnpikes, parkways." That's how we developed the name parkways rather than turnpikes. We just tried to bottle it a little better.

Lawrence Wetherby   I had built a toll road and Chandler complained about it. . . . It was the first toll road in Kentucky in modern times. Chandler made the toll road an issue in the campaign and he called Combs "Toll Road Bertie" because, he said, "He's going to build toll roads all over the state just like Wetherby started." Well, mine turned out to be so successful that Bert was not afraid of it, and he did start the toll road program—the Mountain Parkway and later . . . the West Kentucky Parkway.

Jo Ferguson   Combs is very imaginative in the things that most people think count. Program-wise he was certainly one of the top governors we've ever had. . . . The turnpike program in itself was a great program. It might have been carried on a little bit too long by other governors succeeding him, but certainly the concept of building these turnpikes was a major factor, I think, in bringing new industry to Kentucky and opening up the state.

Cattie Lou Miller   The biggest handicap that Kentucky had prior to the time that he became governor lay either in roads or education. He did so much about both that it was a changing time for the state. Kentucky had not had good east-west access and he built the Mountain Parkway, the West Kentucky Parkway to Princeton, and he got the decision made and the bonds sold in order to build the Bluegrass Parkway to link them. With those and the miles of the interstate highway plus fifty or so miles of other four-lane highways he opened up over two hundred miles of four-lane highways in the state and that made a terrific difference in simply opening up the whole state not only to itself but to commerce and approach from people in other states.

Harry Davis I think that . . . on the short haul . . . the toll roads might have opened up part of Kentucky, but [they] are a big expense to us now. With the interstate system, that should have been completed before we started a toll road system as big as we started. I think some of the toll roads are not economically feasible. I think that might be one of the bad things of his administration. . . .

I don't think you can give him as much credit for state parks as you can Henry Ward and Earle Clements because [Combs] may have built a few extra plush buildings in them, but the park system was developed under Clements with Henry Ward. I think it would be wrong to give Combs more than nominal credit for keeping them up.

Ed Easterly Overall my feeling is that Combs's major accomplishment was to help Kentucky think big and act big. Combs was for progress for Kentucky. No one opposed progress, but they might differ on how you went about it. Keep in mind that we just didn't have enough money in the cash register to finance a lot of things that needed to be done. That's why we had to float some bond issues. If it hadn't been for Combs I wonder if Eastern Kentucky yet would have something like the Mountain Parkway because really the Mountain Parkway opened up Eastern Kentucky. You had a four-lane highway to Campton and then a three-lane highway from Campton to Hazard, and Campton over to Prestonsburg. I wonder if Governor Chandler now would not rue the day he made the remark that that's the road to nowhere.

Jack Matlick [The small lakes program] was entirely Combs's idea as far as I know. The highway engineers, state and federal, said it was impractical, you couldn't do it. And we had an awful time getting the Highway Department, federal and state, to go along with the idea when we were building one of these roads by a community that needed a water supply. Combs's idea was we ought to make that highway fill serve as a dam to supply water for industrial, municipal, and recreational purposes to that community. Just everybody said it couldn't be done. But he thought it could and as I became

The Combs Administration   117

acquainted with his ideas I agreed. It was a shame not to do it because we had it figured out that it would save money in the construction of the highway.

You see engineers had been taught in school that you build a culvert or bridge under highways big enough to take an anticipated fifty-year rain—the largest rainfall that you have in fifty years—and get it through there without getting it up on the highway fill itself. Well, Combs's idea, the one we explored and developed, was that you didn't have a culvert or bridge or either one. You surfaced the upper face of that highway fill, [made] it waterproof with clay compaction and then you backed water up to an area of maybe fifty or one hundred acres. When you have a rain, it takes an awful lot of rain to raise the water level one or two inches over one hundred acres, don't you see. Now we had a trickle tube that went down and under the highway fill and that water would just run off easy-like— no erosion or anything. It would take it several days for that rain to get there where it went through all at one time with the old system.

I don't know where he got that idea. I think mainly he saw a need for water because people were running out of water and hauling water by train and everything else. Although Kentucky has an annual forty-five inches of rain, many places in Kentucky would just dry up and [people] didn't have water to drink. We have a lot of examples of how the program works. Down there at London we saved $200,000 on the cost of building a culvert and got an eight-hundred-acre lake as a byproduct and saved money doing it.

John Ed Pearce Bert was very smart. Let me give you an example. Bert got $10 million out of the legislature for parks—an unprecedented amount. Furthermore, he got their permission to issue another $10 million in revenue bonds for the parks. With this he proposed to renovate—just to remake the park system, to change the whole thrust and nature of it.

It was a tremendous burden for a parks commissioner. He had at that time a young professional guy named Ed Fox as parks commissioner. He really needed something a little different in addition to the usual technical man to oversee this thing—to supervise the expansion program. So he [appointed] three men to a parks board which he had created by the legislature. . . . He chose three editors—Herndon Evans of the *Lexington Herald;* Henry Ward of the *Paducah Sun Democrat;* and me from the *Courier-Journal.* In that he got three men of fairly mature years who were very interested in conservation and in the parks and in tourism. . . . But he had something better. He had pulled the teeth of the three biggest newspapers in the state when it came to criticizing him. From then on it became very difficult for us to criticize him for anything he did with the parks because it was our baby.

Bert was capable of that, very shrewd. . . . We were given $20 million and we were told to spend it in a year. We were told to get out there and expand this park system. The commissioner, Ed Fox, had drawn up plans pretty much for the overall system. He knew where to locate new parks. Each of us took a park or two and went out to find architects and get plans drawn up. We had tremendous authority.

Appalachia

Bert Combs (Interview 6) Being a native of Appalachia, I naturally had a personal interest. I thought that it was the section of Kentucky that had the greatest need at that time. I thought that we couldn't have a modern, progressive state unless every area of the state was doing well economically. So I was very receptive to any sort of suggestion about what could be done for Appalachia.

As I recall, I don't know whether it was my idea or John Whisman's idea or Governor Millard Tawes's idea. Governor Tawes was the governor of Maryland. He had an assistant who had come from Kentucky [and] . . . had caused Governor Tawes to be interested in programs for Appalachia—a little out of the governor of Maryland's sphere of influence—but . . . he and I talked about it . . . and out of that conversation came the idea for an Appalachian Regional Governors' Commission.

I went to Maryland and . . . met with Governor Tawes about this subject specifically. We agreed that we would form an Appalachian Regional Governors' Conference. . . . We asked all the Appalachian governors to meet with us and we told them what we were thinking and asked for their cooperation. Millard and I decided who were Appalachian governors in an arbitrary way. We were thinking about the heart of Appalachia—I was. Millard had a little broader notion, mainly because Maryland ordinarily wouldn't be considered strictly Appalachia. But we selected, as I remember, eight or ten governors to meet with us. They all agreed that it was a good idea and they agreed to cooperate. So we followed through from that.

The Combs Administration

[John] Kennedy was to come into office soon. I don't remember the sequence of events, but we did get an appointment with President Kennedy. I remember Dave Lawrence, the governor of Pennsylvania at the time, was much interested. The governor of West Virginia, Wally Barron, was interested. It so happened that at the time most of us thought that Lawrence and Barron had more rapport or influence with President Kennedy than the rest of us, mainly because they had both been active in his campaign. So we made it a point to get both of them there.

We had a very cordial meeting with President Kennedy. . . . Kennedy thought it was a good idea. . . . Out of that, then, grew the Appalachian Regional Commission. We governors realized that we had to have some sort of close liaison with the federal government because that's where the money was. So we came up with this notion of a regional commission. The governors were supposed to be very active and very influential in the commission but we had some federal people who would have authority also. It was supposed to be . . . almost a co-equal group representing the federal government and the governors. But we made it very clear that we didn't want it to be the usual federally-dominated commission. We wanted it to be different and I think it was different in that . . . it was a pilot program and worked rather successfully with the federal government . . . having some authority but those people recognizing that the governors were more familiar with the area and had greater knowledge about the programs that were needed.

The idea was that the commission would approve the programs and the governors in their respective states would give solid support to [them]. . . . It was understood generally by the commission that the [federal] government would have a strong voice because it furnished the money. . . . That was the genius of the Appalachian Regional Commission and very shortly more governors wanted to get in because they could see some benefits coming to their state. I can remember we were a little surprised and had a joke or two out of the fact that Governor Nelson Rockefeller of New York beat the doors down to get in. Alabama wanted to get in, and so did Georgia— though Georgia was not that far removed from Applachia. . . .

We had to decide what would we concentrate on first. It was the general consensus that transportation and health were the two greatest needs. Education was vitally important, but [we felt] that we could move faster on transportation needs and health needs. Consequently, much of the money that came through the ARC first went to highways. . . . Some of the reporters and columnists thought that we should have concentrated on something else—housing, education, or something besides what we had concentrated on. Of course, I heard a few times, "Well, highways are great but you can't eat highways." Of course, you can't eat books. You can't eat houses, but you have to have them.

My guess is that Kentucky got a big proportion of the money. . . . I was chairman of the commission for two years and John Whisman was there as the governors' representative. Of course, he was in touch with me and I was in touch with him. Then, too, we had Carl Perkins as a congressman, who was effective and interested. With that combination, I think Kentucky certainly got its full share, if not more. We tried to be fair about it, but we also made certain that Kentucky didn't get slighted. . . .

John Whisman is a native of Powell County. . . . I think John had been secretary of the Eastern Kentucky Regional Commission. That was a group of public-spirited citizens in Eastern Kentucky who were attempting to do—but not making much progress—the same sort of thing that the ARC later did do. I was on that commission. I wasn't all that active in it, but I knew the leaders in the group and I knew their objectives. . . .

Out of that Eastern Kentucky Regional Commission grew the idea for the ARC. I think they thought—that commission—that transportation and health needs were the two greatest priorities in Eastern Kentucky at the time. They had the notion that if we could get modern highways, get some basic health facilities in Eastern Kentucky, we could get new industry, small factories. That hasn't worked out to any great extent, but the population has not continued to decline. . . . I think ARC did a great deal to stop that and we were fortunate that the coal business came along and Eastern Kentucky was in much better position to take advantage of it by reason of having the Mountain Parkway, the Daniel Boone Parkway, and some other connecting roads. . . .

I think the ARC . . . has been of great benefit to the southern Appalachian region. I know you hear a lot of criticism about [how] we haven't done enough [and] the conditions are still not good, and that's all true. The point is that you have to compare present conditions to what they were a quarter of a century ago. And we have made, I think, very definite progress in . . . transportation, basic health facilities, and . . . education. I think the educational system in Eastern Kentucky, as much as it needs to be improved, is vastly better than it was a quarter of a century ago. I think people in Appalachia don't have as much feeling of resignation, of being isolated, of being passed by—not nearly as much as they did twenty years ago. I think the people feel that they are part of the economy and the life of this country, that Eastern Kentucky is competitive, and I think that it will continue to improve.

Robert Cornett He was responsible for the Appalachian Regional Commission. John Whisman did most of the digging—it couldn't happen without John. But it couldn't happen without Governor Combs either. Not many governors would have been concerned with something that wasn't going to bear any fruit until they were gone.

The Truck Deal

The Combs administration legislated the first billion-dollar budget in Kentucky history, with little or no corruption attached to it. The one event that came close to being a scandal was the so-called "truck deal," first publicized in the spring of 1960.

Anticipating a stepped-up highway construction program because of the federal interstate program as well as campaign commitments, the Kentucky Highway Department began early to expand its capabilities with more equipment and manpower. Thurston Cooke, a Louisville automobile dealer and a finance chairman for the Combs's campaign, contracted to deliver thirty-four used trucks to fill the need. The trucks were secured in Alabama and some had been delivered, but not accepted, when Courier-Journal *reporter Kyle Vance revealed that the run-down equipment was worth next to nothing—certainly not the $346,800 due to go to the Louisville Equipment Rental Company for their use. Complicating the matter was Cooke's statement that he sold the trucks but had no connection with the planned lease to the state. Even when Governor Combs himself stepped in and cancelled the contract, suspicions persisted[4] because no one seemed to know who ran the rental company.*

Thus, though the state never lost a penny, newspapers, and particularly the Courier-Journal, *continued to act as if a cover-up had been effected. The principal focus was upon Earle Clements, whose appointment as highway commissioner the* Courier-Journal *had found "troubling" and symbolic of factional politics when first announced:*

"It raises the question of his role and influence in the administration outside of highway matters," the paper cautioned.[5]

Apparently convinced that Clements's political practices somehow or other tarnished the otherwise pure image presented by Combs and Wyatt, the Courier-Journal *kept up the pressure. When Clements resigned in August to assist Lyndon Johnson in his campaign for the vice-presidency, the paper fired off another blast describing his departure as a contribution to Kentucky because he had become "the governor's greatest handicap." Although admitting that Combs owed Clements much for helping him win in 1959, the paper reiterated the charge that "petty mistakes" and "politics as usual" in the Highway Department severely undermined the progressive character of the administration. "Governor Combs and Lieutenant Governor Wyatt," the editorial suggested, "promised something much better than politics as usual during their election campaign, and as long as Mr. Clements pursued his traditional course, the result appeared to be a repudiation of all that Combs and Wyatt had promised."*[6]

Out of the turmoil that began with the truck deal revelations evolved a rift between Combs and Clements that caused the former United States senator to oppose Wyatt's [U.S.] Senate hopes in 1962, embrace Chandler against Breathitt in 1963, and work against Combs in 1971.

Bert Combs (Interview 7) The first I knew about it was about the time it appeared in the newspapers in the Louisville *Courier-Journal.* Mr. Cooke was at the point presumably one of the more respected people in Louisville. He had this big Ford agency in Louisville. He was one of the big Baptists in Kentucky. I had no reason to suspect that he was anything other than what he appeared to be.

He had had some position in the fall campaign of the Democratic ticket. So I learned that he had delivered some of these trucks to the Highway Department, I think to the garage for inspection or maintenance or what have you. And that was in compliance with a bid that had been awarded to him some time previously. All that, of course, was within the Highway Department. There was no reason for the governor to know about it, and I didn't know about it.

It turned out on investigation that at least some of these trucks were not suitable for the purpose the Highway Department wanted them for. The paper made a big deal about that and it was a front-page story for three or four days at least, maybe longer. After I got into the thing, I learned . . . that some of these trucks were not suitable for the purposes they were being purchased for, so I cancelled the deal. . . .

I think it should be kept in mind that these trucks had not been accepted at that time. They had been delivered. No money had been paid to Mr. Cooke, and no money ever was paid to him. The truth is that a disgruntled employee tipped off the newspaper reporter and the paper thereby got ahead of the administrative procedures in the Highway Department. In my judgment, these trucks would have been rejected, would not have been paid for, and it would have been handled internally. As it was, it was handled on the front pages of the newspapers at the same time we were handling it administratively. It did turn out that Mr. Cooke had made this bid in the name of a newly organized company—a corporation—and had given an address . . . [that] was fictitious. The purpose in doing that, I don't know. The truck deal alone would not have created that much of a newspaper story, but shortly after that some of the banks in Louisville learned that Mr. Cooke had been giving them fictitious mortgages on automobiles that he claimed to have in his storeroom, but did not have. I think that's about the long and short of it.

These banks then—the prosecution authorities, no doubt at the request of the banks—moved against Mr. Cooke. He was indicted not for the truck deal, but for giving these fictitious mortgages to the banks. He was tried and convicted and served a sentence for the mortgages that he had given to the banks. That created, of course, headlines for many weeks—for many months, for that matter. Every time a trial date was set, when the trial was held, when the jury came in, when he went to jail—all of that was headline news here in Louisville. And every time they talked about Mr. Cooke going to jail for his activities with the banks they rehashed the fact that he had also delivered some used trucks to the Highway Department which were apparently not suitable for the purpose. The so-called truck deal was identified in the minds of the average person as an integral part of the fraudulent mortgages. So people, I am sure, came to believe that the truck deal was just as bad as the fraudulent mortgages. Actually, there is a very definite distinction and I would emphasize that Mr. Cooke was never paid any money by the state. He was not even close to being paid at the time of the first newspaper stories. In my judgment, the truck deal would have been handled internally by the Highway Department in the usual routine with maybe a one-day story, or something like that, rather than to be magnified as it was into a big scandal of a sort. . . .

Senator Clements was highway commissioner at the time. The papers were critical of him personally for permitting it to happen, for permitting it to get that far along. He was chairman of the department and I don't know how much he knew about it or whether he had any opportunity to learn about it before it was broken in the newspaper. I don't blame him for that, but he was head of the department and just like as governor I was responsible overall, he was responsible, in the minds of the newspapers anyway, for the affairs of the Highway Department.

As I mentioned, after several days, after I had made a judgment about the situation, I cancelled the whole arrangement. . . . At the time I thought Senator Clements was in agreement that I should cancel it. Later it developed—and I'm talking in part from hearsay, Clements never told me this—his friends convinced him that I shouldn't have done it, . . . that that made him look bad, that perhaps he should have cancelled. You get into a matter of mechanics there that apparently grated on his sensitivities—and, again, I speak from hearsay because he never told me that, never has told me that.

Then at the next session of the legislature I asked the legislature to investigate this whole situation. I think that somebody convinced Senator Clements that I was attempting to shift the blame to him. . . . I had no such intention . . . for that to happen. But I did want the thing to be investigated while it was comparatively fresh in the minds of everybody involved and before the witnesses got scattered and before the persons who had been involved had died or moved on. . . . I tried to get an independent committee to make this investigation. I do recall that a member of the legislature from Senator Clements's county was on the committee. I was convinced that the committee would find no fault on my part, on Senator Clements's part, or on any person connected with the administration. I was convinced then and I am convinced now that Mr. Cooke just attempted to perpetuate this deal with the Highway Department in order to . . . get his hands on some additional money. I think it was his fault and I think it would have been learned about and would have been straightened out before any money was paid to Mr. Cooke.

Apparently Senator Clements had some resentment about that. I don't want to get into too much detail as to what Senator Clements thought. I'm at a loss to talk too much about Senator Clements's and my relationship in regard to that situation because actually we have never talked about it in detail. I have heard plenty from other sources that he had deep resentment. Whether it was because I cancelled the truck deal, I repeat, I did have his permission to cancel the deal. I asked him if he had any objection. And he said no. He might have thought I was in a position to apply a little arm-twisting, or coercion. He might have thought that I shouldn't have put it to him that way.

I heard much later that he was very bitter about the newspaper stories and the criticism in the newspaper of him and that he thought there was something I could have done about that that I didn't do. I don't know what to say about that. I never directly or indirectly made any statement, insinuation, or innuendo that he was guilty of any lack of duty or any fault in regard to the truck deal. I think he would have stopped it before any money was paid. Now, Wilson Wyatt was lieutenant governor and Wilson Wyatt's firm was counsel for the *Courier-Journal*. I do think that the senator always thought that Wyatt could have done something with the *Courier-Journal*. I don't think he could have. I think that [was] demonstrated before that incident, and subsequently, that Wyatt couldn't have done anything about it . . . [T]he truth is that the newspaper and Senator Clements had not been on good terms for many years. The newspaper's management didn't think Senator Clements should be highway commissioner. I thought the paper was mistaken. I thought the senator would make a good highway commissioner. I think he did. I think he had a very sound administration of the Highway Department.

Those people [who were surprised by his appointment] forgot that Earle Clements had been a county sheriff. He had been a county clerk. He had been a county judge, state senator, governor, and U.S. senator. Earle Clements was a man who liked to get things done. That was his way of life. In fact, that was his main interest in life. . . . And if this had worked out, if Earle Clements had remained as highway commissioner, I think it would have been a good thing for Kentucky. . . .

There was no prior understanding that Clements would later join the Lyndon Johnson campaign. Actually, as far as I know, and I think I know, Earle had no thought at the time he became highway commissioner that Johnson would be running for the vice-presidency. He knew Johnson hoped to be nominated for president and to the surprise of I would guess 90 percent or 95 percent of the people of this country, he accepted the vice-presidency. I'm certain that Senator Clements had no thought when he became highway commissioner [that] he would be in the Johnson campaign. When it did happen, after Johnson became a vice-presidential candidate, he called on Earle to come and help him run his campaign. I knew when he called him about it. Earle told me he had been requested to come into Johnson's campaign and I knew how close he and Lyndon Johnson were. I knew it was a critical campaign for the Democratic party against the Republicans. The senator said to me, "I don't see how I can fail to go into Johnson's campaign. I think I have an obligation to do that." I said to him, "Why don't you take a leave of absence?" I had not thought that the truck deal made him an ineffective highway commissioner. I thought he was still very good. I had no reason to believe that he would not or should not complete four years. But my recollection is that he said, "No, I don't think I ought to take a leave. I think I ought to resign." I said to him, "Of course, it's your decision, and I will abide by your decision. If you do intend to resign, who would you suggest as your successor?" And he gave me two names. One I guess I don't need to mention . . . because he didn't become commissioner. But I contacted Henry Ward and . . . I told Ward what I would expect of a highway commissioner and he told me in general the sort of relationship he would want with the governor if he became commissioner, and within a very short time he accepted the position of highway commissioner.

Earle at that time had not left the Highway Department and we had a little reception for Henry Ward. I recall that Earle was there. Everybody apparently was on good terms. The truck deal, as I recall, was not mentioned by Senator Clements or by me at any time between the time Johnson asked him to come to the campaign and when Henry Ward reported as highway commissioner. Senator Clements did go into the Johnson campaign. Ward became the highway commissioner and served for the remainder of my term. . . .

I have no doubt that many people—many informed people—thought that I would be subservient to Senator Clements and they no doubt thought that with him there as highway commissioner, in perhaps the most powerful cabinet position, that it would make it much easier for him to dominate me. Well, I'd known him I guess since 1947—twelve or thirteen years. I don't know whether you call me a newcomer at that time, but Senator Clements no doubt had some voice in my being appointed judge of the Court of Appeals. He knew about and participated to a considerable extent in my race for judge of the Court of Appeals. I had been on the Court of Appeals and saw him occasionally—not in any intimate fashion, of course. Then I had run for governor in 1955 and was closely associated with him during that campaign. If there's any way you learn about a person, it's being associated with him closely in a political campaign. It's like going fishing with him and playing poker with him. You really learn a person in a political campaign—whether he's strong, whether he's weak, what his weak points are, what his integrity is, what his tenacity is, and so on.

I had enough ego that I didn't think Earle was going to dominate me or even try to dominate me. I don't think he would. I thought he wouldn't try for two reasons. Number one, I thought he knew me well enough to know that I wouldn't be dominated because I had taken an oath of office and he knew my feelings about that. Number two, I think he knew that I would listen to his advice and counsel and give it such weight as I thought it was entitled to but that I would not be any sort of rubber stamp. I think, for that reason, he wouldn't have tried even if he had wanted to otherwise. . . .

So I had no fear about that and I think Earle thought that that would not be a problem. But the press could never believe that Clements, being a dominant personality . . . wouldn't attempt to dominate me. I think Earle intended to run the Highway Department. I think he believed that I would give him a pretty free hand over there. I think that he thought that it would be a lot of satisfaction to him, and perhaps some recognition by fellow citizens that he had made—I'm sure he wanted to make—the best highway commissioner that the state had had.

He was the best qualified person that you could think about. On hindsight, it probably was a mistake for him to come in as highway commissioner. Perhaps it was a mistake for me to agree to it, but I was thinking about it on a relationship of Clements and Combs and I think he was. Both of us should have known that you have to consider the press. You have to consider the appearance of things almost as much as the actuality of a situation.

William May Governor Combs, Louis Cox, Governor Wetherby, and I were at White Sulfur Springs for a weekend of golf when the truck story hit the papers. A friend of ours called him and told him about it. It was on Sunday, the day before we were coming back. He got the message and turned to the three of us and told us about it. They called him off the golf course to receive the phone call. He said, "There's some things you can't do anything about and that happens to be one of them. Let's go back and play golf." Then, on our way home, we learned more about it. You picked up a newspaper, it burned your fingers—the papers were loaded with the story. . . .

I was in Louisville the night before Senator Clements either resigned or was asked to resign. . . . I was with Governor Combs just before bedtime when he had made his mind up he did want [Clements] to leave. . . . I really don't remember the mechanics—whether he sought Clements's resignation or whether Clements volunteered it. At first he was inclined to ride it out, but the story unfolded more and more about the condition of these trucks, things of that sort. At first the story indicated they were of good quality. Then the newspaper people went down to Alabama where they were and looked them over, and they weren't, and it just grew like Topsy.

Robert R. Martin Senator Clements insisted that the truck deal was not what the break was over. . . . [T]here was a harsh editorial the day after he [resigned]. The *Courier-Journal* said he'd done many things but the greatest thing he'd ever done was to leave, and intimated that he'd been fired. Clements insisted that what he really objected to was that Combs never did set the record straight. So he said that was the thing.

Wilson Wyatt It really surprised me that [Clements] was interested in serving [as highway commissioner]. It seemed to me that his position in the party and all was senior to that and I was surprised that he wanted to. I never have been close to him. I don't know why, but our wave lengths have not been that close. . . .

I knew nothing about the truck deal. It unfolded to my surprise. After it exploded it was something everybody gossiped about, but before that I'd never even heard of it.

Ed Prichard I think that the *Courier-Journal's* hostility to Clements influenced Combs's split with Clements. They did not want Clements to be highway commissioner. That's all I know. . . . Then the truck deal came to light and they said this is the typical thing we most feared about Clements's administration of the Highway Department. They played up this Cooke deal very, very heavily. I think to some degree this was influenced by Wyatt, who in 1955 hadn't been all that active but who felt somehow that Clements was a threat to him. Wyatt was very close to the *Courier-Journal* and my own opinion is the truck deal was much more a Combs and Wyatt deal than it was a Clements deal. . . .

I know that the truck deal was first broached at a meeting of the Finance Committee on Sunday afternoon in Louisville. . . . On Sunday afternoon Bill May, I believe maybe Lawrence Wetherby, a couple of others, showed up with Thurston Cooke and Murrel Robertson with the proposition that they become the finance chairmen in the fall election campaign. Now I was not at that Finance Committee meeting. I wasn't a member of the Finance Committee, but I believe firmly that something about the truck deal was broached at that time—that Cooke had certain things he wanted to get done.

Murrel Robinson had the loan on those trucks. His bank had the loan on them. Now I think that Cooke, much more desperate than anyone has ever realized, got a kind of commitment from Combs and Wyatt. During all the period when the truck deal was under consideration, the pressure was coming from the governor's office and the lieutenant governor's office. Clements did it not as a deal of his own and . . . really with great hesitation because he was trying to accommodate the wishes of the governor and the lieutenant governor and he performed what he thought was an obligation. And, in addition, I think Combs at that time didn't realize the condition the trucks were in.

They had put in also a man named [Harry] Klapheke as the director of Equipment, a former employee of Thurston Cooke. Klapheke was brought from Louisville by May, Wyatt, and some others and was suggested to Clements as director of Equipment. On the face of it he had a pretty good record. Clements accepted him though he was not Clements's choice for that. Klapheke gave him a report that he'd gone down to Alabama where these trucks were and that they were in first-class condition. It turned out when they started to deliver the trucks that they weren't in first-class condition and Clements had refused to accept delivery of those first trucks that came in.

But by that time the story [had broken] in the newspaper and Combs jumped in and canceled the contract when Clements already had Cooke waiting over in Bob Martin's office to come in and volunteer to give up the contracts. I think that [Clements] felt that Combs was trying to unload on him something that was really much more the child of Combs and Wyatt than it was his. I think that it exacerbated the feeling between Clements and the *Courier-Journal*, which had played up the truck deal very heavily, and it cemented with Combs the support of the *Courier-Journal*.

Dix Winston When this break came up, there I was administrative assistant to Combs. Actually they were both wrong. We had one person there who got the thing out of kilter and I was in the governor's office where I could hold on to Combs's hand, but Clements was a telephone away and it wasn't always the easiest thing in the world to get Clements on the phone. So as this thing was going on back and forth I was trying to keep everything down and hold it together and I just couldn't get back and forth on the phone fast enough to Clements. That was most unfortunate. Both of them were upset with each other.

Samuel Van Curon The truck deal was the only thing that he really had a bad scandal about. The state didn't lose any money but it was the cover-up—trying to hide something. Clements just happened to be highway commissioner. Clements didn't have a thing to do with that to my knowledge. I've talked to Bert about it. I've talked to Wilson Wyatt about it. I talked to Earle Clements about it. I talked to people in the Highway Department about it.

I think it was done in the Equipment Department, although Clements signed the papers. I think it was presented to him in a way by someone he trusted. He thought the trucks would be helpful in increasing highway construction. As that turned out the amount that the state was to pay was exactly what Cooke owed to the Bank of Louisville. I don't think Earle Clements had anything to do with it.

Arthur Lloyd I don't know whether Bert understood why Clements became bitter. I understood it, I think. Bert Combs had a judicial temperament. He was right cautious in making up his mind. He wanted to look at all factors before he fully made up is mind—which is good. I can't fault that. His natural mountain cunning would cause him to look around at all sides of a question before he came to a conclusion.

When this truck thing came up—what most governors would have done, what I would have done, as a matter of fact, I would first announce immediately that I had great confidence in this man I just appointed as commissioner of highways and if it required corrective action, we'd take corrective action. Bert didn't do that. He didn't say anything. He waited and waited and I think every day he waited Clements got madder and madder. I don't think Bert ever really thought Clements was behind that deal. I think he probably regretted Clements's getting angry.

Barry Bingham, Sr. The investigation in this case began to turn up facts and figures that we thought the public had a right to know about. Editorially, we then came in on this, not with any great feeling of rejoicing that we were exposing something, but we felt this had to be discussed and the public had to know about it. It was not a happy chapter in Kentucky political history.

I'm told that Clements felt he had been left out on the political limb by Governor Combs. He felt that he'd been exposed to the blast of public scorn unfairly by Combs. Also, I'm sorry to say, Governor Clements always felt that our papers had somewhat pumped up this issue of the truck deal and that we'd done it more to injure him than to support the public welfare. I assured him that was not our motive but I think he always did cling to that idea—that we were really trying to hurt him.

Robert Lee "Slick" Combs I wasn't associated with Clements as much until he became highway commissioner under Bert. [He wanted the appointment] because it was the best appointment, the best they had in the state. The highway commissioner has more influence over more people. I had the impression, and I think I'm right, that he was actually building up an organization for Lyndon Johnson through his contacts as highway commissioner. I'm sure of that. Before that he came back and managed Bert's campaign, so naturally he would ordinarily get the position that he wanted, so he took the Highway Department. That was a big question—who Bert was going to appoint highway commissioner and a pretty well-kept secret right up to about a month before the end. But I'm pretty sure that he wanted to become highway commissioner so that he could build up an organization for Lyndon Johnson.

Albert B. Chandler I don't know anything about it except that Clements has told me that Combs tried to put it on him because that broke them. Of course, Clements took Combs from nothing to something. Combs didn't have a chance without Clements. I know what they think of each other. They won't even sit by each other. Clements wouldn't even sit by him at a public gathering. I outrank them all. Clements wanted to get me to change seats because he didn't want to sit by Bert Combs. They're civil with each other but Clements is never going to get over that.

J. David Francis   I think the thing just got into a rash of misunderstandings and the press writing about it and blowing it out of proportion got it into a posture where it couldn't be resolved other than with some kind of adversarial confrontation. I think really that this is one of the mistakes that Governor Combs made in his administration. I don't think he meant to mistreat Clements and I don't know who was giving him the information he had to go on, but you no doubt recall it came up to be a hearing before the [Kentucky] Senate, but . . . by the time they had the hearing . . . it was all moot. It was all over. I was terribly sorry that happened. It hurt our administration. Just at a time when we needed public support and the public with us something came up that didn't look right.

Jo Ferguson   Combs was to a degree Clements's protégé when he first started. The defeat of Clements for reelection to the [U.S.] Senate I guess is the thing that began the troubles. Clements was a very active man and very politically minded, but I suppose he probably knew that he couldn't come back and be elected governor, so by backing Combs for governor in 1959 I suppose that he thought that he would play a big part in the Combs administration.

He then asked for the job of commissioner of highways. I suppose that Combs couldn't refuse it to him but it was not a good idea—a former governor, especially one with as much power as Clements had been used to exercising, couldn't become a second man in an administration very well. So I think the situation was impossible to begin with.

And then they had that so-called truck scandal which was not nearly as much a scandal as it was made out to be. The subsequent conviction and imprisonment of Cooke had nothing to do with the truck scandal whatsoever. He was kiting paper. It had nothing to do with the trucks but Cooke was in trouble and I suppose trying to find a way to bail out and he persuaded them to buy these great big trucks which the Highway Department probably didn't need.

The *Courier-Journal* made a great deal out of it and Clements felt that Combs threw the whole blame on him when I think Combs certainly had known what was going on. The nastiness that finally resulted was an accident. None of them knew that Cooke was guilty of what he actually was doing—that is, borrowing three times on the same piece of equipment. That was certainly not Combs's or Clements's fault because they didn't even know about it.

Robert Bell [When Clements became highway commissioner] it certainly introduced into the political framework there in Frankfort at the time an unusual situation. You had the governor with all the traditional powers of leadership that the governor has; a rather dynamic lieutenant governor more active and more involved, perhaps, than any other lieutenant governor has been, [and] with the consent and blessing of the governor; and then you had the third power center that was located in the Highway Department in the person of Earle Clements, who certainly in the early stages of 1960 helped the Combs administration get off the ground and pass their legislative program. . . . I wonder without Clements's help if they would have been successful and I doubt that they would have been. Just a personal opinion—I doubt that the Combs-Wyatt beginning would have been as successful without him although it did create certain problems that came to a head later in the year.

Tommy Carroll [When Clements became highway commissioner] I thought it was one of the most horrible mistakes he [Clements] could have possibly made. He didn't ask me but here you had a man who had been congressman, governor, U.S. senator—not only a U.S. senator, but one in a position of high leadership, and one who even then was very close to the leadership of the Senate—Lyndon Johnson particularly. I had been to Washington with Clements. I knew how those people felt about him. I thought that he was making a terrible mistake to take any appointive state job—particularly one as dangerous as highway commissioner, because back in those days the commissioner of highways had so much pressure for jobs, for bridges, for roads, for equipment purchases, for contracts, that I could see no sense in Clements doing this. And he didn't need the money.

I think that Clements thought that he was going to be a surrogate governor. I think that he thought that all he had to do was to pull the strings and he had a puppet over across the river. Bert Combs was not that type of governor. Bert was his own man and Clements, in my opinion, totally underestimated Combs. . . .

The truck deal destroyed him politically. It destroyed him politically as far as Kentucky was concerned. Of course, when Kennedy was assassinated and Johnson became president and Beth, his daughter, became the official hostess in the White House, Clements had a great deal of influence in Washington. At one time he was not only the top man in the American Tobacco Institute but also the American Merchant Marine, as I recall. Clements could open both the front and back door[s] of the White House. But as far as local Kentucky politics were concerned I think the Thurston Cooke matter and his acting as commissioner of highways destroyed him politically in this state.

Harry B. Miller [The truck deal] was a comedy of tragic errors. The reason I say that, I do think that Mr. Cooke knew better, but I think that Earle Clements, whom I still consider a good friend, put too much trust into Mr. Cooke. There was no collusion. There was no impropriety on the part of the administration at all. There certainly was impropriety on the part of Mr. Cooke, more than likely. I say that simply because subsequent events proved that he wasn't completely straight up.

Earle, unfortunately, was the sacrificial lamb, but there again that took a lot of courage on the part of Bert Combs because Earle Clements was really his first mentor and it took a lot of guts for him to clean out the department where there was a hint of scandal. I hated to see it, but sometimes good judgment is just as much a part of his job as proper administration. Earle just unfortunately put trust in the wrong man, but there was no question that Combs had no part of it. There's no question in my mind that Earle really had no part in it. He just was careless. Bert never fell out with Earle. Earle fell out with Bert which is the best way I know to put it.

John Palmore That was a decision that sort of flabbergasted me—that Senator Clements chose that particular job with the Combs administration. I thought he would probably make another race for office in Washington. I guess I really didn't realize his interest in roads. [I felt that here was] a man that really and truly in his heart wanted to do everything that could be done for the state. He wanted to do things for people.

I'm sure that Clements felt that Combs was pretty green and that Combs would need his advice and counsel—close advice and counsel—in administering the affairs of the state in the early days at least. Of course, he couldn't be expected just to occupy an office down here in the capitol outside the governor's office. I suppose that was as important a post as he could have occupied and still be close.

There's another phenomenon—a fact of life. When a man becomes governor, with each day's passing he becomes more independent of the people who put him there and he becomes more and more the king in his own right. This was probably happening with Combs and Clements. Combs's personality is such that you don't see what he is thinking and I rather imagine that it was a great surprise and shock to Clements to realize just how blame independent this fellow was—how quick he was to assert his authority.

I think there was a lot of psychology in that breech. . . . I think really that they had discussed when Clements would leave state government and instead of calling Clements in and talking this over with him before he did—You see, Clements heard it from some other source first, and I don't suppose he'll ever forgive Bert for that. He is a proud man.

I don't think anybody ever realized how tough Combs is underneath because he's a mild-mannered individual. He's not a forceful speaker. He doesn't speak with vigor and pound his fist and all that. In fact, he's about the most emotionless person I believe I've ever seen in my life. I think that's the real secret to his success. He doesn't let emotions get in his way. Most all of us, our guts get in our way. But they don't get in his way. He doesn't get mad. He doesn't get excited. He's very cool. He thinks things through. This is a great source of his strength, it really is.

John Ed Pearce I was surprised at Earle. I always thought that Earle Clements had the greatest political intellect that I've ever seen in Kentucky. I still think that. He was a man who saw the result of the result of the result of the move. He thought at least two moves down the road and yet he let, I think, this hope of electing Lyndon Johnson to the presidency get ahead of him and he used the Highway Department to organize this state for Lyndon Johnson and not for Bert Combs. He just couldn't see that he was hurting Bert, and he was. It was unusual because he liked Bert and he was his mentor.

Earle Clements never touched on crookedness, theft, dishonesty, but he let his friends get away with things like that. And then he wouldn't back up on it. He forced Combs into intense embarrassment as governor. The papers here were screaming at Combs day after day, "Cancel the truck deal," and Combs was waiting for Clements to do it. Clements would not cancel and finally Combs had to do it himself, which led to the break between them.

Earl Powell I hated to see [the break between Combs and Clements] happen, but I felt then and I feel now that Judge Combs was correct. He made the right decision. It was pretty harsh for Senator Clements, but at that time I don't think he had any choice.

I was surprised that Clements became highway commissioner. I thought it was too much of a down-step for a former governor. I just didn't think he would be interested. And I didn't much think that Combs would want on his staff, on his team, underneath him a former governor. I thought it was a mistake to appoint him and yet if the fellow wanted it Combs was certainly obligated to Clements. He had helped him. The fair thing is to be big enough to accept him.

Lawrence Wetherby I know Clements did not understand what Combs did. I think there was a lack of communication between Combs and Clements at that time when the so-called truck deal exploded. I think the publicity of it scared Combs to the point that he felt he had to do something. But he did it without communication with Clements. I think had he discussed it all with Clements there never would have been any feeling.

J.R. Miller After this split, and [after] Clements had gone back to Morganfield prior to the time he went to Washington, he called the newspaper editor Clyde Watson and me to come down to see him. We did. He asked if we would be willing to go up to Frankfort. We were trying to get him to get over his mad. We knew that Combs had sent Ned Breathitt down to see Clements and that he had no success with him and other people had the same experience. Combs was trying everything he could for whatever reason to try to bury the hatchet. He wanted to get this thing over with.

We did go down to visit Clements and implored him to get this thing over with because both were too decent. We did everything in the world with Clements. He was just as infuriated as he could be that we would even ask him to do this. Finally we got around to getting him to name four or five or six points that if Combs would make concessions in these areas that he would be willing to sit down and discuss it.

So Clyde and I flew to Frankfort one Sunday morning and met with Combs in the mansion. After some discussion Combs said, "I'll do anything, I'll give Earle Clements anything that I have the power to give him to get this thing settled and over with, because he's wrong about it and perhaps I handled it wrong, but I want to get it over with." He was very compassionate. So he agreed to the several items. So we called in an AP reporter and Combs had a press conference and he covered each one of these specific areas. The press release was out the next morning. . . .

We jumped in the car and ran down to Morganfield because we were so excited about it. And we got the cussing of our lives because we were in collusion with that "dirty lying S.O.B." So we decided we couldn't win. . . . I decided then that my dog wasn't in that fight. I was going to be a friend to both those people. I liked them both. I admired them and I just thought I'd leave it alone.

Election Campaigns

Though personally attracted to John F. Kennedy in 1960, Bert Combs endorsed Lyndon Johnson out of deference to Earle Clements's wishes. Most Kentucky delegates joined with Combs in this, but not all. Among the election reforms pushed by the governor and addressed in 1960 was elimination of the unit rule. This allowed some like Wyatt to support Adlai Stevenson and others like A.B. Chandler and John Breckinridge to endorse Kennedy.

Combs worked hard for the Kennedy–Johnson ticket in the ensuing election, but Kentuckians for the third straight time voted Republican in a presidential race. In part this may have been due to a low ebb through which the administration was going. The sales tax, in effect since the first of July, had not yet produced the attractive benefits apparent later on—only irritations at having to pay extra for purchases.

By 1962, however, the image was much improved and Wilson Wyatt, for one, felt confident that he could wrest Thruston Morton's [U.S.] Senate seat from him. Thwarted in this effort, Wyatt and his aides felt that Combs had undermined his campaign by introducing Ned Breathitt as a gubernatorial choice prior to the end of the senatorial struggle.

There was a parallel here to 1954 when Governor Wetherby held off naming a successor until after Alben Barkley had defeated John Sherman Cooper in a senatorial race. Thus it may be that Wyatt would have secured stronger support, enough to win, had Combs put off naming Breathitt. On the other hand, Combs believed deeply in the importance of continuing programs he had begun and recalled quite well that his own late selection by Wetherby gave him less time than he could have used to prepare in 1955. He wanted Breathitt to have more time than he had and so felt justified in announcing his support early.

Breathitt's success in 1963 over A.B. Chandler was a victory for the Combs administration as much as for Breathitt himself. Just as in 1955, Chandler's main thrusts were aimed at those dissatisfied with the incumbent governor and to that extent the majority of the voters apparently were pleased with what they had experienced. Over half a million Democrats voted and Breathitt was victorious by more than sixty thousand votes.

In fact, the victory was so overwhelming that less care was taken in preparing for the fall campaign than otherwise might have been the case. Up-and-coming Louie Nunn of Glasgow, who had masterminded Thruston Morton to victory twice and headed successful Kentucky campaigns for Richard Nixon and John Sherman Cooper, was the Republican candidate. Breathitt was just as eloquent and attractive as during the primary, but a civil rights issue threatened his campaign. On June 26, 1963, Combs issued an executive order banning racial discrimination by any state-licensed business, preceding by over a year statutory action along similar lines at the federal level. This order seriously eroded Breathitt's support, but he still secured a narrow thirteen-thousand-vote victory.

Bert Combs (Interview 10)   Wilson and I had sort of a tentative understanding, and I considered an agreement by me, to support him for governor to succeed me. That was, I thought, the understanding that Wilson and I had. I think that if Kennedy had not been elected that Wilson would have wanted to go that route. But I think that when Kennedy was elected president and there was glamor and the excitement of a Democratic president, a Democratic Congress, that Wilson had second thoughts and decided that he wanted to be a [U.S.] senator.

I didn't know that he was having those thoughts, for one reason or another, and he had a perfect right to do it. I wasn't the first or even one of the first people that he told he intended to run for the Senate. He had checked with other people. It may be, and I don't know because we have never really talked about it—there wasn't any reason to talk about it after it was over—that he thought perhaps I wanted to run for the Senate and that it was best for him to stake out his course of action before he talked to me. I just don't know. I didn't have any particular desire to run for the Senate. I gave it a little thought. I knew as every governor knows that there was no future in being governor after four years, but I never had any desire then or ever to go to the United States Senate. But I often wondered if Wilson didn't think that perhaps I did, and that is the reason that he set his sails before he told me. He told me days or weeks before he announced, but there were these speculations, articles in the paper, which had to have some sort of foundation. I knew that he was giving it a lot of thought and perhaps had made his decision before he talked with me.

I repeat, he had a perfect right to do that. I do think on hindsight, and he might agree, that if he had told me in advance and if we had worked together to set the peg and make the plans, and checked with a number of people who were close to me that he hadn't checked with, that he would have had a better chance to win. But that's hindsight, and it may be right and it may be wrong.

In any event, at the time he told me, I did tell him, and I think I told him before, that we had, or I had, to make an all-out effort to elect my successor. Otherwise it would be Happy Chandler. Regardless of how I felt about Happy—and I didn't have any personal animosity towards Happy, but I just thought that his philosophy of government was just so opposite to ours—that he would tear down the programs that I thought were important to Kentucky and that we had got off the ground during my administration. . . .

I knew Happy was a creature of habit. I knew that Happy had gone by the rule . . . that you can't announce too early, and he was, from the time I was elected, running for governor to succeed me. So I told Wilson—he may have forgotten this and we've never mentioned it—and later his friends thought that I contributed to his defeat by doing some things for Breathitt, letting Breathitt announce before the Senate race was over.

Ordinarily that is good political strategy—only run one race at a time. But I thought this was so unusual and so important that we had to make an exception in this case. I want to make it clear—I told Wilson that and he agreed—at least, he didn't object. . . . There was a very reputable citizen of this state present when I spelled it out in specifics that, yes, I would do everything I could for him for the Senate, but I had to lay some groundwork for Breathitt in the meantime. I had designated Breathitt as the candidate to run for governor—thinking back on it, I guess I didn't give him Breathitt's name. I do know that I told him I had to lay some groundwork for my successor—the man I wanted to be my successor. Before the Senate race was over Breathitt was announced.

I would be willing to admit that it might have cost Wilson some votes. I don't think it was decisive. I think what was decisive was that Wilson was a Louisville man—sophisticated, articulate, capable person—but never was able to establish rapport with [the] people out in the state that he needed to get elected to office. That's no reflection on Wilson. Perhaps it's a poor commentary on the people of this state. But I think that's part of it.

Morton had a different personality—a completely difference personality. Morton was able to go to Hazard or to Elkhorn City and even take a drink or two, or admit he took a drink or two, tell an off-color story, and to identify with those people better than Wilson. That is just a fact.

Perhaps the decisive thing—well, there were two decisive things. One, I don't think that Earle Clements was ever very much for Wilson Wyatt. Earle never told me that, but Earle was bitterly opposed to the *Courier-Journal* hierarchy and he considered Wilson as part of that group. I don't think Earle knocked himself out for Wilson. Whether he did anything in opposition I don't know, but we needed all hands because we knew that Happy Chandler was against Wilson. . . .

Happy at that time was strong as a candidate for governor. He had a lot of influence. At that stage people were pretty confident that Happy was going to be the next governor. People thought Happy was invincible at that time. He had demonstrated that he was almost invincible. So that hurt Wilson. . . .

[Wilson's] defeat was a great disappointment and then his friends convinced him—maybe not maliciously, but they convinced him, I think—that if I had kept Breathitt from talking about the governor's race, if I had devoted my full time, it would have been different. I think the criticism, severe criticism, was hindsight about permitting the governor's race to interfere.

I don't believe Wilson and I have ever discussed it. If we have, I don't recall it. I heard it from others—some of Wilson's close friends, and I think it has been stated in the press. I think I've seen it in the press, "Well, let's not make the mistake that Combs made in trying to run two races at once." Wyatt's friends thought it was a mistake, a goof-off, that I shouldn't have made, that [it was] violating one of the basic rules of politics. But, as I say, Happy was running. That's the reason.

Wilson Wyatt Combs said he would be all for [my running for the U.S. Senate]. I think he would rather for me to have run for governor. I always thought that he would have rather run for the Senate. . . .

I think that Breathitt's race was the single thing that cost me the Senate race. Ned was a part of our team, Bert's and mine, and when it was announced by the governor that he was supporting Ned Breathitt for governor, when that announcement was made during my Senate campaign, it immediately squared off the forces and I was running two races. I was running against my Republican opponent and was also finding that the Chandler people were opposing me because they felt my election to the Senate would mean Ned's election to the governorship. My defeat would be helpful to them. I know that's true. They've even told me that. If the Breathitt [announcement] had been held off until after November then we would have won both.

I mention this frankly. I don't have any animosity about it because I'm happy now that I wasn't elected. All the things I've done since, I've enjoyed doing. . . . I mentioned to Bert—not mentioned, I specifically stated to him in advance of his announcement about Breathitt, "I hope you'll not announce for Ned until after my race is over. If you do, I think it will cost me at least fifty thousand votes."

Then one morning Bert called me on the telephone and said he had to tell me something he didn't think I would like to hear, "I've announced for Ned Breathitt for governor." I told him I appreciated his calling me, but "I'm afraid you've cost me fifty thousand votes with what you've just told me." He felt this was the only way that he could be sure to elect his successor—by stating it early.

Then it meant Chandler forces started working against Ned Breathitt immediately. That meant in August, September, October, the very time I was running for the Senate, there were ads run in the state in different papers saying, "A vote for Wilson Wyatt for the Senate is a vote for Ned Breathitt for governor next year. Be sure and support Wilson Wyatt. We can't have Chandler winning the race next year." It automatically brought the Chandler group in opposition.

Robert Bell I guess as part of a group of people who had been close to Wyatt I maintained a personal communication with him and was one of a group of maybe a dozen or fifteen that he called over one evening, not to get our advice about going to the Senate, but more to tell us that he'd already made the decision.

My recollection was that most of us felt he'd made a mistake. His political ambitions would have been better satisfied had he not made the race for the Senate and waited and run for governor to succeed Combs. . . . I think he would have been in a very preemptive position in terms of gaining that nomination and probably getting elected as governor. I don't mean there wouldn't have been problems, but overall Combs and Wyatt maintained a very good relationship during the entire administration and it would have been very difficult for another candidate to have gotten Governor Combs's support in the 1963 governor's race had Wyatt waited. His loss in 1962 eliminated him from the possibility of running for governor and also eliminated some of his desire to be a candidate. I don't . . . recall Wilson Wyatt ever making any overt effort to be considered as a possible candidate for the governor's race in 1963. I think the Breathitt announcement was considered by a lot of people who had been active in Wyatt's campaign to have created a lot of difficulty for the senatorial race.

Gil Kingsbury (Interview 2) We went every week down to the lieutenant governor's home in Frankfort to plan Wilson Wyatt's campaign. We were trying to keep the governor's race out of it. . . . Other people had ambitions to be governor and when Combs anointed Ned Breathitt those people moved away from Wilson Wyatt because Breathitt and Wyatt were hooked together.

June Taylor I don't think the Breathitt campaign interfered with Wyatt's. . . . It's easy to blame somebody when you lose. I worked in Mr. Wyatt's campaign and I heard it all the time about Breathitt. I was very much for both of them but I felt that each race could stand on its own. They were entirely different races. . . .

Incidentally, Governor Combs is the one who asked me to go work in the Wyatt campaign. He called me in the office in March and asked if I would like to go down and work for Wilson in his senatorial campaign. I said, "You know I have a lot of respect for him, but I really wouldn't like to work in this campaign, Governor, because I just got married last year and I don't want to leave home." And he turned and looked out the window and said, "Well, you're going to have to go anyway."

The Combs Administration

J. David Francis Quite frankly, I was terribly disappointed when Lieutenant Governor Wyatt decided to run for the Senate in 1962. I knew he was going to run for one or the other and I was disappointed in the choice he made.

I have no quarrel with it. It was a terrible loss that Wilson Wyatt wasn't elected to the United States Senate because he was really more in the national scene . . . and probably better known and understood on the national level than he was on the state and probably could have been more effective there. It was a terrible shame that he wasn't elected to the Senate, but what I really wanted him to do was run for governor in 1963.

It was discussed at the merger and agreed that he would have the administration's support for either the Senate in 1962 or governor in 1963. Yessir, that was a very firm understanding. He decided to go for the Senate and that, of course, freed Combs to select whoever he wanted to for governor.

Bert Combs (Interview 10) I didn't suddenly decide who [the 1963 gubernatorial candidate] would be. . . . I would have preferred and would have felt an obligation to be for Wilson still. Wilson could have run for governor, and Wilson and I talked about it, but I was convinced and I believe that Wilson had grave doubts whether he could win against Happy Chandler, having just come out of a losing race for the Senate. I wanted the person that I would support to have two qualifications. They were very important and about the only requirements that I had in mind. One, would he have a good chance to win, to defeat Happy Chandler? And, two, did he have in general the same philosophy of government that I had? So I looked for people who would meet those qualifications. I don't know which I put first. They were of equal importance to me. But certainly, very importantly, who could win.

I talked to Bill Natcher. I talked to John Watts. Both of them were strong at the time. Both would make a good candidate. . . . I gave a lot of thought to Henry Ward. Natcher and Watts were not interested in running. They had secure positions in Congress. They thought it would be very difficult to beat Happy Chandler and they didn't want to make the race. . . . [A]lthough I never completely removed [Ward] as a possibility until the very last day, I never thought he could win and I thought that was something that we just couldn't take a chance on. I thought Ward would be a good governor and his philosophy, his beliefs about programs, satisfied the requirement, but I never thought he could win. . . .

I talked to Jim Gordon who then was a federal judge. I thought Jim Gordon could win. . . . [A]lthough it had never been spelled out, I thought I could take a chance on his philosophy. I've forgotten if I talked to anybody else. I certainly considered others. But it boiled down in my mind to two people.

One was John Palmore, who was then judge on the Court of Appeals, and Ned Breathitt. I had campaigned with Breathitt when I ran for governor. I had campaigned with John Palmore when he ran for judge. I had high regard for both of them. I knew that Palmore was an able judge, had been a good commonwealth attorney. [But] I . . . was not fully satisfied that he had the personality or the willingness to make the kind of campaign I thought had to be made to beat Happy Chandler.

So I considered those two more than anybody else during the weeks preceding my decision. Judge Palmore did get around a little to family reunions and church meetings, things like that, and of course Breathitt was irrepressible. He was all over the state. I finally decided that Breathitt was the man with the best chance of beating Happy Chandler. I was a little afraid that John Palmore, having been in the judiciary, would not be able to unbend enough to meet Happy in the trenches and perhaps defeat him at his own game. . . .

A little of the reasoning that I had was that you couldn't beat Happy with just a good citizen. I thought you had to have something a little different that would counteract some of Happy's gimmicks, charisma. I thought Ned possessed some of those qualifications. One, because he was young, different, and, two, I thought the surprise element would be psychologically important to us. The average person knew very little about Ned Breathitt. I think that psychologically it did have that effect. Ned came on, you know, as a big handshaker, backslapper, joke-teller, and so on, and he had a good name. The name Breathitt had a lot of prestige in Kentucky—even Eastern Kentucky.

So those were the reasons why I went for Ned Breathitt, and I might say there were some business people . . . who were influential in raising money and in Democratic politics who were opposed to John Palmore because of some opinions he had written. John by that time had become known among knowledgeable people as a progressive, liberal judge. That didn't concern me. I thought that was good. But I had to get back to keeping the people that I thought would make it possible for us to beat Happy Chandler. Breathitt hadn't done anything much. He'd been in the legislature. He'd voted right enough to have a pretty good image. He'd been on the Public Service Commission, hadn't done anything very controversial. He had served as personnel commissioner in my administration for a few months early on. But he had no bitter enemies to speak of. . . .

I controlled the money so I had a hand in the major decisions and the major strategy of the campaign. I wanted that role and I think he wanted me to act in that role. I tried not to project myself too far out front so I'd make myself the only issue, but Happy did run against me just as I had run against him. I tried to minimize that as much as possible but certainly as the controller of the purse strings I was active in having an impact about the decisions and what he would say about this issue or another. . . .

I thought [Ned's victory] was a vote of approval of my administration. It was certainly not disapproval. Now, I think Ned could have been the most popular candidate in the country and if I had had a very unpopular administration I think perhaps he couldn't have won. On the other hand, if I had been extremely popular, my administration well-accepted, . . . we still had to have a good candidate. I think it took those two things to defeat Happy, and I believe that was the bottom line in that election—that people generally accepted . . . that the Combs administration was a good one, comparatively speaking anyway, and they liked Ned Breathitt.

We darn near lost it by overexposing it. We thought, and I think rightly so, that Ned was better on television than was Happy. That is, I think, something of interest, that Happy Chandler with all of his charisma . . . has never been good on television. When television came along, Happy apparently mistrusted, distrusted, didn't want to get on television. I've always thought it was because subconsciously he didn't like television. It may be that if they had a live audience for Happy he would have been much better on television. But that's a facet of Happy's personality. . . .

In any event, we thought that Ned came through on television well . . . and we almost overexposed him. By the time the primary came around we had about worn Ned out on television. And then it showed up in the general election more markedly, I think. We probably overexposed him more [in] the fall campaign, which was one thing that contributed to his small majority. . . . We had him on TV with the same script too often.

Ed Fossett Two years before the primary there [were] Judge Palmore, Henry Ward, and Breathitt—all hopefuls. Of course, there was Chandler hovering in the background. I think without being present at the conversation that there was an understanding with those people in sensitive jobs in the Combs administration that there would be only one administration candidate . . . to oppose Happy—that they could not beat him if they had two or three running. I think it was a pretty good understanding that anyone who didn't want to play the game that way should make it known now and get on out. . . . [I]t came down to . . . which one had the best shot. Once that was determined it was fully understood by all the rest of them that [they] would play the game.

John Palmore [Combs] called me one Sunday morning and asked me if I wanted to go up to Pikeville with him to a reunion of a family up there. So I flew up there with him. We came back and he and I sat out there behind the mansion and he asked me if I had ever considered running for governor. He said he thought I ought to consider it because there weren't many sources for qualified material to make the governor's race and he discussed several people and their pros and cons. . . . He wanted to know if I would object if I got invitations to go various places and speak and I said I would do that. Frankly, I really wasn't interested in running for governor. I had just come on the court. This must have been in 1961—two years before the election. . . .

Combs didn't say anything to me about Henry Ward. He did not at that time consider Henry Ward to be a viable candidate, I can guarantee you that. I don't remember discussing anything about Wilson Wyatt. I've got my doubts that Wilson could have beaten Happy Chandler. I really doubt that. Now Ned Breathitt was young and is a friendly, open person. He had a lot of fine attributes as a candidate. He speaks well and he's friendly. He's a marvelous public relations individual. He did a good job in that race. . . .

John Ed Pearce For a long time [Combs] thought that John Palmore was going to be an ideal governor. As everybody has always said, he looked more like a governor than anybody who ever stood up in public in Kentucky. He had a fine voice, fine head, good mind, good background. Combs tried him out . . . in the state quite a bit. Businessmen didn't like him. He had delivered on the court of appeals half a dozen decisions that businessmen didn't like. They wouldn't take him so Combs went back to Ned—not that Ned was as impressive a candidate, but that he was clean. He had no marks on him. He wanted somebody who would win. Ned went pretty good. As it turned out he was better than he looked. He came on as a very scrappy campaigner. I don't recall that Henry Ward at that point was seriously considered.

Ed Farris [During the 1963 campaign] I was in Breathitt's headquarters. I would evaluate Combs's role as being very effective and as being total commitment to Breathitt. . . . I give Combs high marks—very, very high marks. . . .

William May Combs was just determined to have [Breathitt]. He liked him and considered him a devoted protégé. Ned offered a good clean Eagle Scout look with a fine young family. . . . Bert had his mind made up. I was not too sure that we could pull it off with Ned.

Cattie Lou Miller I don't recall being particularly surprised [when Combs picked Breathitt]. Breathitt was an excellent person and was a very clean candidate. He was intelligent. He had a good mind, legal mind. He had had good standing at the university. He had been a very active member of the legislature. He was a splendid speaker. He made a good appearance. He had great enthusiasm.

I think there were many people in Kentucky who thought that he was such a different cut in the respect of being the young man not-too-many-years-out-of-college type of candidate than Governor Combs had been, that I think it surprised them somewhat that Combs had not picked someone who was deeper in politics than Breathitt appeared to be—although Breathitt was certainly no political novice.

Chandler was a formidable candidate. He had a great personal following and he ran a campaign that had all the color and entertainment that a Chandler campaign has. Breathitt just simply ran a slightly better campaign.

Earl Powell I knew Ned right well. I did not expect him to be the candidate in 1963. You might say that when Governor Combs selected him I was surprised and was fearful that he would not be able to stand up to Chandler. I thought Governor Combs had picked a poor candidate and I told him so. I thought [Breathitt] was too mild, too buoyant, a little too youthful. I just could see Chandler beating him around and clubbing him, but he fooled me. . . . Breathitt turned out to be a much better candidate, much more aggressive, than I thought he would be. Also, the Chandler wounds from 1955 [and] 1959 were still there and Breathitt could reopen the sores.

June Taylor   I guess I knew [about Breathitt's selection] so far ahead that it wasn't surprising to me. He helped Combs at the beginning as commissioner of Personnel. Then he was on the Public Service Commission. For a long time Combs asked everybody who came in who they'd like to see named governor. He tested everybody. He had a lot of balloons flying around. . . .

As soon as the Senate campaign was over . . . Breathitt came in and asked me if I would stay and work for him, which I did, because I could remember a long time ago when I'd say I hoped Ned Breathitt would be governor. The Breathitt headquarters was the same place as Wyatt's in the Seelbach. We never closed the doors. [But] it was not the same people necessarily.

Dix Winston   I was not greatly surprised by Ned's choice because he had a tremendous image and to me he came across to the public a little bit like Billy Graham—his speech, mannerisms, and everything. I accused him once or twice of trying to copy Billy Graham. So I saw him as a real potent candidate. By the time that got underway I was down here, back in western Kentucky. Of course, as it finally resulted, I was doing a little night work for Breathitt. I happened to run into Clements on one night occasion. When Clements saw me he got quite upset. So he started out on me that I should get out of this Breathitt thing and not be fooling around. I wouldn't agree with him and I tried to reason with him. "Earle," I said, "It's incomprehensible to me how you can support the man that cost you a whole career." He had a few choice words in reply to me and went on—he was in his cups and he was getting terribly emotional so finally he pounded the table and glared at me and screamed all at the same time, "One thing I want you to do is keep out of Union County."

Course, I'd been playing around in the home front. I said, "I've got some other things to do but also will be in Union County by nine o'clock, Senator. If that's the way you feel, I'm sorry, but that's the way it's going to be." You'll recall that Breathitt did beat Chandler in Union County, Clements's home county. For two years he didn't recognize that I existed.

Bert Combs (Interview 10)   We thought the primary would be the hard race and that if we got past the primary the general election would be a snap. But then some things happened—of course, they always happen in a campaign—that created new problems. We almost lost the general election.

The civil rights issue wasn't the only thing, in my judgment, but most people who you talk with now would say it was the big thing. I thought we handled it poorly and that's one place where the campaign people disagreed with me about it and, I thought, mishandled it. Since I was so involved and since I had signed the order I thought that I was probably not objective about it. I didn't attempt to strong-arm anybody. But I think if they had faced up to that order and just said that's the way it should be and decent people know that the order is not going to harm Kentucky or injure Kentucky people, that it wouldn't have been nearly as significant. When the headquarters people almost denied it and tried to get as far away from it and as far away from me on that subject, I think people thought, well, hell, it must be bad. Otherwise why would they run from it?

J. David Francis   [When Combs issued the executive order] he called several of us over there. Now, he'd already issued the order. . . . But before it was in the press or on the radio he called several of us over there and told us about it. I guess he gave us copies of it. I was one of those several. I remember thinking at the time that, "Combs, you're right, but you've blown the election." I think this kind of demonstrates Combs's style. He's not a sort of fellow like George Wallace of Alabama. He doesn't walk around with a chip on his shoulder or his lower jaw stuck out all the time. But when it's time to bite the bullet he can bite the bullet. I think he did in this instance something that he felt deeply was the law and should be the law of Kentucky—that the proper way to do it was to face it and not saddle it on somebody else—to do it himself, which he did. I am extremely proud of him for what he did and I hold that opinion to this day that he did it right.

William May   [The civil rights executive order] cost Breathitt some votes in the Confederate part of the state. It went on to affect Governor Breathitt in the November election. We had polls indicating he was running far better than it finally turned out he was running. We had to go back in our analysis and decide that was the secret no pollster could get a fellow to say—"I'm a racist." We had to attribute the low majority to that.

Ed Prichard I really think that [Combs's executive order] was more of a response to the Kennedys than it was to Louisville. Combs was always very close to the Kennedys. He didn't support him in 1960, but in his heart he was for Kennedy. Clements's closeness to Lyndon Johnson more or less foreordained that Kentucky would be in the Johnson column. But Combs quickly became an ally of Kennedy. I know that when the Kennedys were proposing the civil rights legislation . . . Bobby Kennedy and President Kennedy asked all the governors to issue executive orders or effect state action along the same lines. And I think Combs was responding to that as much as anything.

Leadership

Bert Combs (Interview 9) A governor, of course, can only set the course and announce the policies and perhaps oversee the implementation of the highlights of his program. He doesn't have the time—no one man does—to implement programs that are necessary to have a progressive or efficient government. So he has to rely on his cabinet, the heads of the departments that are members of the governor's cabinet. . . . So the governor has ten or twelve, maybe fifteen, cabinet members. And those people for the most part either make or break a governor. And again that's where knowledge of human nature, being able to work with people, determines in large part how successful a governor will be. If that governor appoints as members of his cabinet mediocre, inefficient people who are not interested—dedicated I suppose is a better word—to making that governor's administration a success, it will not be a success. Loyalty, not necessarily to the governor individually, but loyalty to the objectives and the goals of that administration [is important]. Without that it just won't work.

And in state government, and I'm certain this is true at the national level, one of the big problems a governor has is getting first-rate people to come into government, knowing that they will be subjected to the criticism, the viccisitudes, that public servants are subjected to, particularly if they have to come at a big financial sacrifice. In Kentucky, thirty years ago it was even worse than now.

The state could not compensate cabinet members on a level that they could demand in private industry. Consequently, it was necessary to find a dedicated person who was willing to sacrifice four years from his own profession or from his own industry in order to make a contribution to state government.

I think I had on balance a high-caliber cabinet. I didn't know all of them [initially]. I can't recall how many I knew personally before I started thinking about them as cabinet members. I would guess I knew half of them—some of them better than others, of course. But a governor has to be able to look at a man's background, look at his personality, look at his acquaintances, look at his track record, and make a judgment whether that person is the proper one to head up a certain department of government. It's still a gamble and everybody will guess wrong, but it's one of the most important attributes that a governor, or a president for that matter, must have. Unless a governor is able to have a cabinet of dedicated, capable people who are willing to sacrifice, and sacrifice their own convenience and sometimes their own interest, for the good of the administration, the administration will just not be successful. . . .

It's difficult to differentiate between loyalty to the governor himself, to be specific, and loyalty to a governor's program. . . . I think I had one or two of those who didn't agree with me personally but thought that I was doing something worthwhile for the state and were willing to go along with me, go along with my programs, because that person thought I was advancing the state. . . .

I didn't want anybody close to me that was unwilling to freely express their opinions about whether I was doing something that should be done, doing it in the right way, or doing it in the wrong way. I think that's basic. I think any government officer who is unwilling to have his cabinet members and those who work with him disagree is inviting disaster. There [are] not as many of those people as you might think.

I heard continuously, and I heard before I was governor, that a governor is isolated. He doesn't know what's going on out in the state. He does not know what people are thinking or saying because the people who come to see the governor are always prone to agree with him or to say to him things they think he wants to hear. . . . But anybody who is capable enough to become governor usually is perceptive enough to know that the people who come asking for favors are not going to come to antagonize him. And he's going to discount the compliments and the sugar-coated sayings of those people; and then, too, if he's capable of being governor he's going to have some people that he knows will tell him what to think.

So this business of a governor being isolated is greatly exaggerated, in my opinion. I'm sure we have had some governors who didn't like to hear any criticism, and who avoided people who were prone to criticize them. [But] after all, the governor gets hundreds of letters per week, and he gets them from people all over the state.... [H]e gets a pretty good cross section of what the people of the state are saying. Then, I repeat, if he's capable of being governor, he will want to make certain that he gets people around him who are willing to freely express their opinion....

I think that the press is an indispensable facet of government. I think the press, like every other profession, could be more proficient, could be more objective, could write with more of a perspective, and particularly could dig deeper and write with more knowledge. Admittedly they are in a hurry because they're always trying to meet a deadline.... I do think that reporters, because they're always in a hurry, fail to do as much homework as should be done. I think there is sort of a philosophy among reporters that you do it quickly, you do it as it comes along. If you're good, you don't have to do much homework.... I think the press has improved in that respect. I think the press on the whole is more responsible than it used to be....

I'll have to say that the *Courier-Journal* in our state, in my judgment and during my career in public life, at least attempted to be fair and objective. Now I know it didn't always accomplish that objective. I know that it has people in its organization and reporters on its staff that were not objective. But I think this state has been fortunate in having the *Courier-Journal* as the one statewide newspaper.

Robert Bell As I look back on his administration I think he was a very innovative governor who had a peculiar ability to develop public support for his program. I don't think he knew or cared a lot about the internal structure of the state government. So you had some problems in respect to his housekeeping. I think he was more concerned about ideas and general broad programs and developed public support for them. I think he was very successful at doing that.

There were problems in the Combs administration between certain department heads that largely relate[d] to their personalities and their styles—some of which I think could have been solved with a little clearer line of authority. But I don't think Bert Combs was that concerned about structure of state government. Governor Combs on occasion reached down into the bureaucracy in order to get something done and to move on something a little faster. He would violate all the normal concepts of line of command and that create[d] some problems . . . that might not have happened or been necessary had some of the classical concepts of administration been followed more closely.

Unquestionably, it encouraged many to go directly to him. Bert Combs was like a lot of governors, a political animal—took great stock in political loyalties of various people that had worked in his campaign and never discouraged them from staying in contact with him. I think even the maids at state parks could reach Bert Combs on the phone at the mansion, which was a tribute to his loyalties to his friends but made life kind of unbearable for whoever was commissioner of Parks.

Robert Cornett His instincts were different than any governor that I've worked for or been around, and I was around a whole lot of them when I was over at the Council of State Governments. The governors tend to be preoccupied with their own term. They tend to think almost exclusively of their relationship with their voters during that term—they've been successful if they're popular.

Governor Combs seemed to go in with a totally different perspective. He seemed to go into office with a set of notions about what he wanted to do with the office, and I'm no psychologist but I suspect that he had already made it in his own mind as a career. He'd been a respected judge. He probably was satisfied with his role in life. He didn't want to be governor. He wanted to use the office. And usually people want to be governor. They'll figure out what to do with it later. This meant that he did think in terms of what is going to last. Even while he was driving everybody crazy by mixing the politicking and the administrative he made steady progress on everything.

Martin (Mike) Duffy, Jr. When Combs became governor, we had the opposition of the Chandler people in the [Kentucky] Senate just like Waterfield had the opposition of the anti-Chandler people when Happy was governor. But Bert was his own man. You could depend on him. He was always polite, always courteous. He didn't run roughshod over anybody. But when he told you something he would back you up. Breathitt was about as nice a man and about as philosophical and idealistic as any governor could have been, but Ned vacillated. . . . He tried to be all things to all people.

Ed Easterly He lived and slept being governor because he was enthused by it. There were so many things he wanted to do for Kentucky. As a result he just wanted to meet all the people he could who could help him in that objective. He worked at all hours. It was not unusual—I'd be at home maybe at 10:00 P.M. and I'd get a call from the governor. "Ed," he'd say, "I've got an idea. Will you come over and talk with me? By the way, I'll have a scotch and soda waiting for you." I'd go over there and the governor would have some project and the first thing you know we'd work until midnight or one o'clock in the morning. I'd need additional information and I'd be on the phone calling commissioners getting information the governor needed right then. On many occasions I'd meet him for breakfast. We'd discuss things. He applied himself twenty-four hours a day to that job.

Most of the time I gathered that the ideas he had were his own. But he was in a position to pick up ideas because he enjoyed talking with people and I have never known a person who made such effective use of the telephone as Combs did. When Combs gave his support to a bill in the legislature it was almost certain that that bill would be approved. People wondered about his remarkable batting average in recommending legislation. It worked like this. Somebody would ask him to support a piece of legislation and Combs would get on the phone and call various people around the state who were interested in the particular legislative project and ask them what they thought of it. He used them as a sounding board and from their composite opinions he would decide whether or not to support the bill. If there was a lot of objection to it, unless it was something extremely important, Combs would not throw his support to it. But when he did throw his support he knew that people around the state were in support of the proposal and it usually went through. . . .

Combs was very sensitive to the need for public relations, the need for informing the public, and one of the things that we organized when I was with Combs was statewide press conferences whereby we invited the managers of the radio stations and the newspapers, editors, all to come to Frankfort. We met in the [Kentucky] House of Representatives's chamber and the governor was there surrounded by his cabinet. The newsmen were able to ask any question they wanted to. Combs either answered them or for elaboration he referred the questions to the commissioner representing that particular department. We also threw a dinner for them which became an annual event.

Jo Ferguson As an administrator . . . he was at the beginning extremely inept. I don't think he had any administrative concept. He'd had no administrative experience before. I always remember joking about how he would ask anybody who happened to be in his office to undertake a task for him whether it had any relationship to his work or not. I remember right after he got in he asked me as attorney general to fire a member of the State Fair Board. And I did. He would do that. He would see somebody from one department and he would tell them to do something in another, which finally would get worked out.

Ed Fossett At times we suffered from lack of direction. He'd give you a job without much direction to it. At times I got much of the governor's mail. At that time I guess he was averaging seven hundred pieces of mail a week. Much of it would be referred out to departments for an answer. The biggest judgment problems in working both as a legal assistant and later as administrative assistant was what items do I discuss with the governor? I'd say 80 percent of the correspondence you could handle but . . . I would keep a running list and would travel with the governor at times and try with my list to get as many answers as possible. . . .

I've always had great admiration, respect and esteem for Bert Combs. I think he was a great governor, but maybe as an administrator it was too foreign to him. At times when he wanted something done, whoever was standing next to him got the assignment. Maybe that's better than not getting it done at all but it sure gave headaches to some of us in the department because I'd find myself in personnel matters or something that normally would flow to someone else. But he liked when he had a problem, a project to work on, he liked to get right on it and he gave it to someone to work on. . . .

I found him very conscientious in his job. I think he added quiet dignity to it that maybe had not always been there in the office. He was very conscious of the dignity of the office of governor. I've seen him get angry. He did not pound the table. Usually a steely look came into his eyes. As far as mistakes of his commissioners and his staff, he was very tolerant of that. He didn't like mistakes any more than anyone else likes them. Sometimes he would get angry over . . . situations if he felt that someone had been less than honest with him, or had been devious, or had not kept a commitment to him. [Those were] the times I noticed he became angry. I would say you had to know him a little bit to tell when he was angry. It didn't come through in his language or anything like that.

He was always thinking about working on big projects. . . . Sometimes a good administrator gets so bogged down in details that he loses sight of the big programs. I thought Combs had a great perspective in that area. Certainly it's frustrating to any assistants to an executive when you want a decision directive and you don't get it. Or when you get, "Write a nice letter" and you don't get the answer, yes or no. It's frustrating. But in his case I always thought he was putting his time and emphasis and his thoughts on bigger projects. You couldn't call Bert Combs indecisive. Sometimes it's better not to make a decision until you've got all the facts or until the controversy seasons a little more.

Walter Gattis I have never in my life had a more satisfying work relationship than I had with him and four years with Governor Breathitt. That doesn't mean there were not frustrations and pressures and heat and all that. But at a final showdown I always had the knowledge that if it was a hard-core, legal, right-or-wrong moral question, Governor Combs would back me. I've had people say they were going back to the governor's office and get me fired because of my bureaucratic meddling, keeping their people off the payroll.

I've seen him on political platforms at political rallies at Jefferson–Jackson Day dinners and what not. He had a mystique. He'd just walk into a room of ten thousand ticket-paying Jefferson–Jackson Day diners and almost his presence would bring people to their feet. I've never known a man with quite that mystique. And yet he was basically humble. I think maybe that's one thing people related to. He was never to my knowledge arrogant. He had a temper. He could express himself. He was head of the party and governor and he performed in both areas, and I think he performed well.

Polly Gorman (Interview 2) My activity as appointments secretary never did ease up, which was a surprise to me. The whole time that I was there, there was not ever a time in the outer waiting room, when the governor was in, that there was not somebody waiting to see him. There would be some times when nothing was scheduled but these were people who just dropped in. . . .

If he was coming in at all, he came in pretty early. He would start at eight o'clock in the morning along with everybody else. I always had to go to work before eight o'clock in order to get anything done—the things I had to do to get the schedules out. Then later on we decided that it would be helpful if he knew the day before who was coming in that day. . . . I gave him a general schedule at the first of the month—appointments outside the office, the days he was going to be in. By that time I had put down specific individual appointments. Then I gave him a weekly schedule, and then I gave him a daily schedule. Of course, the daily schedule was the one that was the most accurate. . . .

I think he really liked to talk to people. He felt like he had been elected by everybody and that every individual had as much right to come to him with some problem, great or small, as the next one. He tried not to exclude anybody.

Robert Matthews He was dedicated to the cause and he had a lot of personal loyalty among his friends. I was very loyal to him and still am. He had other friends extremely loyal to him on a personal basis because of his concern for people and his liking of people. But he was not truly a gregarious person. He's not an outgoing, back-slapping kind of fellow. So you had to know him pretty well to understand him. He's reserved in that sense. I don't know if that's a weakness, but being reserved is not a particular plus. He was a hard person to get to know—still is.

Cattie Lou Miller The Combs administration made a very strenuous effort to make information available to the press and to be accessible to the press. Governor Combs began having at least once a year an . . . all-day session where all the press people in the state were invited into Frankfort and were provided with a chance to ask him and his full cabinet . . . any question they wanted to ask. There was no effort to avoid any questions. The friendly members of the press asked friendly questions. Those members of the press who were more enterprising sought to ask more probing questions and were probably delighted with the governor's response and the response of others. I think all of that was a plus.

Governor Combs personally took a very active role in trying to get closer to the newspapermen and see that they understood him and that they would understand better what he was trying to do as governor. My approach to public information work, and I certainly think that Governor Combs and Governor Breathitt concurred in this, is that if something's wrong for heaven's sake go on and admit it. No governor's perfect and no administration is perfect. There are going to be errors. There are going to be mistakes. Don't go on the offensive. Go on and admit it and say what you're trying to do to correct it. I rather think this was a relatively new approach.

Earl Powell He was sort of like a blotter, too. He absorbs things. He was a great one for osmosis. I don't know how frequently he did this with other cabinet members, but he would call me on the golf course on a Sunday afternoon. I'd be playing golf, not him. He'd leave word at the pro shop for me to call him back. I'd promptly call, and he'd say, "What are you doing?" My reaction would be, "What do you think I'm doing, I'm playing golf." Then he'd say, "Come by this afternoon."

I'd go by—leave the golf course and go by—and maybe sit out in the back yard at the mansion. And he might just want to talk about bits and pieces, and when I left there, we hadn't accomplished anything. He didn't really ask me real specifics, but I had the feeling he was always probing and searching. Maybe he had other fellows ahead of me that day, but he was always sucking up something, and learning something.

Julius Rather Governor Combs was a remarkable person—just remarkable. He's extremely intelligent and extremely quick—has an attentive mind and a certain amount of wisdom. He was not swayed by bull—all that kind of stuff that people give a person in high office, blowing smoke. There is a great deal of that around a governor and even some on his staff. However, it just slid over him like water off a duck's back. He kept his feet firmly attached to the ground.

William Scent I recall [that the working relationship between Combs and his commissioners] was very good. I know it was as far as I was personally concerned. Combs has a tremendous capacity to just have a summary of whatever a problem is. You would give it to him in an orderly short memo and he could get right to the root of the matter. He [would] see what the problem [was] and usually come up with a pretty good solution.

Jay Spurrier I think he surrounded himself with very capable people. To be honest, he stayed right with government. I think this is the key. He knew the workings of it. He had good people around him. He had Fontaine Banks, Ned Breathitt, Bob Bell. He brought in a lot of young people that turned out to be very capable. . . . Probably his ability to get along with people and to keep them . . . motivated to try to do a good job [was his strength]. Maybe he was better at that than he was an administrator, but that made his administration move smoothly. He could motivate people and people would do anything for him.

Wilson Wyatt I'd say Combs was an effective governor which to me is a little bit different from saying he is an effective administrator. I've never thought that it be necessary that a president be a great manager or that a governor be a great administrator. It is important that he be able to general forces and if he does that and has other people doing the administering, then he's doing his best job. I think that Bert was a very effective governor. Whether he would have been an effective administrator in charge of a department making sure the personnel records were all accurate and straight and the budget was balanced, prepared in advance, the paper work in order, reports held in a regular time and all, I doubt [it]. I don't think that was his bent. Had [it] been I don't think he would have been effective as governor, as he was. When the chips were down he could be forceful and, thank heavens, that's true.

Taking Government to the People

Bert Combs (Interview 5) I heard as I went across the state in the primary and the general election, and I believe I did cover every county, people say, "We're glad you're here. We're going to be for you. That's fine, but we probably won't see you anymore. We haven't had a governor visit here in so many years. We see the candidates, but we never see the governor."

So I thought that it would be something a little different and perhaps symbolical of our desire to stay in touch with the people if we could develop a program whereby we would select one community across the state to have a headquarters of state government for that day. We called it "Taking Government to the People."

I don't know if it was new, but certainly it was new for Kentucky. We did that throughout my term. We visited forty-five different communities. It was not too difficult. As I say, it certainly was symbolical. It gave department heads and my staff, each person, an opportunity to talk to people that otherwise we would not have talked to.

We would take half a dozen department heads—those that we thought would be of most interest to a particular community. If we had a little town that was particularly interested in highways we would make certain that we had enough top highway officials on that particular day. If they were interested in parks, we would concentrate on parks people. If it was education, we would try to have some top education people go.

We'd get in two state airplanes. We didn't have many airplanes then, but the Highway Department had a pretty good airplane. I had a twin Beech, which is a six-passenger plane, assigned to me as governor. So we would usually fly in the morning—early morning—of state government day to a designated town and we'd by prearrangement set up headquarters. I would be there. My staff would be there. The department heads would be there. Anybody who wanted to come, make a complaint, make a recommendation, just sound off whatever was on their mind, was welcome. . . .

We didn't work any miracles. . . . We tried to have some appropriate announcement if possible for each of these days—something that the community would be interested in. It did tend to focus in our minds the need for a particular highway or a particular park or a small lake or whatever. So it worked both ways. Certainly it was good for me and my staff and department heads because it kept them from getting too far removed from the thoughts of the people.

Fontaine Banks I'll never forget, we were at Hazard. We were in a small room and a well-dressed black lady came in very quietly and registered and stood for probably an hour until her turn came. Back in those days you were having problems all over the country. Some of my people became a little agitated and concerned about her being there and wondered what she wanted to do. She asked to see the governor. I was the one that led her to the governor and introduced her to the governor and he shook hands with her. She sat down and very calmly and quietly explained to him that she just wanted to come and thank him for all that he had done for the black people. The conversation lasted two or three minutes. She stood up, he shook her hand again, and she moved toward the door. Just as I opened the door she screamed at the top of her lungs, "He shook this big fat black hand." She went out shouting with joy and crying, scared everybody to death, but some of the ladies on the staff and I got her calmed down. She was overjoyed that her governor would shake her hand and talk to her. I assume she was from Hazard. . . .

Ed Easterly The presence of the governor in the community was something. The fact that someone was able to sit down and talk with him and even to shake hands with him was a great experience in their lives. I'm sure it had a great impact not only upon a person in the community but on the state. Combs enjoyed talking to people and the humbler the person the more he enjoyed it. I think he recognized what it meant to some of these people to talk with the governor. The fact that their governor would go to Maysville and Mayfield or Manchester, Corbin, or London, or any place like that, that was *something*.

Polly Gorman (Interview 1) I don't know anything I enjoyed more than what we called state government day. I remember we went to one up in Letcher County. It was a mining camp, and I recall that we went down on the school ground at recess when the children were outside playing, and many of the children came up and shook the governor's hand and were glad to see him. One little fellow . . . kept turning somersaults over [an] iron fence all by himself. As we were walking out the gate Governor Combs went up to him and said, "Young man, do you know who your governor is?" He said, "My pap says we ain't got none." He told it on himself any number of times, so we know he didn't make that one up. We used to accuse him of making them up on the spot, but he didn't make that one up because I heard it. He could tell a joke on himself better than he could on anyone else. He definitely could laugh at himself.

Cattie Lou Miller There were differences between the Combs and Clements administrations in that some time had gone by. There was much more movement out in the state by the governor by the time that Governor Combs became governor. And it was his style to move greatly about the state. The Combs administration was not very popular in its first year, partly because of the enactment of the 3 percent sales tax, and I believe it would be correct to say that he felt a great need to stay close to the public as he had been close during the campaign, and to try to get across to the public what he was doing and what results were coming from his effort and from state government efforts—to try to somehow make that transition from the fact that there was a new tax being collected to the fact that new results were being achieved.

So Combs traveled a lot about the state. He undertook programs that were entirely different from what Governor Clements and those others had done in that he began actively bringing government to the people. . . . He enjoyed these trips tremendously in that he was . . . aware that it's very easy for a governor to get barricaded behind the mohogany in Frankfort and to be out of touch with the large middle economic group of Kentuckians as well as others. It's sort of like an in-office campaign insofar as being directly available to the public, and this is more so even than in the campaign.

In the campaign a candidate is kind of shaking hands with this one and looking on to the next one, but in the government-to-the-people project the governor was seated, the people talking to him were seated, they had plenty of time to say to him what they wanted to say. He had people taking notes to make sure he didn't forget what their project was. The citizen had his choice as to whether or not the press would hear what the conversation was, and it was simply an opportunity for persons to really talk to the governor about something they were interested in. Sometimes people would stop by and say they didn't want anything except they wanted their little boy to shake hands with the governor. Or they might just say they thought he was doing a good job.

Innovations

Bert Combs (Interview 6) I got the idea for the floral clock at Niagara Falls, Canada. For some reason, and I don't recall why, I had occasion to be in Niagara Falls and I saw the one which is across the river in Canada. It occurred to me, why couldn't we have something somewhat similar on our capitol grounds? So I mulled it over. I sent one of my aides to Niagara Falls to inquire about that floral clock and make a drawing of it to find out just what the mechanical features were.

From that I thought I would get some idea about the cost of it, and the feasibility. So after I got that sort of information, I called one of the watch companies and asked this company if it would donate the mechanical part and it said it would. Then I thought that we can build it with prison labor and the cost will be nominal. I should have been a little more wise. As soon as the word got around that I intended to build a clock with prison labor, the labor unions said, "No, oh no. We'll picket. You can't do that."

Well, I didn't want a picket around the capitol grounds so I had to come off of the prison labor thing and then about that time I was called back by the watch company and they said there was a federal code and they couldn't donate the works. I had already announced that I was going to build it so I felt like I had to go through with it. So it was let to a contractor. The mechanical parts of the clock were purchased by the state, and the clock was built amid a lot of conversation, some of which amounted to criticism.

I didn't have too many people in favor of it. Aides thought it would be the death of us politically. Of course, Happy Chandler, at that time getting ready to run for governor for the second time, immediately started making jokes about it, jibes—came up with the saying, "Well, they don't say it's half past ten in Frankfort anymore. They say it's two petunias past the jimson weed." That sort of thing.

Fortunately, the Garden Club of Kentucky got interested in the project. Of course, I courted them very hard. . . . The Garden Club agreed to come over and help dedicate it and to make it the Garden Club project for that year. That sort of took the sting out of it.

Then we proceeded with the idea of putting gold fish, turtles, that sort of creature, in the pool around the clock. We started calling it a wishing well and people started throwing coins in the pool. We said we'd use the money for handicapped children, which we did. So Happy and most of the critics came off of it and started talking about something else.

Fontaine Banks I remember the clock business. Wendell Ford and I were on the governor's staff at the time. Combs had talked about building this floral clock. Wendell and I thought at the time that this would be a real political issue and that we weren't sure that he ought to do it. We felt . . . Happy Chandler was going to run again and this would be just the very thing that Happy would make a great issue out of.

Wendell and I were standing in front of [Combs's] desk and [Combs] looked out the window—always when he looked out the window we kept quiet because he was either making a decision or he was about to chew us out on something. He turned around and said, "I'm going to build my damn clock." He told me later after he left office that he had come very close not to doing it, but had made the decision that moment to build that clock. . . . He got his clock. I don't recall that on anything of major consequence he changed his mind in midstream. . . .

He was very strong on the beautification of the capitol grounds. I have seen him many mornings walking around . . . the capitol grounds looking. After he got the clock built, we were in his office one day and he was looking out his window and he said, "I've got to do something with that other corner to balance off the clock," and I just almost went through the floor and thought, "Oh no, not another situation like the clock." "Oh," he said, "how about a rose garden, Banksie?" He put a rose garden on the other side.

Ed Easterly Combs proposed to build a floral clock. All the politicians were against it. Frankly, I was too, because I was thinking of the effect politically of the governor spending twenty-five or thirty thousand dollars to build a floral clock when the people of Kentucky and especially Eastern Kentucky needed jobs, money, and things like that. I thought Combs would be crucified over it. Combs said, "No, drive right ahead," and he built the floral clock and I understand the floral clock has turned out to be the number one tourist attraction in Kentucky. Everybody praises him for it.

Sara Combs Kaufman He wanted people to come to Frankfort. He thought that we had a lovely capital and they should be more aware of what went on there. . . . I think it was Kentuckians he wanted to come there—not necessarily tourists from out of state. He was trying to get the people of Kentucky to visit and be proud and interested in their state capital.

Gil Kingsbury (Interview 2) I was called down by several of his friends telling me what Bert was going to do [about the clock]. Cattie Lou Miller was one who called a lot. They said he was spending $50,000 on this thing and it would just cause trouble. He enlisted the Garden Club of Kentucky to get on it and nobody is going to complain about the Garden Club, and he got it by all right. It's all right. I haven't any great love for it, but I think he made capital out of something that could have been a real liability. Bert showed some pretty good public relations sense in that particular thing.

Earl Powell He talked to me about [the floral clock]. I guess he talked to everybody. I told him I thought it was a stupid thing. I would never spend that money to put that thing up. He put it up and

I think it turned out to be quite a tourist attraction. So his judgment was a heck of a lot better than mine.

Potpourri

Fontaine Banks I think he was always looking out for ways to do things a little differently to show appreciation for those who worked for him and he came up with this varmint dinner idea. Some of the things they cooked, although edible, I could never get up enough courage to eat. They became enjoyable events and he had many of them.

Most of them were down at the clubhouse at Stag Distillery, which could accommodate three hundred or four hundred people. You get enough varmints in to cook for that many people [and] you have a lot. Possums, squirrels, rabbits, venison, bear meat, wild boar, elk, antelope—over a period of time they had a little bit of everything.

He invited mainly people from state government and different groups from out in the state. It got to be a great honor to be invited to one of his varmint dinners. He always tried to have an emcee. He'd get up and crack a few jokes. Everyone had a good time. It was very relaxed. And on those occasions he was very, very approachable. He probably spoke to everyone who attended every night which I know is a task but there's no question in my mind but that he spoke to everyone.

Barry Bingham, Sr. I think he left a kind of tradition in Frankfort of utter personal integrity which is something that will not always be observed, but it's something for people to use as a benchmark. I think that Bert Combs really was a governor who established that kind of reputation and it's a very valuable thing not just for his administration but something you can always point to.

Wendell Butler Combs had a great sense of mountain humor. His background and training reflected his personality. He had a lot of wit. I remember one time he met a man on the road somewhere in the campaign. He asked the fellow to vote for him. This man said, "Judge, I wouldn't vote for you if you were Saint Peter." Combs said, "You couldn't vote for me. You wouldn't be in my district."

Robert Lee "Slick" Combs I remember one time when he was on the state Court of Appeals he was up here quail hunting. . . . I kept a couple of dogs and he began to like hunting—doesn't shoot worth a damn, but he liked to get out. We went hunting up there in Clay County once with the game warden and my brother-in-law Troy Savage, assistant attorney general at one time. We got through and were driving back in. . . . Bert . . . looked at [his license] and said, "Can you fish and hunt both on the same license?" I said, "No, you have a hunting license for hunting and a fishing license for fishing." Well, he'd been out all day with a game warden with a fishing license. He said, "What am I going to do?" I said, "Well, we'll stop up here at the Standard station and I'll call the county clerk and have him to issue you a license. It's still the same day." He said, "That's a good idea." So I called the clerk and got up to my father-in-law's. I was living in Harlan then. I was telling this license tale on him. After I told it two or three times he called me off in another room. He said, "Slick, I know that's a good tale. But don't you think we've heard about enough of that?"

Harry Davis I think that Combs was a good governor. His weakness was his friends. He had several friends around him who were feathering their nests rather than serving Combs or serving the people. He wasn't vindictive. He was an easy fellow to talk with when he was governor. I would say that he just carried out the duties of his office well. I do think his big weakness was that he did select some people who were not as honorable as he was. It's real difficult for a governor to be on top of what is going on because there are so many things. It's like a three-ring circus. But I think he did a good job.

Ed Easterly In 1960 we went out to the Democratic convention in Los Angeles. Kentucky wasn't on very good terms with the Democratic National Committee. I guess we owed them some money and hadn't paid it to them. The result was they gave us a hotel way away from the coliseum where the convention was being held. It was what some people would consider ratty. The elevator service was terrible. It was just an old-fashioned hotel called the Commodore, and people like Bill May and well-to-do people from Kentucky were delegates out there and to come and stay in a hotel like that made them outraged. Jo Westpheling, newspaper publisher from Hickman, quipped that it was the first hotel she'd been in that had hole-to-hole carpeting. They were very unhappy.

The governor's suite was no bigger than my living room and there was a good deal of grumbling. So Combs called a breakfast meeting and we got everybody together. He said, "I know our accommodations here are not what a lot of us are accustomed to. I might say they're probably better than a lot of us are accustomed to, but we're stuck with them. The hotel management is doing the best it can to improve service and be helpful to us. So let's just be good sports about it." That lifted their morale. They figured we might be staying in a rat's nest but that's all right. It's like camping out. When anyone asked where we were staying after that, we told them it was the Commodore Hilton Hotel. You could just feel the spirits of the crowd rise at that breakfast conference when Combs told them to be good sports.

Polly Gorman (Interview 2) [When he discussed policy with people] I think he was looking for real advice in that he was seeing if they knew something that was strong enough evidence that he shouldn't go the way he was going. If they convinced him that he probably shouldn't do that he would have listened to them. . . .

I do not think Combs liked power. I never got the feeling that he felt the power. If it was something that he had to weigh one way or the other, because he could do it was not enough. I think he was more apt to do something because he should do it, not because he just simply had the power and could do it. I think he backed off often because of any feeling of power he had.

Sara Combs Kaufman I think Bert enjoyed being governor, but I think that he was very available to the public which perhaps made it more strenuous. . . . I've heard him say that he thought the governor's residence shouldn't be so near the capitol, because he had no privacy. In those days if you sat out in back, the drive went right past. We would be out having a picnic or something and have the public walk in. This is all right for a short time, but when you have four years of it, twenty-four hours a day, it is strenuous.

Gil Kingsbury (Interview 2) My wife, Sylvia, and Mabel Combs got along real, real well together. We went to the Derby with them one year. Sylvia and Mabel would split bets on the horses. Mabel was a shy person. We got along with her real well. She wasn't shy with us. I would see her at parties at the mansion wandering around all alone, not mixing with people. . . . There was some entertaining to be done, but I don't think she was ever at ease, unlike Bert's second wife, Helen. Helen enjoyed it and Mabel didn't.

Jack Matlick I knew his children very well. My daughter was about the age of Governor Combs's daughter and he called my daughter and Lois in. "Now, this summer [1960] during your vacation, I want you girls to go work in the state parks." Neither one of them wanted to go and wait on tables. He kept insisting and finally he said, "I'm going to send a trooper over there to pick up your daughter and my daughter is going to be in there and we're going down to Cumberland Falls State Park."

At that time my daughter was only five-foot and we just couldn't imagine those girls running around carrying those great big trays of food around. So they'd been down there about a month. And he said, "Now, I want you girls to go down to west Kentucky to Kentucky Lake and work down there."

Neither one of our girls wanted to go. They had met all these boys and people down there at the other park after working hours. They played games and had a lot of fun and they didn't want to go. But he insisted they had to go down to west Kentucky so they spent a month down there. They made fifty cents an hour plus their tips and I remember when my wife went out and picked up my daughter, who flew in from Kentucky Lake, she handed her purse to her and the purse was so heavy it took her way down to the ground because she had all those tips.

But it was a good education. I think that was something for the governor to send his daughter out and get some first-hand experience waiting on the public in the state parks.

J.R. Miller I don't think Combs . . . was as much of an introvert as the public would perhaps think he was. One-on-one he's not. He's not an extrovert in the sense that I am. He's not enough of a private person that I would class as a real introvert. He's an interesting fellow to sit down and visit with. He has varied interests. He's a good fisherman, good hunter, good mixer with people. He's a good sportsman and I enjoyed hunting with him. He does like people, but as I say, he's prone to take advice from people he trusts whether the advice is good or bad, and whatever their motives might be for giving him this advice.

Julius Rather I've seen him once get angry. He never yelled. He never raised his voice. In fact, he didn't say anything. And I think Fontaine Banks could remember the instance. He got awful quiet. You could tell that he was awfully angry. It involved something he wanted done very much—something he had a right to ask of a person in state government who said that he would do it but without saying anything to him this person did something different, making him look pretty bad.

Bobby Combs Rehm One thing I have never found Bert to do is talk about himself or his problems or his day-to-day life. I think that's one of the other things I admire him for. He never seemed when he was governor or when he was judge or whatever or on a campaign—he never gives the impression that he doesn't have all the time in the world to listen to you or that he has any problems he needs to be working on. . . . Whatever you ask him he always acts as though he has all the time in the world and is thinking of nothing except what you're talking about.

June Taylor I think he had his finger on what was going on pretty well. And that's very difficult for a governor to do. He would give you an assignment—you wouldn't be the only one who had that assignment. He might have five others of us out here doing the same thing. Then he'd gather all that information. He did this with many things so he'd be sure he'd be getting all sides of the story. I think he had in mind what he'd like to do but he wanted to be sure and also I think he wanted to draw these people in and make them think that they'd had a part of it.

Dix Winston I think Combs is one hell of a fellow. He's painful—his honesty is painful both to himself and to his friends. I saw a lot of people that were very close friends of Combs when he was governor. They would approach him with this shenanigan or that shenanigan that they wanted and if it had any taint to it Combs would let them know that we "taint going to do it."

He had tremendous sense. He could sniff something out way ahead of it. When someone started talking to him, he would listen rather intently, although you might not realize he was listening intently, and before they got through all the proposition, you'd see him start shaking his head and wrinkling his brow a bit because he could start smelling something before anybody else. Combs was a rare commodity politically and becoming more of an endangered species each day.

Chapter 5
Aftermath

Law and Politics: 1963–1967

With the expiration of his term as governor in 1963, Bert Combs returned to private law practice, this time in Lexington, Kentucky, where he and Mabel purchased a home. Early the next year his former legal assistant in Frankfort, Julius Rather, joined him as a partner. Combs scrupulously avoided cases that concerned state agencies and he refused all personal service contracts offered by Governor Breathitt. In short, he made an energetic effort to avoid the appearance of being surrogate governor, and it was not easy.

A considerable number of people in Breathitt's administration were carry-overs from the Combs period. Democrats throughout the state and particularly those from Eastern Kentucky continued to look upon him as the head of the party, the man to see if they wanted something from Breathitt. Newspaper observers as well regarded him as a potential candidate in 1967 despite vigorous statements to the contrary. At Breathitt's inauguration, for example, Combs concluded his farewell remarks by stating that he did "not expect to stand here again,"[1] and when queried four months later about running again retorted, "Not on your life. I'm happy where I am."[2]

Yet political circumstances militated against Combs's ability to separate himself positively from political consideration. Breathitt had problems not experienced by Combs. Harry Lee Waterfield, the lieutenant governor again, was not closely allied to Breathitt as Wyatt had been to Combs and posed an ever-increasing divisive threat. The shadow of factionalism remained whether Waterfield and Breathitt wished it or not. Waterfield symbolized to old Chandlerites their hope for a return to power while many of Breathitt's advisers and associates still identified with Combs.

Whereas Combs had been in a position to improvise, create, and begin anew with a team of his choosing, Breathitt in effect was a caretaker, a guardian of what had been initiated. Eventually the new governor established a measure of control and did expand into new areas, but he never seemed to be in charge the way Combs had been.

In the meantime the state Republican party gained new strength due in part to Democratic divisions but also as a result of G.O.P. successes in Louisville and Jefferson County. For the first time since the 1930s Republicans effectively challenged the dominance of city and county government by Democrats. New and youthful leaders like Marlow Cook and William Cowger gained popularity and Louie Nunn retained and built upon the power base he had established when he lost by a narrow margin to Breathitt in 1963.

Under the circumstances, Democrats in large number came to regard Combs more and more as a kind of potential savior. The fact that he rejected an offer to become federal judge for Kentucky's western district in August 1964 heightened this hope that he would return despite his concurrent denial of any interest in political office.[3] In early 1966, forty political and business friends from nine Eastern Kentucky counties met at Ashland, Kentucky, and called for a statewide "draft Combs" movement. "I have talked with Governor Combs," one Ashland businessman observed, "about the prospects that he might run. He hasn't told me he will run, but neither has he told me he will not run."[4]

At the same time Combs continued making speeches and addressing major issues at public gatherings, and whether he did so to promote an election cause or not, did not matter. It looked like he was campaigning when he told teachers at a statewide Lexington meeting that they ought to receive the full salary increase they had demanded and that Governor Breathitt should "stretch" his campaign pledge of no new taxes to accommodate them.[5]

When the legislature adjourned in April, however, Democrats were still uncertain about the future. They seemed to feel that only a Combs candidacy would keep the party from splitting asunder in a divisive primary. Already state senator J.D. "Jiggs" Buckman had formally announced he was a candidate; the commissioner of highways, Henry Ward, had revealed he was "available"; and A.B. Chandler had said he was ready to go again.[6] But Breathitt hesitated to endorse anyone. He still hoped that Combs would run. "Until he declares himself out," the governor cautioned, "there is a chance" he will run. Combs himself did not help matters by suggesting that it

Aftermath 173

was far too early to proclaim his political intentions though it was the same time frame in which he had announced in 1958.[7]

By midsummer it appeared that Breathitt had settled upon Henry Ward with the understanding that Combs would be named to the Sixth Circuit Federal Court of Appeals. Ward was more than willing but Breathitt again held off by pointing out that the senatorial race between John Y. Brown and John Sherman Cooper required primary attention. At the same time, he repeated his preference for Combs.[8]

October found Waterfield in the race along with Lexington businessman David M. Trapp, swelling the number of candidates to five. Probably because of arguments presented to him by Breathitt as well as others, Combs acknowledged he was reconsidering his decision not to run. "I have agreed," he publicly averred in late October, "to take one last look at it."[9] *The idea apparently was that Ward would run for lieutenant governor on the same slate.*

But ten days later it was over. Combs withdrew and threw his support to Ward who, with administration backing assured, resigned his Highway Department job and announced formally for governor. Combs remained active politically in support of Ward's candidacy through the May primary, which Ward won by a wide margin over his closest rivals, Chandler and Waterfield. By the time the general election took place in November Combs had been a United States circuit court judge for five months.

Bert Combs (Interview 11) A former governor of Kentucky does have problems merely by reason of having been a governor. Kentucky has a sort of a love-hate relationship with its governors, I think. The people are probably closer or feel closer to Kentucky governors than they do in most states, particularly in the larger industrial states.

It has been, too, traditional in Kentucky for a candidate for the office to campaign long and hard. . . . I don't know whether this is a plus or a minus, but Happy Chandler had the knack of causing people to feel very close to him as a person and as a governor. Though he personified that attitude perhaps more dramatically than most, it has been true through the years that people, many people, thought that if they came to the capitol and the governor wasn't in his office that they would just walk on over to the governor's mansion and come in and make themselves at home. All of us in my generation encouraged that, during the campaign in particular, and so when the campaigns were over many people felt that we had meant what we said about coming to the mansion and joining us for dinner, or a cup of coffee.

People expect the governor to be one of them. At the same time I think they feel like he ought to also be an image of strength, and of wisdom, and of sophistication so that he could hold his own with the statesmen of the world, and at the same time be perfectly at home at a fish fry in Letcher County. It takes a pretty good man to meet all those qualifications. I'm sure none of us have done that. But I think people subconsciously are seeking that type of person in their governor.

We have more former governors in Kentucky than other states merely because not many states now prohibit a governor from running for a second term. So we have seven or eight former governors now. Too, people apparently expect a former governor to remain as an emblem of an elder statesman that many . . . resent being in industry, in a profession, or having to make a living. I know that is a little intangible, but a governor, for instance, steps on a lot of toes. He has to make hard decisions. Invariably, after his term of office has expired, if he has to make a living, which I did, he runs into those people who rightly or wrongly feel like that he was not as good to them as he should have been while he was governor. That is part of the problem.

For instance, a Democrat governor has created an image of being a partisan Democrat. You almost have to create that image in order to get elected on the Democratic ticket. And Republicans, hard-nosed, hard-rock Republicans, don't have any great love for a liberal Democrat. I think it's been a handicap to me by reason of having an image of a liberal Democrat. Most of the industrial leaders, most of the establishment, are Republicans. They don't feel too comfortable with someone who has acquired an image of being a liberal Democrat.

A former governor has certain handicaps as well as perhaps certain plusses when he gets back in his profession. I would think that most former governors have had, or are having, that experience. . . . Many people think that having been governor is a tremendous asset in business and a profession. But actually I don't think that's true. Number one, the spotlight is still on you if you get into industry or just practicing a profession and many people think that if a former governor is interested in something that it is a political adventure of some sort or that he's trying to work an angle, get an advantage. Your friends, if you have friends still in office, they are afraid to even give you a fair shake because the news media or their critics would say that the former governor was getting an advantage or attempting to get an advantage. So your friends are afraid to do anything for you and your critics, your foes, are not going to do it. . . .

Ned Breathitt and I had somewhat of a unique relationship. Our relationship went back to the time when I first ran for governor in 1955. Ned at that time was in the legislature, or he came shortly after that. In any event, I knew him as a member of the legislature. He was actually for me in the 1955 campaign and also in the 1959 campaign. He was my personnel commissioner and then later a member of the Public Service Commission. But Ned was young and he hadn't had extensive experience in government. He had some. He had very little name recognition when he announced for governor. So I worked closely with him in his campaign. So we had a very close relationship as a friend—personal friend and political friend. The last thing I wanted to do was for Ned's critics and my critics to say that I was attempting to get too much influence over the Breathitt administration.

On the other hand, I had to live in Kentucky. I had to make a living and state government touches almost everything. Even a college professor or a man who's running a restaurant over here—he has to have a license of some kind. So you don't get along too well unless you are at least on friendly terms with a state administration. I knew it was somewhat of a difficult situation for Ned and for me. . . .

But the problem about that sort of relationship is not between the two individuals. The problem is that the aides and the staff of each of the individuals become jealous, envious, or they are so concerned about the person they work with, and work for, that the staff members churn this sort of thing. I'm sure that some of the Breathitt staff members wanted to go to extremes to avoid any possibility that the press or the people would think that Combs was having too much influence with the Breathitt administration.

On the other hand, I had many friends, and many of them remained in the Breathitt administration. I don't know whether it's good or bad, but the fact is that Breathitt had a built-in program that he was obligated to follow—programs started during my administration. My friends thought, of course, that I ought to have a tremendous influence with Breathitt. If one of them wanted a job, if one of them wanted something, some sort of honor, maybe it would be a highway, all sorts of things, they thought that I should be able to pick up the telephone and call Ned Breathitt and say, "Ned, I'd like you to do this." . . .

Invariably there's a great deal of overlap and Ned and I never had any real problems. I like to think that I was very circumspect in not placing him in that position. I'm sure some of his close advisers would say that Combs did try to exert too much influence. In any event, both Ned and I were attempting to strike some sort of balance.

For instance, I didn't practice any law before any of the agencies in state government. I never went to the Revenue Department. I go now occasionally, and most lawyers do, on tax problems, severance tax problems, income tax problems, inheritance tax problems. But I very studiously remained aloof from that sort of law practice and the truth is while I established an office in Lexington I curtailed my law practice a great deal for that reason. . . .

When I got out of government I got a job representing Southern Railway. I became special counsel—I represented Southern in Kentucky and when I went on the circuit court of appeals, I recommended that Ned Breathitt—at that time he was out of office—be employed by Southern when I had to give up the position. Ned is now a vice-president of Southern Railway and I am division counsel for Southern Railway which means chief Kentucky counsel. I mention that only to show the relationship that I've had with Ned Breathitt. I do think that we're probably unique in that we have never had any sort of disagreement. Most politicians somewhere along the line have some sort of a hassle. There was a four-year period there where we did have many opportunities to disagree. . . .

Yes, Ned strongly urged me to run as his successor. He had some polls made. By that time polls were relied on, and his polls showed that I was the strongest candidate to succeed him. And I do think that at that stage in my career I was rather popular. In any event, the polls that Ned had made convinced him that I was the strongest candidate. He did attempt to persuade me to run as his successor, the alternative being Henry Ward and two or three others. But I think it was generally understood that if I didn't run, Ned would be for Henry Ward. Ned had high regard for Henry Ward and I had high regard for him. Most people who knew him well did regard him highly, but we also knew, as politicians, that Henry would have a very difficult time getting elected. Henry had wanted to run when I first ran and he didn't attempt to hide the fact that he would like to be governor of this state. He was my highway commissioner the latter part of my term and continued as Ned's highway commissioner.

So having these grave doubts about the electibility of Henry Ward, Ned wanted me to run. I considered it seriously and probably would have run at that time except for a personal family situation. But I finally told Ned that I wouldn't run under the circumstances and so all of us got behind Henry Ward. Of course, you know the history of that race. My decision was well in advance of the time for anybody to announce so Ward had enough time to prepare.

Ed Fossett [After Breathitt was inaugurated] Combs did not come to Frankfort much. I recall on the day of the inauguration they had a big reception in the capitol. Combs wasn't there so I gave him a call in Lexington. He said, "Mabel is in cooking some beans and I'm sitting here with my shoes off. We're really enjoying it. This is Ned's night. So let him have all of it."

J. David Francis I saw Combs here and there [after 1963]. There were several of us got together not long after that. He invited me to join the group. There [were] Governor Wetherby, Governor Combs, Don Sturgill, Harry Miller from Lexington, and several more. We got together and built a Ramada Inn on the north end of the belt line just past . . . Paris Pike. We tried to meet . . . once a month and have dinner together. We didn't make it every month but we did several.

Sara Combs Kaufman After 1963 I knew that he was engrossed in politics and would always be interested. I also knew or perhaps he had said that he was not interested in going to Washington. He wanted to stay in Kentucky. I feel sure jobs were offered to him. I wondered if he was interested in the federal court or if he was approached. I honestly don't know. So many people would come to Bert and say, "Why don't you do this?" So I honestly don't know whether he sought the position or they asked him.

Robert R. Martin I've heard Combs talk about [Breathitt's administration] many times. One of the things after Breathitt was elected some people were objecting to this or that and he said to me, "All I told them was he could be elected. I didn't tell them that he'd be a Boy Scout after he was elected."

William May I would see Combs frequently [after 1963]. He had young Julius Rather as a law partner with him. I saw him frequently and had some law work for him then. We got on different sides of the lieutenant governor's race between Wendell Ford and Bob Matthews. If he ever really criticized me to my face, which he did very strongly, it was when I and Louis Cox and Governor Wetherby supported Governor Nunn's sales tax increase. Although Bert Combs was the author of this sales tax he seemed to take real exception to that. It didn't affect our relation of seeing each other at all, but it was a subject he spoke very frankly to me about. He said that we had betrayed our side.

Ruth Murphy During the Breathitt administration Bert and Ned were personally very, very close. Ned looks on Bert almost like a father and I think Bert feels that Ned is like a son. . . . They spent a great deal of time together on a personal level, not in an official capacity. Some holdovers continued to look to Combs as governor, but it didn't cause trouble because Ned didn't have a jealous bone in his body. He was almost unbelievable in that respect. . . . I don't ever think that Breathitt resented people looking upon Combs as being the greatest because I think Ned feels like he was. Combs didn't want to be a bother and he didn't want Ned to feel he was dictating to him in any way. I think Bert really intentionally kept his distance from a political and governmental standpoint.

Julius Rather People from the mountains, . . . if they wanted something out of government, tried to stop off and clear it with Combs, who honestly was trying to keep his hands off and let Breathitt be governor. It was not always possible. I was in the governor's office one day and Governor Breathitt was very sensitive about it and these people had stopped off and got Combs to say it wasn't such a bad idea. When they got into the governor's office, Governor Breathitt was against it. One fellow just got furious, got madder and madder and couldn't convince the governor to go along with it, I don't remember what it was. He finally got so mad, he looked right in his face and said, "Goddam it, Ned. I checked this out with the governor." That actually happened. . . .

[Combs] did tell a story in Frankfort one day that I was leaving late in the afternoon when he was coming in and asked me where I was going and I told him, "to get a haircut." He looked at me and said, "On state time?" I looked at him and said, "It grew on state time." But that's not really true. He keeps telling it anyway. He loved a story on himself. . . .

We had maybe not a typical law practice and it was basically his practice. I didn't bring in any big clients. We did a whole lot of appellate work. That is, we did work before appeals court, writing briefs, making oral arguments, and that's not a whole lot unusual because there are a lot of lawyers in rural Kentucky that are shy about that. They don't like to write or they don't have that much experience. And Governor Combs is a good writer. They don't have that much experience on their feet. Combs was very good on his feet. We did a lot of that.

One thing we didn't do was what's called "influence peddling." We represented insurance companies. We contracted personal injury accidents, deeds, wills, things of that sort. I remember . . . Governor Breathitt told me he wanted to give me whatever I wanted—a personal service contract. Governor Combs said, "Now, I don't think it would be a very good idea if we took a personal service contract. Do you?" I said, "Well, no." So I've never had one, though it was there for the taking. There were times when I guess I could have used one, perhaps. I can understand the feeling that you're independent, not tied—you don't have an obligation, and it would have really sort of looked bad. You are in this world what you hold yourself out to be.

June Taylor Some people still looked to Combs as the leader after the election, but I don't think it ever really caused a problem with Governor Breathitt because he had such high respect for Governor Combs and he really did seek Governor Combs's advice on many things. He made his own decisions on many things, but just because he was elected governor he didn't say to Governor Combs that he didn't need him anymore. He was very loyal to him and to this day he feels that loyalty to him.

Tommy Carroll In the late fall of 1966 Breathitt called me one day. He was governor, of course. He said, "Combs has finally agreed to go. We met at the mansion last evening and he and Mabel and Frances [Mrs. Breathitt] and I discussed it. He's going to run and Ward is going to run for lieutenant governor. Have you got somebody you can trust down there to get some bumper stickers to spring when we're ready?" And I said, "Yes." And he said, "Get them."

J.R. Miller I don't think there was [a possibility of Combs running in 1967]. I talked to him about it. I don't recall why but we were down at Kentucky Lake about the time Combs was going to be appointed federal judge and we flew back into Lexington and I drove out to Spindletop with him. We had a real heart-to-heart talk enroute out there about taking the judgeship and running for governor. I believe he could have been reelected in 1967.

John Palmore In 1967 I think he wanted to run. I have the impression from talking to people like Bill May that Combs wanted to make the race for governor in 1967, but that Mabel put the quietus on it. He at this time was having difficulty—may have been separated from Mabel. . . . She was very jealous of him and I have heard—I don't know if this is true—that she simply threatened to sue him for divorce if he made that race for governor. I do know from some of the people I know here in Frankfort who are close to him that, say on Friday, they thought he'd decided to make the race and on Sunday he suddenly had changed and said he just couldn't do it. That's when they let Ward have it. Had Combs run in 1967 I think he would have won, assuming that there hadn't been any scandal or anything. In other words I think that if she had agreed and he had run, he would have won.

The Federal Court

The official announcement that Bert Combs had been nominated to serve on the Federal Court of Appeals for the Sixth Circuit came early in January 1967 ending permanently any remote chance he might yet be a gubernatorial contender at that time. It also removed, according to the Courier-Journal "from Kentucky politics one of its most colorful, popular and respected figures. . . . There will be many in both parties who will regret to see him leave the conflict of the political arena for the judicial calm of the federal bench."[10]

In early April Combs won the endorsement of the United States Senate Judiciary Committee and confirmation by the full Senate followed the next day. He delayed official swearing-in ceremonies at Cincinnati until June 1, 1967, however, to allow him to help with the May Democratic primary.

Though no longer a participant in Democratic party strategy and tactics, Combs could hardly be expected not to be an interested ob-

server. Henry Ward's defeat at the hands of Louie Nunn disappointed him and Wendell Ford's election as lieutenant governor, making him titular head of the party, did not enthuse him, but the general continuation of basic programs begun in 1960 must have been gratifying. He was upset by Louie Nunn's addition of two cents to the sales tax. Whether the addition itself bothered him the most, or the fact it came about because of key efforts by Democratic friends, is not clear.

During the Nunn years Democratic party chairman J.R. Miller and Lieutenant Governor Ford worked diligently to rebuild and strengthen a party organization disrupted by Ward's defeat. Combs played no role in this and may not even have been aware of all the efforts that were made. What he did become increasingly aware of as time went by was the continued tendency of the party to divide into factions. Kentucky House Speaker Julian Carroll of Paducah emerged as an ambitious seeker of political power, paralleling the equally ambitious goals of Lieutenant Governor Ford. With a Republican in the governor's mansion, competition between Ford and Carroll boded ill for the future of the party. Marlow Cook's victory over Katherine Peden in the U.S. Senate race and Richard Nixon's wide margin of victory in Kentucky in the 1968 presidential election served further to confirm the need for a more cohesive Democratic party.

Meanwhile Combs was learning rapidly that being a federal circuit judge was not his cup of tea. The strict rules of the court required that he sever all his business and bank investments. He had to resign his position as general counsel for the Southern Railroad. He could not belong to clubs or socialize actively with his old friends. The relaxation of hunting, fishing, and golfing with associates was sharply curtailed.

The job itself, moreover, became increasingly burdensome because it necessitated constant study of briefs, no contact with live witnesses, and writing of opinions to which the Supreme Court paid little if any attention if and when cases were appealed beyond the circuit level. Nearly everything about his work and his lifestyle became more and more distasteful so it is not surprising that he was attracted by opportunities to do something else. When a friend invited him to join a leading law firm in Louisville, he found the prospect tempting and ultimately made plans to do so in 1970. At the same time he found an increasing number of political associates urging him to come back and save the Democratic party from destruction by running for governor. Such an action, many suggested, would defuse the explosiveness of the Ford–Carroll rivalry and create a new togetherness in the party.

By the time the 1970 general assembly convened rumors were flying all around Frankfort that Combs would enter the 1971 gubernatorial race and that neither Carroll nor Ford would challenge his nomination.[11] Julian Carroll, in fact, announced for lieutenant governor even before Combs left the court and indicated he would run in tandem with the former governor. Though Combs did not plan to make his resignation official until June he did react publicly. "Julian is a fine young man . . . ," he offered, "I think he would make a good lieutenant governor and it would be an honor to run with him."[12]

Disinclined to retire to private life and convinced by polls he could win, Ford did not wait until June to announce his candidacy for governor.[13] It only remained for Combs to indicate publicly what had long been expected—that he would indeed be a candidate for a second term in 1971.

Bert Combs (Interview 11)   I did think about [the court] as perhaps the last job I would ever have. I had been on the Kentucky Court of Appeals when I was in my late thirties. I liked it very well [but] I didn't think I wanted to spend the rest of my life there. Then, too, I was in a doubtful district which might have prevented me from staying there all my life even if I had wanted to. That's an open question. . . .

But I thought if I were older I'd be more satisfied to stay on a court of that type. So after I had served as governor and after I'd practiced law for two or three years in Lexington there was this vacancy on the Sixth Circuit Court of Appeals where Shackelford Miller of Louisville had been on the court from Kentucky and had become chief judge of that court, a very able and respected judge. Anyway he died and that vacancy was there.

Many lawyers think that to become a federal judge is the epitome of a legal career. I've never thought about it in those terms. I've never been that strong in that belief but . . . I was fifty-five at the time and I thought, having reached that age, that I would enjoy being a federal judge, this position being considered, I suppose, about as good as the average lawyer aspires to—a prestigious position and one that most lawyers would consider as a fitting manner in which to end your active working career.

So I decided that I would like to have that job. About all I needed to do was to tell Ned that I was willing to take the job. He had told me that if I wanted the job he would recommend me to the president. So I debated several months, as I recall, two or three months anyway, whether I would run for governor or go on the Circuit court of appeals.

As I mentioned, Ned really wanted me to run for governor because he thought I was the best candidate. By reason of my family situation, personal problems, my age—on balance, as they say, I decided that I wanted to go on the court and I told Ned that. He immediately called President Johnson and Johnson, as I recall, said, "All right, if that's what you want." Of course, I had been strong for Kennedy and Johnson. There were no Democratic senators to worry about. Johnson became president while I was still governor so I knew him. . . .

There was one possible cloud on the horizon. That was Earle Clements, who still was very close to Lyndon Johnson, and who had a very low opinion of me at the time. But I didn't think Earle Clements would resist, object, that I be appointed to the court. And I later heard that he said to Johnson, "I wouldn't appoint him, if I were president, but I'm not president and you ought to appoint him." So I was appointed and confirmed by the Senate without any hitch at all. Thruston Morton was senator from Kentucky and John Sherman Cooper was the other Kentucky senator at the time. They were both very helpful. Either of them, of course, could have put in a blue slip which would have made it difficult. Thruston Morton said facetiously, "Hell, I'm for you. I want to get you out of Kentucky politics." . . .

As I said, it is a prestigious position. They had then and they have now very high-class people as judges. I enjoyed the personal relationship and certainly didn't dislike the work, but the federal appeals court is somewhat isolated. You rarely see a client. You rarely see a litigant, I should say. Ordinarily, the litigants don't even see the court. The lawyers come and the lawyers argue the cases. You decide the cases from briefs and arguments of counsel, and they had a great deal of work. . . .

The truth is the appellate court on important issues, constitutional issues, is more of a conduit between the district court and the Supreme Court. They do decide, of course, many important law suits that the Supreme Court doesn't grant *certiorari*. But you know that if it is an important constitutional question that there is at least a possibility, if not a probability, that the Supreme Court will grant *certiorari* and decide the case without any consideration about what the appellate court has done. They rarely mention what happened in the circuit court. If they do, it's merely because they want to explain how the case got to the Supreme Court.

So I really didn't have a feeling of accomplishment on the sixth circuit and although I enjoyed the work and it was pleasant—certainly you had security for life—I finally decided that I would resign. In the meantime, John Tarrant of this law firm had been a friend, more than a friend, for years, had talked to me about resigning from the court and practicing law, coming into the firm as a partner. He'd mentioned it on two or three occasions at Derby parties, that sort of thing. So I knew, thought I knew, that I could come into this law firm if I wanted to. I guess I decided that, facetiously, as some judge said, that I would rather talk to a bunch of idiots than listen to a bunch of idiots.

Everybody, practically everybody, thinks that I resigned from the sixth circuit to run for governor. I really didn't. I didn't resign for that purpose. I thought at the time that I would come into this law firm and practice law. I like to practice law. In fact, I enjoy practicing law more than anything I've ever done except the time as governor. You do get a feeling of challenge, a feeling of being in position to do the things that you believe should be done. On the other hand, there are a heck of a lot of headaches, a lot of dips as well as peaks in being governor. But I like the challenge of practicing law. Of course, the financial consideration was important. I was making at the time $42,500 as a judge. I knew I could make much more than that as a lawyer. . . .

In any event, after some consideration I decided I would just resign. By the time I had made up my mind it was close enough to three years that I just thought that would be a good time to make my resignation effective. So I sent my letter of resignation to the president and it was several months before my resignation was announced. I guess I probably sent it in about April and made it effective June 1 so he would have an opportunity to decide who he wanted to nominate as my successor so there wouldn't be a hiatus in the position.

Polly Gorman (Interview 2)   I wasn't surprised [at his appointment to the court] because I knew that the application had been made and that Governor Breathitt had talked to the president about it. I expected it. Combs made a strong effort to secure the appointment. He appeared to really want it. When he first started thinking about it, I couldn't tell you, but I do know that he did make a strong pitch for it.

J.R. Miller He didn't say anything . . . about why he wanted the circuit judge job. I think Combs had so many frustrations in his domestic life that the judgeship seemed to be sort of a haven for him where he could go in and just hide from some of these things. That's my judgment because he later divorced, and he had the son who was retarded. I think that Combs sincerely wanted to hold his marriage together although I probably don't have sufficient knowledge to make this statement. But Mabel, his first wife, couldn't stand the public. She was just an introvert.

John Palmore I've talked to him about [the federal bench] probably more than anybody has. You know I wanted that job myself and I talked to him about it because I didn't want to apply for it if he wanted it. The word was that he wanted it and we went to somebody's funeral, maybe Parker Duncan's, and I remember talking with Bert about it and my own reelection would have been coming up fairly soon in 1966. He said he was interested when I asked him. So I said, "If you decide you're not interested would you then support me?" and he said he would.

Eventually he did decide to go for it and he did get it. It's funny though. He never really would tell you outright. For example, he told me, "Well, I think I might be." Then he would advise me that I ought not to make any racket about it because I had my own election coming up the next year and if people got the idea I wanted something else that I might encourage opposition. This was the pitch he made to me. He's real sly, you know. He's got an indirect method of coming at you always. Very seldom is it a frontal attack. In the military he would have been great on winning things like the Navy took the Pacific with island hopping. They never did make a frontal assault on a strong position but they blocked them out. This is his style.

Fontaine Banks I think Combs felt the federal court was a culmination in his life, but I felt from the very beginning that he would not be happy. The federal bench limits your associations and what you can do. He was not the type who could be limited on who he played golf with or who he had lunch with. I don't know why he wasn't aware of this when he took the job and I've never asked him. I think maybe he just felt this was going to be the final chapter of his career, and he'd stay there a few years.

Tommy Carroll   Combs quickly became a very lonely man in Cincinnati. He was miserable in that position. Julie Ann, my wife, and I would frequently drive to Cincinnati to have dinner with him. By 1969 Combs was telling me that regardless of what he did in the governor's race in 1971 he was going to resign from the federal bench. He didn't like it. He didn't like being away from his home in Louisville at that time. He didn't like the work. The work was tedious. It was boring. As the youngest judge on the court he was being literally swamped with these appeals, which prison inmates themselves prepare. Because the Supreme Court of the United States had become so particular as to the rights of prisoners, the lower courts had to be meticulously careful with every piece of junk that came across the table. And Combs was just miserable. He was not getting what a district judge gets, which is the fun of the witness, the fun of the lawyers in the sense of the questioning and the arguments, the jury and everything like that—the courtroom drama.

Robert Lee "Slick" Combs   He told me enough so I knew what his aims were, and that was if he went to the sixth federal circuit court and made a pretty good judge and President Johnson was still in the White House, if things broke right, he had a chance to go on the Supreme Court. He didn't tell me that in so many words, but I know him well enough that I know that was what he was thinking.

He told me the reason he resigned [was] he wasn't interested in the sixth circuit court for the simple reason that they'd already been tried in your district court and when it got back as far as the sixth circuit, no matter which way it went it would be going on to the Supreme Court. He said all they did was sit there. They had no say-so. It'd already been passed on. And I think along with that he missed being with people, socializing with them. He couldn't go to the race track. He couldn't be the director of any bank. He couldn't be in a corporation because they might have litigation in court. He had to dispose of all that. So he decided to get back in the mainstream. He did tell me that.

J. David Francis   I didn't think Combs liked his job and I didn't think he would before he took it. It's funny about Judge Combs, and a lot of people don't seem to understand this. He's quiet, reserved, but he's very gregarious. I think he liked his work as far as—he loves the law. He's primarily a lawyer. He loves to study law and he liked that. He didn't like to be closed in a room with a great big record and I don't either—to read that record and come out with an opinion. I told him at the time if he wanted to be a federal judge, be a federal district judge. You at least see members of the bar, your old friends.

Sara Combs Kaufman He did say to me that it was a very monotonous job and being a new judge he was assigned cases that were not terribly interesting. I guess he said to me that it was an assured income for life. He said that you worked by yourself and I think he missed the contact with people and I think it was difficult for him to remove himself from politics, which one had to do. He also said that being a judge even your best friends were apprehensive about approaching you. Perhaps you were going to be doing a case involving them.

Earl Powell After 1963 Combs came to Lexington and practiced law and I was in Lexington and I still kept in contact with him—dropped by his office and had lunch with him, talked to him on the phone. When he went on the federal court I saw him fairly often. I would go up there to Cincinnati maybe once every two months . . . to have lunch with him. I don't think he liked his job. When he took the job, I thought that was the end of him politically. Never again would he be involved. Not only would he not be a candidate, he would no longer participate.

But I would go up to his hotel and we'd have lunch in the hotel, maybe have dinner. I'd come back to Lexington eleven or twelve o'clock at night. I did that several times. Of course, I was one of the people who agitated him and encouraged him to come back and run against Wendell Ford, but I didn't think he would.

The 1971 Gubernatorial Primary

Before an overflow audience in the Flag Room of the Kentucky Hotel, Bert Combs announced for governor and explained that he had resigned from the court because he had been forced to sit "in isolation and silence while the problems of this state have multiplied with traumatic force." Pollution, urban decay, unsatisfactory teacher salaries, and student unrest were the major problems. Not content to sit in idleness on the court where he could not even express an opinion about them, he decided to run for governor.[14]

The possibility that a new factional split of the Democratic party might emerge seemed real. The fact that it never materialized is probably the most significant factor about the primary. To be sure, there was clear evidence of division between the Democrats supportive of Combs and those who backed Ford, but it did not persist long after the campaign.

Combs vigorously promoted more money for education, supported professional negotiation legislation, and encouraged political activity by teachers. Ford did favor more money for the schools, but only if the state could afford it and sharply criticized the development of educational politics. Neither candidate openly advocated more taxes, although Ford frequently charged Combs with making promises that would require more revenue. The candidates differed little on other issues. Both favored a severance tax on coal, continued restrictions on strip mining, improved home rule for Louisville, and other state aids to the city and Jefferson County.[15]

There were, to be sure, some personal attacks leveled by each contender at the other. Each referred to "fat cats" supporting the other's causes.[16] When Ford, age forty-six, suggested Combs, age fifty-nine, was too old to run, the latter retorted that "Combses have a tendency to get gray before they are thirty."[17] Combs called Ford an "ineffective lieutenant governor"[18] who permitted the Democratic party to "flounder" for three and one half years.[19] "The ex-judge," Ford retaliated, "is so confused and desperate . . . that it would not surprise me that before election day he will be promising, if elected, to take off in 1972 the sales tax he promised not to put on in 1960."[20] Yet nothing came close to the biting invective and slashing assaults prevalent in earlier primaries with which Combs had been associated. What did distinguish the candidates were what one newspaper reporter referred to as iceberg issues[21]—those that voters thought about, perhaps discussed with each other, but with which the candidates did not deal extensively.

Ford was younger, came across better on television, and attracted many youthful supporters who, not being battle-scarred veterans of previous political wars, were more enthusiastic and hardworking than were Combs's people. The former governor, moreover, had divorced his first wife in 1969 and remarried only a month later, and *this may have influenced Catholic voters in northern Kentucky and Louisville. Most damaging, however, was that Combs had resigned a lifetime job paying $42,500 to contend for a four-year post paying only $30,000. People just could not understand why he would do such a thing unless he had an ulterior motive.*

Perhaps the most important hidden factor of all, though, was that an overwhelming number of Kentuckians, including many Ford backers, believed Combs just could not lose, and it showed up most vividly on election day. Only 445,000 of 1.5 million registered Democrats showed up to vote.[22] Overconfidence may well have kept many Combs supporters away.

Described as a "stunning defeat" by the Courier-Journal, *which had endorsed Combs, the election did not signal renewed factionalism. The former governor conceded early and graciously. He congratulated Ford and indicated without rancor that it was "the end of the road . . . politically" for him.[23]*

Combs had known before he decided to run that he could join a Louisville firm and return to active law practice. It is probably what he would have done four years later if he had been nominated and elected in 1971. The big difference following the 1971 primary was not that he would be inactive politically, but that the pressure from others that began in 1955 to run for public office was at an end. He was now free to pursue his basic love for law while participating from time to time in the political world without being regarded as a candidate for anything.

Bert Combs (Interview 11)   Some people who were influential had talked to me maybe a year before about resigning and coming back to run for governor. But I brushed them off. As events transpired that was a big mistake because they were some of Wendell Ford's close friends. I thought about it in a rather arrogant way. I wasn't ready to think about it. I've made a number of mistakes like that in my life and that was one of them. I was somewhat surprised that they brought it up.

J.R. Miller, Louis Cox, Bill May, or Lawrence Wetherby came to Cincinnati and we had dinner and talked about it. I did, I guess, have suspicions, but I wasn't certain whether they wanted to talk about somebody else. I'm sure I knew pretty well that they wanted to talk about the next governor's race and at that time J.R. Miller was undecided about Wendell Ford. J.R. wanted Wendell Ford to have a honorable, respectable position. He was Wendell's friend and felt he had some obligations to Wendell and he wanted him to be treated fairly.

If I had played my cards halfway smart, Wendell would never have announced. The truth is after I resigned and after I came back to Louisville, after I started talking about running for governor—it gets back to this thing that there always are some people who are talking for you, people who are unselfish, who think that it would be good for the state, it would be good for the individual. Then there are those who just like to say "I was an early supporter—I was in on the ground floor." And so you have those kind of people.

Anyway, J.R. Miller and Wendell and I had two or three meetings about whether Wendell should run or whether I should run. I think J.R. had some doubts about whether Wendell could win or not and had some doubts whether I could, although I did have at that time a proven track record. J.R. was the Democratic chairman at the time. If I had agreed with J.R. that I would be for Wendell for the next [U.S.] Senate seat—we knew that Morton might not run at the time, we knew John Sherman Cooper was getting to the age where he might not run, so people were thinking toward the Senate seats—I'm convinced if I had been willing to agree that I would support Wendell for the Senate Wendell wouldn't have run for governor. Again, I was bullheaded and thought a governor ought not do that sort of thing. I was still filled with the spirit of judicial ethics. So I said, "No, I won't promise."

Again, I didn't use very good judgment. My polls showed that I was not substantially ahead of Wendell going in, but some several points ahead of him. He had a poll made by J.R. that showed him about even with me, as I recall. I overlooked the fact that Wendell was young and didn't have the same name recognition, didn't have people already fitted in to a position. In other words, I guess everybody for Combs knew that they would be for Combs at the time, but there was a tremendous undecided group and Wendell got most of the undecided.

Wendell Ford and Bob Matthews had had a pretty bitter race [in 1967 for lieutenant governor] and there was that division between the Matthews people and the Ford people, but I don't think that was a major factor in the race. I think, myself, that a great many people concluded when I became a federal judge that I was finished with Kentucky politics—logically would have thought so. Many of them then were looking for a different connection, a different home, so to speak. A great many of them—people who perhaps would have been for me—became obligated to Wendell while he was lieutenant governor. He looked like the logical person to seek the governor's office. I think that was a factor.

Then, too, the fact that I would have been making more as a federal judge than I would have as governor was something that we never could put to rest. So many people think that if a fellow who's making $42,500 is running for an office that pays $30,000 that he's getting ready to steal something. I think it's just about that simple. Why would he be doing it otherwise? So that was an important factor.

But primarily the reason I lost, I think, was that the last few days of the campaign—the primary campaign, certainly the last few weeks—Wendell's supporters started talking about Combs's sales tax. We had sort of put the sales tax to rest—we thought, anyway—during the Chandler campaign. That was another mistake I made because we hadn't put it to rest. We had put it to rest temporarily. But when Louie Nunn came along and raised the tax to five cents that reopened all those old wounds and the trauma set in once more.

When we look at the returns, it's easy enough to see that I lost the election in places like Louisville, Lexington, northern Kentucky—densely populated areas where the housewives and so-called low income groups—and I say that as a descriptive word—had bitterly fought the sales tax. Handbills, not heavily publicized, appeared in Louisville. "If you are against the sales tax, vote against Combs." The timing, and I'm not critical of that because J.R. Miller is a smart operator, [was good]. Of course, Earle Clements was advising with him. Earle, I think, was a significant factor. Again I'm not critical. It's history. . . . So those are the reasons, I think, why I lost. Of course, I should have anticipated the situation. The truth is I shouldn't have run until I had been back in the state long enough to set up the organization.

Tommy Carroll In February 1970 we had our annual Jefferson–Jackson Day dinner while the legislature was in session. At that time Julie Ann [Carroll] and I were seated at the same table with then–Lieutenant Governor Ford. [She] made some comment to Wendell, "What are we going to do?" Wendell said, "Well, we can't do anything until the big judge makes up his mind what he's going to do."

The next few weeks there was almost a continual series of meetings and negotiations. At one time Louis Cox, J.R. Miller, and I flew to Cincinnati and had dinner with Combs. After dinner we went out to the airplane and—I remember distinctly because I damn near froze to death—we sat in the airplane and talked for about two hours. Combs said that he would make up his mind. J.R. Miller, in effect, said he had to make up his mind. "It's not fair to Wendell. You've got to decide what you're going to do."

In late March of 1970, I remember this like it was yesterday, J.R. and I . . . met with Combs in his offices at the Federal Building. In essence, Combs said that regardless of what happened he was going to resign as federal judge effective June 1. He had all he wanted, all he was going to take. But he had determined almost 99 percent in his mind to run for governor. J.R. said, "Is that a commitment?" Combs said, "Yes," and J.R. said, "Then I'm going to go to Frankfort tonight and tell Wendell so we can get the air cleared and you can run and Wendell and I will be for you." . . .

The next morning J.R. telephoned me and he said to me, "Wendell is going to run. He's just gotten a poll which shows him only four points behind Combs with considerable undecided." I think [the pollster] was John Craft because J.R. was a great believer in Craft. He said, "Wendell has been apprised that the undecided vote is soft, that Combs's popularity is not nearly as great as people think it is, and he's going to run. I have got to be for him. He is my home-town boy. He's been a friend for years and there's no way that I can turn my back on him." These, in effect, were his words.

He then called Combs and told Combs the same thing. From then on we knew which way we were going. I was going to go with Combs and J.R. was going to go with Wendell and it never in any way affected any of our personal relationships. But that was the turning point in the 1970 thing. Combs made a final decision which he communicated to people all over the state and Wendell made a final decision. There could not have been a misunderstanding on the part of Ford about Combs's desire to run. Combs resigned from the court on June 1 and about a week later in a rally at the Kentucky Hotel he announced for the governorship.

[The campaign] was the most inept, poorly run, disorganized political campaign I've ever had the misfortune to be involved with in my life. By the summer of 1970 I had the feeling that we were being outorganized, outmaneuvered, and that we were going to walk right down the road to defeat. I tried to get it across to Combs. Helen [Combs] wouldn't listen. She was of the opinion that Combs was going to be coronated, not elected, and I knew what J.R. was doing.

I also began to pick up this business of resentment against a federal judge. Combs's divorce was hurting. Helen was hurting. Combs wasn't doing anything. It was just a fiasco. . . .

I think that the average person in the street, even though he wasn't going to vote for Combs, thought up until almost the very last that Combs was going to win it. I think Combs thought he was going to win it. As far as I was concerned personally, I was so deeply devoted to Combs . . . that it was a rather traumatic experience for me because I knew what was happening.

J.R. Miller I spent almost full-time in Frankfort to try to keep Wendell Ford and Julian Carroll apart. They were both ambitious. . . . I liked Julian and I liked Ford. It was a full-time job to try to keep our heads above water during that 1970 session of the legislature and keep these fellows from cutting each other's throats. This was an everyday event. There was no leadership emerging. It was just going to be a shootout and I knew this.

So I went to Combs and begged him that summer of 1969, before the session, to come off the bench. . . . I knew he wasn't happy and . . . I'd already heard rumors he was not going to stay on the bench. . . . I did everything I could to convince him that he had to come off the bench and assume leadership of the party. If he wanted to run for governor, good, and if he didn't, support somebody else. I told him if he would come off the bench, Wendell Ford would not seek the governorship and Ford had told me this and he told me to tell Combs this. And I did tell Combs that. But for whatever reason he did not resign at that time.

Then during the 1970 session, I saw all of this stuff boiling—the summer shootout coming. I went to Cincinnati on two different occasions with different people—Louis Cox, Ed Prichard, Thomas Carroll—to talk to Combs about our inability to get these guys apart. Somebody had to demonstrate some leadership and he needed to come off that bench and come down here and get with it and I told him Ford would support it. Apparently that didn't take.

I was trying to get Ford to visit with Combs, and they may have met, but if they did I was unaware of it. I don't think they did. I think the relationship had become a little strained because by this time Combs was showing some partisanship for Carroll and this came about by virtue of the people around Combs, who did not believe that Ford had the weight to run and they were telling me he didn't have. This included Ed Prichard, Louis Cox, Wetherby, Julian Carroll, and other people who were Combs's so-called followers.

I finally went to Combs and told him that it would be a mistake for him to take out and run against Wendell Ford. This was shortly after the 1970 session. [I said] that he had been out of office too long, that he had been on the bench, had been sequestered, that we had organized the party around Ford, and that without Ford's support he could not win. I knew by this time that he was pretty well committed to run. . . .

I don't think the people around Combs gave him good advice. I think they gave him bad advice and I think it was kind of self-serving. I don't think they had confidence in Ford. They weren't close to Ford. These people, while they had helped us, did not have the feel for the political situation in Kentucky at that time.

William May   The question was continually raised—is Bert Combs really going to run? So I don't know why he wanted to stay on the court those succeeding months, but Carroll was a candidate for lieutenant governor much earlier than Bert Combs was an official candidate for governor. And Carroll was campaigning over the state as a candidate that was going to run with Combs. It was a very awkward situation hard to understand. Of course, J.R. Miller went right up the chimney on it. I think Combs thought that Ford would never run against him. I think that's what Combs was trying to do with the Carroll vehicle, . . . to get Carroll out front with the message, "Yes, this fellow is going to run, and Ford, you take notice and your friends take notice that he's going to run." But it didn't work out.

Cattie Lou Miller   I was somewhat surprised that he ran for governor [in 1971]. I was in the office of Lieutenant Governor Ford, who had made it widely known for a long time that he intended to run for governor. As rumors began to come along with the press and others that . . . Judge Combs might be interested in running, there was a lot of speculation about it.

I recall talking with Governor Ford about it, and he said he didn't think that was any possibility. "It's just not likely to happen," he said, "but I can tell you one thing that, even if that happens, one thing that won't happen is that Bert Combs and I will be candidates in the same race."

John Palmore   At this time [in 1970] . . . Wendell Ford was wanting to make the race. He didn't want to run if Combs was going to run, but Combs didn't make up his mind. Combs kept saying, "Just keep your powder dry"—one of his favorite expressions. People were pressing Wendell to get in the race to run. As J.R. Miller explained it to me, "Dammit, we couldn't get Combs to say and the time came we just decided we couldn't hold Ford any longer." There was no place for J.R. Miller to go except to be for Wendell. I think if Bert Combs had made up his mind a little bit sooner about making that race—he is a great one for letting things ripen. Lots of things work out of their own accord, you know, and he is the great waiter. He waits to see how it goes. But, you see, that cost him the election. . . .

Bob Matthews was Combs's campaign manager in 1971 and snatched defeat from the jaws of victory. That was a poor choice. Combs can be mistaken in his judgments like anyone else. He just picked the wrong man there. I like Bob Matthews. He's a gentleman, an excellent loyal friend, but he was just not cut out for that. He doesn't have enough drive.

Robert Matthews I think one of the problems we had in the 1971 campaign was . . . the TV tube. Combs ran against Wendell Ford. Not only did we have an age problem on a comparison basis between Combs and Ford, but we had a reserved person against an apparently outgoing, gregarious person like Ford. And Combs came across as more reserved and older, and didn't have the appeal that Wendell Ford did, and the TV tube picked that up. It's hard to project on a TV tube unless you are outgoing. It makes a difference. . . . I think the question of why he resigned from the appellate court to run for governor when he'd been there one time before was never satisfactorily explained to the people. Maybe there wasn't an answer. I don't know whether there was or wasn't. His idea was that he wanted to come back as governor and do something for the people, but I don't think the people ever bought that in the sense that they couldn't understand why a person would give up a $60,000 [*sic*] job to come back and run for governor. We just never did get it explained properly.

Fontaine Banks A lot of us were really alarmed when he announced and appointed his campaign chairman. When Wendell Ford and Bob Matthews ran for lieutenant governor, many, many of the Combs people ended up being very active, including myself, for Wendell in the last couple, three weeks. It was a very close race and

Bob Matthews was very bitter about it. Then when Governor Combs announced his candidacy and appointed Bob Matthews, we felt that this was a terrible mistake and so told him, but the decision had already been made.

I think that it had a lot to do with the direction of the Combs campaign. I'm not so sure that Bob Matthews was really interested in being a state campaign chairman. He was still bitter . . . at some of us that helped Wendell beat him. I know I was in headquarters one time during that campaign and only went there because Combs wanted me to be there and [I] did not feel welcome. None of us did.

Gil Kingsbury (Interview 1) I remember going down to headquarters in Louisville in the campaign and it was run like a bank—all sedate and quiet. I think a campaign headquarters should be organized confusion. I went down to ask advice and bring down my advice for whatever it was worth and pick up some campaign material. I don't think the campaign was run very well, but that's hindsight.

Robert R. Martin He lost the primary because his organization wasn't as strong. He'd been out of office for eight years. A lot of people had grown up who hadn't known him. Ford was lieutenant governor at the time and had been working four years building for it. Many of the people who had been his supporters were committed to Ford.

Robert Bell I wasn't particularly surprised [that Combs ran in 1971]. I think the office of governor is probably so much more personally satisfying and challenging than to hold a seat on the federal bench that I wasn't surprised. And then Combs had such a large political following of supporters who were anxious for him to run again and Bert Combs always felt an overriding loyalty to the people that were his friends and his supporters. I expect that he made that race and probably rationalized it a lot that it was to their interest for him to make the race. He owed it to them.

Barry Bingham, Sr. I think it was probably a mistake for him to run again, not because he lost, but I think it was not in the cards that he could be reelected governor. There was the old sales tax issue which was used very heavily against him. . . .

As I said earlier, I never thought that Bert Combs was obsessed with power and therefore couldn't resist trying to get back into the governorship in order to exert power. There certainly were certain issues that he had pursued in his first administration that he probably thought he could go back to in a second administration and make more progress on. It would be unnatural for any man to be governor of this state and not want to continue certain things that he had started through another administration. But in this case it just didn't work out that way. I think after that defeat he was perfectly willing to go back to private life and lead a useful life as a lawyer.

Ed Farris There was some tendency on the part of Combs to revert back to the 1955 campaign style. He did not have the drive, enthusiasm, the spark that he did in 1959. I do think that he'd like to be governor, wanted it again, so I'm sure he had his heart in it. I just think that he . . . got on the defensive a little bit and could never get rolling. The campaign didn't take off. I'm not certain I've ever been able to determine in my own mind what was the most salient factor of his defeat. I was absolutely surprised by his defeat. I was very strong for Combs and I'd have to say that I was absolutely shocked.

Ed Fossett I did work in Frankfort for him, but I also, in conjunction with his campaign headquarters, went to five or six counties and made surveys and talked to people to see how things were going. I realized as a result of those that things weren't going very well. As I recall, it was about two or three months before the primary. There was concern over his changing jobs and there were a lot of people who don't believe that any governor should be governor a second time.

I also found that the Combs people thought it was won and weren't really working. The Ford people were working very hard, very diligently. Perhaps they were hungrier. Ford had a tie-in with the Jaycees, who were younger. Other than that I don't know that you could say the older people were for Combs and younger people were for Ford. I think we cut across those lines.

J. David Francis I thought he was crazy [to run in 1971], to tell you the truth about it. I was involved in the election very heavily . . . in that we were talking frequently. I was in his home, I was in his office, he was in mine. Everywhere we talked about campaign strategy and things of that kind. . . . He made up his mind rather early to run and try to win. I didn't have the impression that he wasn't clear on whether to run or not. The other side had by far the best organization. Combs had the worst organization I ever saw. He had no organization.

Polly Gorman (Interview 2)   I didn't expect Wendell Ford to run for governor. It was just like turning on your best friend. I did not think he was as capable as Combs. I felt like Combs did not have a good campaign organization. I think that's what beat him. I talked with him after the defeat. He showed a very stoic nature. . . . Again, he seemed like he regretted what he'd done to his friends more than for his own welfare. I don't know—there were times that I felt that he didn't really care whether he won that election or not. He had much less enthusiasm for it. I don't know that that's true, but that came through to me. It did not seem to me to be the disappointment to him that it was when he lost in 1955.

Sara Combs Kaufman   We were sorry to see Bert become a candidate in 1971. I know that people active in politics were always after him. We felt very strongly that he had been an excellent governor the first time. I said to him, "Bert, at your age, why do you want to get into this again?" and he said he thought he'd give it a try. I don't think—it wasn't a conscious thing that we were not as active, but we weren't. We'd already gone that road before so it's difficult to repeat it. I really felt that Bert and others in the campaign weren't as anxious to be governor again as they were the first time. It's hard to get up the enthusiasm, because this was the *third* time.

Foster Ockerman   [Combs ran in 1971 because] a lot of people encouraged him to run. I think that most of those that encouraged him thought that it would be good for the commonwealth that he would be governor. I believe he did an excellent job when he was governor. I don't think it was necessarily because they thought they would be personally enriched because he did it. I just think they had an honest belief that he would be good for the state.

Earl Powell   I don't know why [Combs ran in 1971]. You've got to remember that he would be succeeding a Republican and maybe there's a little bit of a savior complex. Maybe there's a little bit of a messiah complex. Had he been succeeding a Democrat, I don't think he would have been enthused. I think that was part of it. . . . [Another] thing is he had an awful lot of people like me going to him saying, "You've got to come back and save us. You're the man, we need you." I think a lot of it was that.... If people like me had left him alone and let him go on and be a judge he might just be a judge today. I know personally that I wasn't the only fellow that would drop up there occasionally. I'm amazed that the fellow did any work or wrote any opinions. At that time I wasn't in state government. I had no ax to grind. I wasn't seeking a job. I just wanted him to come back and be a statesman.

Julius Rather As I look back on it now he never did light up a fire. All the people he had—he had everybody he wanted in an election for him, most of whom sat on their duff and did nothing. They were overconfident. They all thought that they had a lock. Everybody thought so. I would have bet my house that he would have won. There were times when Wendell Ford was out of the race, had gone to Florida crying—he just knew he couldn't win. However, he was an awful good campaigner. Combs's marital problems hurt him. The teachers' issue—he made no bones about the fact that he wanted to do something for the teachers. This was a little hard to take for a lot of people.

William Scent He had been out of touch, so to speak, for several years [by 1971] because he served on the U.S. Court of Appeals for the Sixth Circuit at Cincinnati. Being an appellate judge he could no longer participate in what was going on in politics during that stint. Wendell Ford spent his four years as lieutenant governor getting prepared to run for governor. Wendell Ford's a very hard campaigner, very personable. He had just circulated around and gotten himself known.

June Taylor I wouldn't take anything away from Governor Ford or Governor Combs, but I think it really was a lot harder work [that won the primary]. I think that Mr. Miller worked at it twenty hours a day and I don't think our people did. Some of the people that were working in our headquarters were just not as energetic. I don't think Combs was as concerned [after the loss] about what was going to happen to his people as he was earlier. I think he was disappointed. I kind of feel he didn't want to be the candidate. His wife wanted him to be the candidate.

[Combs's leaving the court to run] was the hardest thing we had from headquarters. That was the big thing. It was really hard to explain. Even the people who were for him questioned it. That may have been Ford's strategy in his campaign and our people fell for it. I think it was more difficult for Combs to be humorous with Ford. There were deep feelings he had that Ford would never run against him. He felt that if he ran Ford would not. And it really bugged him.

Robert Lee "Slick" Combs Bert was very disappointed after 1971. He was surprised and very hurt. I don't know whether he felt someone let him down. He felt like he had done enough for Kentucky that he should have been reelected. He didn't try as hard as in 1959.

The Combs Impact

Fontaine Banks I think that the Combs administration really brought Kentucky into the twentieth century. I think he had such an impact on state government and on all of Kentucky that we're still measuring the impact and I think a lot of it will be evident for a long time. The impetus that he started is still going.

I think that he really for the first time made Kentuckians proud to be Kentuckians because of what the state was doing—particularly Eastern Kentucky. Every time I ride over the Mountain Parkway I thank him for doing that. Eastern Kentucky had been a forgotten section and I think . . . that he brought it into the fold—gave it some attention and opened it up.

Robert Bell I think the benchmark[s] probably will be the unusual relationship to the lieutenant governor—working together; sweeping changes in economic development that were broad-based; the concept of treating the Mountain Parkway not as a toll project but as economically feasible—a developmental project that would open up Eastern Kentucky, which it did; [and] his political opportunism—where he seized the opportunity to enact a sales tax based on the veterans' bonus vote and was able to come through the back door, so to speak—introduced a much broader-based revenue situation for the state of Kentucky.

Tommy Carroll Combs had one trait that neither Clements nor Chandler had. Combs can laugh at himself. Neither one of them had that. Combs could control his venom. I never really saw Combs mad in my life. I have seen Clements so mad he was incoherent. . . . I've never seen Combs exhibit any vindictive traits or get even ideas like Clements and Chandler. Combs was able not only to pick pretty good people when he was governor, but he would delegate authority. Clements was not much of a delegater. Clements wanted to have his finger on everything.

Jo Ferguson I still have some contact with Judge Combs both as a lawyer and as a friend and like many people who were a part of his administration I still consider him to be my leader in politics. I'm not an active politician anymore but I do take some interest in it and I tend to support the candidates he supports. He still is a leader in politics. I think he's interested in the good of the state. He's done things for the common schools, for the colleges. He takes a tremendous interest in areas which needed attention. He's been a very progressive leader of our state. He is a man with more parts than one would think. . . . He's a man of broad interests. He and Wilson Wyatt together, more or less, sponsored the establishment of the Arts Commission and making state appropriations to various art projects like the Kentucky Opera Association and various things of that nature.

Ed Fossett I think he left his footprints in the sands of time. He liked the expression and he used it. To me it's original with him. I think he made good decisions. History has shown that—as with the toll roads, which there was clear opposition to. His merit system, his use of the sales tax, all of those things were well done. History has shown that he was a good governor. Certainly he was an active one. I was very proud to have a small part in it. It's one of the things in my life that I take great pride in.

J. David Francis Combs is a very complex person. He's an extremely deep thinker, so intelligent and qualified in nearly everything. He's an exceptionally good lawyer. I love to talk about law with him. I find him very challenging just in a conversational context. I think he would have been an outstanding jurist on the Supreme Court. I think he's probably the best governor we've ever had in Kentucky. I value him very highly as a personal friend and respect him very highly as a lawyer and a statesman and a jurist.

Polly Gorman (Interview 2) I think Combs's impact upon Kentucky was tremendous. I really think that he had many innovative ideas that were perhaps ahead of other people. He had the courage of his convictions. First, for instance, would be the Mountain Parkway. Think what that's done. It opened up that whole end of the state even though they said it went nowhere. The people up there didn't think so. He built many highways. He was very highway-oriented. Kentucky probably finished their toll road system earlier than anyone else because of the push that he gave it.

Jack Matlick   I can't help but feel that he's made the greatest contribution that anybody has ever made. I still say that we'll still be carrying out programs he initiated another ten or twenty years from now, because they make so much sense. The fact that water resources have been developed to the extent they have,—the park system, our highway system. Schools have been improved every year since he started it.

Cattie Lou Miller   I think that he had a strong impact on Kentucky. He moved the state forward in many, many respects in opening the transportation, developing the roads and airport system. He made it possible for many other developments to come. He got the schools off to a great start that in some respects the public schools have not lived up to. He started educational television, which to me has been a great disappointment in the light of what I think the original vision was for it. He got the tourism industry up and going. It's been a plus all around. The parks system has very nearly fulfilled his dream for them.

He did so many other things about the tourism industry other than just the parks. He created the chain of small lakes that became places of interest and he developed the statewide beautification and cleanup program and really pushed them. He developed the Kentucky handicrafts industry which unfortunately didn't survive the onslaughts of the federal hours and wages people a few years later. This made it impossible for crafts outlets to survive. He gave his blessing and backing to enterprises like the amphitheaters, the dramas, the travel advertising matching fund, and so many of those things that were creative and imaginative which some governor with less energy and less money might just have left off. He did so much in the mental health field and the mental retardation field. That was just a night and day difference when he became governor and when he went out of the governorship.

It all reflected his imagination and the drive he put behind these efforts to get the shows on the road. It wasn't too unusual for Combs to start about three people unbeknownst to each other on a particular planning task and then to take whatever ideas they came back to him with and either combine them or pick the best of them.

So there is nothing that plodded along during his administration. It moved along and he moved it along. He was a very aggressive and energetic gentleman who did a lot that made permanent changes in the state. Many, many things were a lot better and a lot more progressive and were set on a track of where they had to be propelled forward for some time to come—long after he went out of office.

J.R. Miller People, when they win high public office, seem to change. They get on an ego trip. I'm sure Combs did too but I have to confess that he showed it less than anyone I've ever seen. But they all think they are carrying the weight of the world on their shoulders and become different people. But Combs didn't show that as much as others. I haven't seen one other as stable as he was throughout his entire administration. He did have fun. He enjoyed people.

John Ed Pearce At the time I don't think that we realized how well-rounded the Combs program was, and how far-reaching. It just pushed Kentucky ahead—just like tourism brought in a lot of money to a lot of places. The park system made possible the program of tourism that he espoused. The new industry produced taxes that were needed to keep these programs going and of course his sales tax, cussed as it has always been, made possible the big jump in education.

All of it was of a part to create jobs, activity for Kentucky, and then he started this program of roads to make all parts of the state accessible. It modernized Kentucky. We're just today living on the secondary effects of his program. When I first came here we had to travel to Pikeville and it was a backbreaking drive, terrifying—the roads were so bad. Now it's so pleasant to drive around Kentucky.

Earl Powell I have the feeling when I think of Keen Johnson, Clements, Wetherby, Chandler, Combs, Breathitt, Ford, Carroll—of the group, maybe because I was more closely associated with Combs, I have the feeling that he somehow was a little superior to most of these people whether it's in brains or genuine interest, character, an overall feeling he tried to do. This doesn't mean that I think any of these other governors were thieves, or crooks, or bums. But somehow he sort of stands out as being maybe a little above them either in interest, or brains, or desire, or whatever it is.

June Taylor   I think he made a great impact upon Kentucky and he has been a good leader. The park system, he did an outstanding job on, and the people who succeeded him have helped to keep that picture. I think he's one of the most brilliant men we've had as governor. He's a very deep thinker and tried to do what he thought would help Kentucky. I don't think he's a selfish person at all. I think he liked practicing law. He loves law. I don't think he'll be interested in any office again.

Wilson Wyatt   [Combs's impact] has been very good. The major impact has been the very things I talked about that represented our consolidated program that we were able to put into effect during those four years—the major upgrading in the educational system; a fortuitously excellent use of what was in theory a very bad beginning—the veterans' bonus, something that made no logical sense at all but the people voted for it, and a sales tax thereby became imperative—not in the size it was, but as long as you're going to have one it was an ideal time to do it. . . .

   [A]s a result of . . . the enormous funds that came from that we were able to move the educational system forward to a tremendous degree. Colleges and universities of the state, as well as the school system, were enormously improved. New schools were built, salaries were improved, we were able to do things on the economic development front that could not probably have been done. And yet we were able to fashion the sales tax with appropriate exemptions in the way of protecting industrial and commercial opportunities that made it possible for us, in spite of the sales tax, to be highly competitive with other states and to attract new industry.

Notes

Chapter 2. The 1955 Gubernatorial Primary

1. *Louisville Courier-Journal*, June 3, 1955.   2. Ibid., August 1, 1955.   3. Ibid.

Chapter 3. The 1959 Gubernatorial Primary

1. *Louisville Courier-Journal*, June 20, 21, and 26, 1956.   2. Ibid., July 1, 1956.   3. Ibid., September 6, October 13 and 22, 1956. 4. Ibid., February 6, 1957.   5. Ibid., January 24, 1957.   6. Ibid., May 30, 1957.
 7. Ibid., January 17, 1958.   8. Ibid., March 20, 1958. Since a majority proved unattainable, many Chandler people in the end voted to reject the bill.   9. Ibid., March 28, 1958.   10. Ibid., April 3, 1958. 11. Ibid., April 10, 14, 22, June 29, 1958.   12. Ibid., February 8, 1959.

Chapter 4. The Combs Administration

1. George W. Robinson, ed., *The Public Papers of Governor Bert T. Combs, 1959–1963* (Lexington: Univ. Press of Kentucky, 1979), p. 7. 2. Ibid.   3. Ibid., p. 9.   4. *Louisville Courier-Journal*, April 15, 1960.   5. Ibid., December 10, 1959.   6. Ibid., August 19, 1960.

Chapter 5. Aftermath

1. *Louisville Courier-Journal*, December 11, 1963.   2. Ibid., April 19, 1964.   3. Ibid., August 19, 1964.   4. Ibid., January 7, 1966. 5. Ibid., February 4, 1966.   6. Ibid., April 8, 1966.
 7. Ibid., April 12, 1966.   8. Ibid., July 30, 1966.   9. Ibid., November 1, 1966.   10. Ibid., January 15, 1967.   11. Ibid., February 9, 1970.   12. Ibid., April 30, 1970.

13. Ibid., May 10, 1970.   14. Ibid., June 14, 1970.   15. Ibid., January 23, February 17, April 28, and May 5, 1971.   16. Ibid., February 25 and March 3, 1971.   17. Ibid., March 26, 1971.   18. Ibid., April 20, 1971.

19. Ibid., April 27, 1971.   20. Ibid., May 7, 1971.   21. Ibid., April 25, 1971.   22. Ibid., May 27, 1971.   23. Ibid., May 26, 1971.

Index

Aberdeen, Md., 16, 18
Administrative Office of the Courts, xvi
Aerojet General Co., xviii
airports, 5, 38, 202
Alcoholic Beverage Control Board, Kentucky, xv
Allen and Co., 113
Appalachia, 118–21
Appalachian Regional Commission, 119–21
Appalachian Regional Governors' Commission, 118
Appalachian Regional Hospitals, xiii, xv
Ardery, Phil, xiii; quoted, 47, 104
Arts Commission, Kentucky, 201
Ashland, Ky., xiii, 172
Ashland Petroleum Co., xiii
Associated Press Editors' Assoc., xx
Austin, Acree, 30

Ballard County, 85
Banks, Fontaine, xiii, 159, 169; quoted, 59–60, 82, 90, 160–61, 163–65, 185–86, 195–96, 200
Bardstown, Kentucky, 87
Barkley, Alben W., 28–29, 47, 51, 53–54, 62, 137
Barnes, Vego, 52–53, 88
Barron, Wally, 119
Beauchamp, Emerson "Doc," 29–37, 67, 72, 87, 107
Beech Creek, Ky., 9, 14
Bell, Robert, xiii, 159; quoted, 72, 82, 95–96, 104–5, 141–42, 152–53, 196, 200
Benge, Martha, 10, 11

Better Roads Council, xvii
Big Creek, Ky., 13
Big Rivers Electric Co., xxi
Big Sandy River Valley, 114
Bingham, Barry, Sr., xiii; quoted, 47, 104, 131, 165, 196–97
Bluegrass Parkway, 115
Bowling Green, Ky., xvi, 66, 80, 84
Breathitt, Edward "Ned," xiii, xvi, xix, xx, xxi, 1, 5, 69, 95, 122, 136–42, 144–49, 153–54, 156, 158–59, 171–73, 175–79, 183–84, 203
Breathitt, Frances, 179
Breathitt, James, 12
Breckinridge, John, xxi, 66, 68, 79, 90, 96, 107, 137
Brighton Engineering Co., xviii, 112, 115
Broadbent, Smith, 67–68
Brown, John Y., Sr., xiii, 103, 173; quoted, 24, 56
Buckman, J. D. "Jiggs," 172
Burke, Bob, 77
Burly and Dark Tobacco Export Assoc., xvii
Butler, Wendell, xiv; quoted, 165
Byrd, Harry, 39

Cammack, James W., 18, 20–22, 32
Camp Atterbury, Ind., 18
Campbell County, xvi
Campton, Ky., 112, 116
Cane Creek, Ky., 7
Carroll, Julie Ann, 186, 191
Carroll, Julian, 6, 181–82, 193–94, 203
Carroll, Tommy, xiv, 193; quoted, 70, 74–75, 82–83, 87–89, 110, 133, 179, 186, 191–93, 200–201

Carter, Henry, 64
Centre College, xvi
Chandler, Albert B. "Happy," xiv, xv, 4–5, 13, 19, 29–31, 33, 35–36, 39, 41–43, 46–59 passim, 62–67, 70–71, 73–76, 80, 82–85, 88–89, 91, 94, 102–3, 111, 113, 115–16, 122, 137–41, 143–48, 153, 163, 172–73, 191, 200–201, 203; quoted, 40, 104, 110, 131–32
Cincinnati, Oh., 74, 180, 186–87, 189, 192–93
Citizens Security Life Insurance Co., Owensboro, xix
civil rights issue of 1963, 138, 149–50
Clay County, 2, 8–10, 12, 13, 15, 16, 20, 22–24, 44, 166
Clay County High School, 9
Clements, Earle, xv, xviii, xix, xxi, 3, 20, 22, 28–33, 36, 39, 45, 50, 51, 54, 57, 62–63, 65–68, 70–81, 83, 87–89, 116, 121–22, 124–37, 140, 148, 161–62, 183, 191, 200–201, 203
Clinton County, 87
coal mine litigation, 15, 18, 58
Cobb, Irvin S., 53
Coldiron, Dr., 19
Combs, Helen Rechtin, 168, 192–93, 199
Combs, LeRoy, 16
Combs, Mabel Hall, 3, 8, 15, 17–18, 31, 37, 100, 167–68, 171, 177, 179, 180, 185
Combs, Martha Jones, 2, 9, 12–14, 16, 22–23, 25
Combs, Owsley Stanley, xxi
Combs, Robert Lee "Slick," xiv; comments by, 13, 23–24, 33–34, 47–48, 131, 166, 186, 200
Combs, Steve, 2, 9, 12–14, 16, 23, 25, 31
Combs, Tommy, 18, 30, 32–33
Combs and Combs, 16
Commodore Hotel, 166–67
Congress (U.S.), xiii, xxi, 51, 54, 62, 137–38, 142–43, 180, 183
Conservation, Kentucky Department of, 98; small lakes program, 116–17; water resources, 202
Cook, Marlow, 172, 181

Cooke, Thurston, 121–24, 128–30, 132, 134
Cooper, John Sherman, 29, 137–38, 173, 183, 190
Corbin, Ky., 161
Cornett, Robert, xv; quoted, 108, 121, 153
Council of State Governments, xv, 153
Council on Higher Education, 7
Court of Appeals, Kentucky, xv, xix, 1, 3–4, 18, 20–21, 23–26, 30, 32–33, 35–36, 40, 55, 57, 63–64, 126, 166, 182
Covington, Ky., 37
Cowger, William, 172
Cox, Louis, 31, 57, 127, 178, 189, 191, 193–94
Craft, John, 192
Creech, Dr. J. L., 11
Crestview, Ky., xvi
Crime Victims Compensation Board, Kentucky, xviii
Crimmins, Bernie, 89
Crimmins, John, xv; quoted, 47, 90–91
Crutcher, Mrs., 12
Cumberland College, 2, 8, 10–11

Daviess County, xviii, 57
Davis, Harry, xv; quoted, 40, 56, 116, 166
Davis, John L., 25
Democratic party, 2, 5–6, 8, 12, 22–24, 44, 51, 60, 99, 107, 137, 172, 174, 180–81, 191; Chicago National Convention, 63; Fayette County Democratic party, xviii; Jefferson County Executive Committee, xiv; Jefferson County Democratic party, xv; Los Angeles National Convention, 166–67; National Committee, xxi, 63, 166; Owensboro Democratic party, xviii; Senatorial (U.S.) Campaign Committee, 63; State Campaign Committee for Kentucky, xiv; State Central Executive Committee, xiv, xviii, xxi, 62, 99
Denny, Edwin, 58
Department of Budget, Kentucky, xv
Department of Health, Education, and Welfare (U.S.), xvi

Index

Duffy, Martin (Mike), Jr., xv; quoted, 153–54
Duncan, Parker, 185

Easterly, Ed, xv; comments by, 94, 105, 116, 154–55, 161, 164, 166–67
Eastern Kentucky, 21–22, 34–35, 37, 50, 57, 92, 114, 116, 120–21, 144, 164, 171, 200; Regional Planning Commission, xx, 120
Eastern Kentucky University, xvi, xvii
Economic Security, Kentucky Department of, xv, xviii, xix, xx, 96, 107
education, 1, 5, 38, 44, 50, 93, 101, 103, 106, 115, 119–20, 160, 188, 204; educational television, 5, 202; minimum foundation program, 47, 57
Education, Department of, xiii, xvi, xx
Eisenhower, Dwight D., 29, 63
elections: 1967, 179–80; 1955 primary, 40–42, 52–58; 1959 primary, 65–72; 1971 primary, 189–200
Elizabethtown, Ky., 84, 88, 112
Elkhorn City, Ky., 112, 140
Ervin S. Cobb Hotel, 44
Evans, Herndon, 117
Excepticon, Inc., xiii

Farris, Ed, xv, 79–81; quoted, 34, 40, 60, 75, 83, 147, 197
Fayette County, 42
Ferguson, Jo, xv, 69, 96, 98; quoted, 25, 40–41, 90, 96, 107, 115, 132, 155, 201
Finance, Kentucky Department of, xvi
floral clock, 162–64
Floyd County, 3, 20, 23, 40, 92; Federal Savings and Loan Assoc. of, 58
Ford Wendell, xviii, xxi, 5–6, 96, 100, 163, 178, 181–82, 187–95, 197–200, 203
Fort Knox, Ky., 15, 17, 91
Fort Mitchell, Ky., xvii
Fosset, Ed., xv, 98, 100; quoted, 68–69, 96, 146, 155–56, 177, 197, 201
Fox, Ed, 117–18
Francis, J. David, xvi, 80, 96; quoted, 41, 79–80, 86, 110, 132, 143, 149, 177, 186–87, 197–98, 201
Frankfort, Ky., xiv, xv, xvi, xviii, xix, xx, 3–5, 8, 12, 14–15, 18, 22–25, 30, 36, 44, 56, 58, 65, 70, 94–95, 99, 108, 133, 136, 142, 154, 157, 162–65, 171, 177–78, 180, 182, 192–93, 197
Frankfort State Journal, xx
Frankfurter, Felix, xix
Franklin County, 100
Franklin County High School, 88

Garden Club of Kentucky, 163–64
Gattis, Walter, xvi, 108; quoted, 98, 108–9, 156
General Assembly, Kentucky, xiii, xv, xvii, xix, xx, xxi, 5, 64–67, 69–70, 101–3, 105–6, 124, 153, 182, 193
Glasgow, Ky., 138
Gordon, Jim, 144
Gorman, Bob, 14–15, 17
Gorman, Chris, 26
Gorman, Polly Preston, xvi; quoted, 14–15, 17, 25–26, 41, 60, 96–97, 156–57, 161, 167, 184–85, 198, 201–2
Great Depression, 8, 12, 15

Harlan, Ky., xiv, 23, 166
Harlan Daily Enterprise, xx
Hatfield, Dr. Henry D., 19
Hazard, Ky., 18, 20, 112, 116, 140, 160–61
Hehl, Lambert, xvi; quoted, 102
Helm, Roy, 18, 20–22
Henderson, Ky., xix, 37, 43, 91
Henderson County River Port Authority, xxi
Hensley, Bige, 11
Hensley, Bob, 13
Hickman, Ky., 167
Highway Department, Kentucky, xiv, 8, 11–14, 38, 86, 107, 114, 116, 121–28, 130–33, 135, 160, 173
highways, 38, 44, 93, 104, 106, 112–17, 120, 160, 202; Daniel Boone Parkway, 120; Kentucky Turnpike, 112; Mountain Parkway, 112–16, 120, 200, 202; road building, 1, 5, 47, 202; toll roads, 39, 116, 201–2; Western Kentucky Parkway, 115
Hindman, Ky., xx
Hopkins, Hoppy, 66
Hopkinsville, Ky., 83

Howard, J. Woodford, 18–21, 58–59
Huddleston, Paul, 66, 69–70
Huntington, W.V., 18–19
Hyden, Ky., 13

industrial development, 44, 79, 93, 203–4
Insurance, Kentucky Department of, xvi

Japanese war criminals, 15
Jefferson County, 44, 47, 63, 68, 72–73, 91, 172, 188; Juvenile Court, xx
Johnson, Ben, 12
Johnson, Lyndon B., 51, 54, 62–63, 122, 125–26, 131, 133, 135, 137, 150, 183, 186
Johnson County, 24
Jones, Libby, 25
Jones, Preston J. "Uncle Pete," 11
Jones, T. T., 12, 31, 37
Joyner, Felix, xxi, 98
Judge Advocate General Branch (U.S. Army), 3, 15, 17
Judicial Council of Kentucky, 20
Justice, Zach, 12

Kammerer, Gladys, 107–8
Kaufman, Sara Combs, xvii; quoted, 13–14, 34, 60, 164, 167, 177, 187, 198
Kennedy, Bobby, 150
Kennedy, John F., 5, 119, 133, 137–38, 150, 183
Kenton County, 43–44
Kentucky Associated Press, xv
Kentucky Hotel, 187, 192
Kentucky Opera Association, 201
Kentucky Press Association, xx
Kentucky State Fair and Exposition, xvii; Fair Board, 155
Kentucky Utilities, xx
Kentucky Wholesale Liquor Distributors, xv
Kincaid, Garvice, 13
Kingsbury, Gil, xvii, 70; comments by, 69, 81, 87, 102, 115, 142, 164, 167–68, 196
Kingsbury, Sylvia, 167–68
Klapheke, Harry, 129
Knott County, 15–16, 19

Lafayette Hotel, 107
Laffoon, Ruby, 50
law practice, Combs's, 15
Lawrence, David, 119
law school, Combs at, 3, 8, 12–13, 16
Leary, Joe, xxi, 62
Legislative Research Commission, xvii, 25, 68–69
Legislature. *See* General Assembly
Letcher County, 24, 161, 174
Levins, Helena, 15
Lexington, Ky., xiii, xv, xvii, xviii, xix, 4–5, 17–19, 22–23, 25, 30, 58–59, 68, 92, 99, 107, 114, 171–72, 176–77, 180, 182, 187, 191
Lexington Herald, 117
Lindsay, Jess, 31
Lloyd, Arthur, xvii; comments by, 24–25, 34–35, 48, 56–57, 94, 105, 130–31
Lloyd, Libby, 25
London, Ky., 161
Lou Harris Poll, 80–81
Louisville, Kentucky, xiii, xiv, xv, xvii, xx, xxi, 19, 26, 56, 60, 63, 65–69, 72–73, 77–79, 81–82, 88, 95, 97–98, 107, 112, 121–23, 128–29, 140, 150, 172, 181–82, 186, 188–91, 196
Louisville Chamber of Commerce, xviii, 75–76, 87, 104–5
Louisville Courier-Journal, xiii, xix, 14, 45–47, 49, 51, 68, 71, 75, 81, 83, 121–22, 125, 128–32, 140, 152, 180, 189
Louisville Equipment Rental Co., 121

MacArthur, Douglas, 17
McLaughlin, Mrs. Lennie, xxi, 79
Manchester, Ky., xiv, 2, 8–10, 13, 16, 30, 161
Manchester Drug Co., 10
Manila, Philippine Islands, 17
Marcum, Louise Combs, 30
Marion Taylor Building, 79
Martin, Dr. James, 16, 45, 106
Martin, Robert R., xvii, 79–80, 86, 107–8, 129; quoted, 41, 60–61, 70–71, 80–81, 86–87, 102–3, 128, 177, 196
Matlick, Jack, xvii, 105; quoted, 98, 105–6, 116–17, 168, 202

Index

Matthews, Robert, xvii, 96, 178, 190, 195-96; comments by, 91, 109-10, 157, 195
May, William, xviii, 112, 115, 129, 166, 180, 189; quoted, 48, 91, 107-8, 114-15, 127, 147, 149-50, 178, 194
Mayfield, Ky., 161
Mayo, W. P., 59
Maysville, Ky., 161
Meade County, 91
Medicaid, 96
Meigs, Henry, II, xviii; quoted, 99-100
Merchant Marine, 134
merit system, 5, 93, 95, 106-11, 201
Metcalf County, xiv
Middlesboro, Ky., 94
Middletown, Ky., 68
Military Affairs, Kentucky Dept. of, 105
Miller, Cattie Lou, xviii, 97, 164; quoted, 26, 41-42, 48, 75-76, 89-90, 97-98, 103, 115-16, 147, 157-58, 161-62, 194, 202-3
Miller, Harry B., xviii, 177; quoted, 42, 48-49, 99, 110-11, 134
Miller, J. R., xviii, 181, 189-92, 194-95, 199; comments by, 42, 57, 76, 81, 136-37, 168-69, 180, 185, 193-94, 203
Miller, Shackelford, 182
Mitchell, Leonard, 82
Moloney, Dick, 77, 80, 82, 95
Morehead State University, xvii
Morganfield, Ky., 70, 136-37
Morris, Hugh, 46-47
Morton, Thruston, 5, 83, 137-38, 140, 183, 190
Mount Sterling, Ky., 77, 79
Muldraugh, Ky., 91
Murphy, Ruth, xviii, 69; quoted, 42-43, 49, 69-70, 81-82, 178

Natcher, William, 143
National Guard, Kentucky, 94
National Youth Administration, 12
Newport, Ky., xvi, 37
Niagara Falls, Canada, 162
Nicholasville, Ky., 94
Nixon, Richard M., 5, 138, 181

Normal School, London, Ky., 9
Nunn, Louie, 5, 111, 138, 172, 178, 181, 191

Ockerman, Foster, xix, 66, 68; quoted, 43, 198
O'Connell, Charles, 64
Officer Candidate School, 16-17
old age pensions, 52
Oneida Baptist Institute, 9
Owens, Doris, 64
Owensboro, Ky., xviii, xix, xxi, 37, 76, 81, 100

Paducah, Ky., 37, 53, 83, 86, 103, 112, 181
Paducah Sun-Democrat, xxi, 117
Palmore, John, xix, 144, 146; quoted, 43, 71, 82, 91, 134-35, 146, 180, 185, 194-95
parks, 1, 5, 38, 47, 93, 106, 111, 113, 117-18, 153, 160, 168, 202-4; Cumberland Falls State Park, 168; Cumberland Gap National Historical Park, 94; DuPont lodge, 66; Kentucky Lake State Park, 168, 180
Parks, Kentucky Department of, xiii
Pearce, John Ed, xix; quoted, 35, 43, 76, 91-92, 106, 117-18, 135, 146-47, 203
Pearl Harbor, 16
Peden, Katherine, 181
Perkins, Carl, xxi, 19, 22, 120
Perry County, 24
Personnel, Kentucky Department of, xvi, 95
Philippine Islands, 3, 17
Pike County, Ky., 69
Pikeville, Ky., 12, 32, 65, 84, 86, 146, 203
politics, 13, 19-20, 23-24; Castro speech, 88-89; Christmas Massacre, 59, 111; crippled goose, 85-86, 89; Cumberland Falls meeting, 66, 68; factionalism, 28-29, 33, 58, 63, 69, 73-74, 77, 188-89; merger, 77-92; rebels, 64-70, 73; selection of Combs to run, 29-33; selection of Breathitt to run, 143-48; $20,000 rug, 55-56, 85-86. *See also* elections

Porter, Dr., 10
Powell, Earl, xix; quoted, 26–27, 98–99, 136, 147–48, 158, 164–65, 187, 198–99, 203–4
Powell County, 120
Preston, Capt., 24
Prestonsburg, Ky., 3, 15–16, 18–19, 21–23, 44, 53, 58–59, 67, 92, 108, 112, 116
Prichard, Edward, xix, 87, 193–94; quoted, 35, 49, 57, 83, 111, 128–30, 150
Princeton, Ky., 115
Public Information, Kentucky Department of, xviii, 97
Public Service Commission, Kentucky, xvi, 95–96, 145, 148, 175
Public Welfare, Kentucky Department of, xvii
Pulaski County, 88

Rather, Julius, xix, 171, 178; quoted, 100, 158, 169, 178–79, 199
rebels. *See* politics
Reeves, Ben, 51
Rehm, Bobby Combs, xx, 13, 25, 40–41; quoted, 14, 169
Rehm, Paul, 25
Republican party, 4–5, 8, 22, 24, 58, 99, 108, 137–38, 174, 181, 183, 190
Revenue, Kentucky Department of, xx, 106, 109, 176
Reynolds, Bob, 77
Reynolds, Jack, 77
Rhea, Tom, 13, 50
Rhodes scholarship, 20
Richmond, Ky., xvii
Robertson, Murrel, 129
Robsion, John, 87, 94
Rockefeller, Nelson, 119
Roosevelt, Franklin, D., xix

sales tax, 5, 31, 40, 43, 45–46, 49–50, 52, 57, 65, 67, 87, 89, 90, 101–6, 112–13, 137, 188, 191, 196, 200–204
Sampson, Flem, 8, 12
Savage, Troy, 166
Scent, William, xx, 105; quoted, 71, 106, 158, 199

Seelbach Hotel, 42–43, 69, 75–76, 81, 95, 148
Shelby County, 44
Shelbyville, Ky., 44, 47–50, 57
Shelbyville speech, 45–47, 49–50
Sixth Circuit Court of Appeals (U.S.), 2, 5–6, 173, 176, 180–87
Smith, Uncle Herb, 23–24, 48
soldiers' bonus, 31, 87, 89–90, 101–5, 200, 204
Somerset, Ky., 84, 88
Southern Railway, 176, 181
South Fort Mitchell, Ky., xx
Spindletop Hall, 180
Spurrier, Jay, xx; quoted, 83, 158–59
Stag Distillery, 165
Standiford Motel, 77, 79, 81, 83
State Board of Claims, Kentucky, xviii
Stevenson, Adlai, xxi, 63, 137
Stewart, Brady, 44, 53, 60
strip mining restrictions, 188
Sturgill, Don, 177
Summer Girl, The, 15
Supreme Court, U.S., xix, 6, 181, 183–84, 186, 201
Swinford, Mac, 65

"Taking Government to the People," 159–62
Talbott, Dan, 12
Tarrant, John, 184
Tawes, Millard, 118
taxes, 44–50, 53, 57, 73, 87, 188; severance tax on coal, 188
Taylor, June, xx; quoted, 26, 35, 49, 61, 142, 148, 169, 179, 199–200, 204
Taylor, Rumsey, xxi
Team You Can Trust, the, 83, 86, 93
Tobacco Institute, 74, 134
tourism, 1, 5, 44, 93, 111–12, 118, 202–3
Trapp, David M., 173
truck deal, 121–37

Union County, 148
University of Kentucky, xvii, 3, 8, 12–13, 20, 37; Bureau of Government Services, xvi; Personnel Department of Kentucky Medical Center, xvi
University of Louisville, 97

Index

Vance, Kyle, 121
Van Curon, Samuel, xx; quoted, 103, 130
Vanderbilt University, xvii
varmint dinners, 165
Versailles, Ky., xiv, xx
Volunteer Officer Candidate Program, 16

Wallace, Earl, 85
Wallace, George, 149
War Crimes Department (Philippine Islands), 17
Ward, Henry, xiii, xxi, 5, 39, 45, 104, 116-17, 126, 143, 146-47, 172-73, 176-77, 179-81
Ware, James C., xx, 66, 69; quoted, 43-44, 70, 102
Warren County, xvi
Waterfield, Harry Lee, xiii, xx, 4, 28, 50-52, 64-65, 68-69, 71-76, 81-84, 91, 94, 153, 171, 173; quoted, 85-86, 103
Watson, Clyde, 136-37
Watts, John, 87, 89, 143
Webster County High School, xvii
Weinberg, Lois Combs, xx, 17-18, 25, 168; quoted, 20, 23, 59, 68, 92, 100

Westpheling, Jo, 167
Wetherby, Lawrence, xv, xviii, xix, xx, 3-4, 18, 20-22, 24, 26, 29-31, 34-41, 45, 50-54, 57-58, 62-63, 73, 79, 84, 112, 127, 129, 137, 177-78, 189, 194, 203; quoted, 23, 31-33, 46-47, 55-56, 68, 111, 115, 136
Wheatcraft, Ky., xvii
Whisman, John, xxi, 118, 120-21
Williamsburg, Ky., 8, 11
Williamstown, Ky., 84
Willis, Simeon, 3-4, 22-24, 28, 35
Winchester, Ky., 112
Winston, Dix, xxi; quoted, 44, 50, 57, 71-72, 94-95, 130, 148, 169-70
workmen's compensation, 19
World War II, xvii, 3, 15, 17, 28, 37, 102
Wyatt, Wilson, xiii, xxi, 4-5, 65, 67-68, 71-84, 86-87, 90-92, 95-96, 102, 104, 106-7, 110, 122, 125, 128-30, 133, 137-43, 146, 171, 201; quoted, 72, 78-79, 95, 128, 141, 159, 204
Wyatt, Tarrant and Combs, 7

Young, Bill, 87
Young, Gates, 66